Here's what people a [W9-BNI-324]
surprise *New York Times* bestseller:

"*Very intriguing . . . insightful . . . informative.*"

"*I loved the book. I couldn't put it down. I read it all in one day.*"

"*It's quite a book. It's what a lot of people should know.*"

"*It's fantastic . . . it gave me chills.*"

"*I can't wait to share it with some other people when I'm done with it.*"

"*Wonderful . . . I wish everyone would read it.*"

"*It's intriguing how so few people could have so much power.*"

"*Eye opening . . . shocking.*"

"*It's about time someone told the truth.*"

"*I had no idea that all this was going on.*"

"Revealing."

"Timely . . . Nice to have someone tie all this together."

"It makes me a little uneasy."

"I hardly ever read or even finish a book . . . I finished this one."

"I knew something was going on."

"I believe every word of it."

"I've promised to loan my copy to four friends."

"It's the kind of book that makes your hair stand on end."

"I didn't know all these things were going on."

"Enlightening . . ."

"President Bush ought to have a copy to read."

THE NEW WORLD ORDER

Other Books by Pat Robertson

Shout It from the Housetops
The Secret Kingdom
Answers to 200 of Life's Most Probing Questions
America's Date with Destiny
Beyond Reason: How Miracles Can Change Your Life
The Plan
The New Millennium

THE NEW WORLD ORDER

PAT ROBERTSON

WORD PUBLISHING

Dallas · London · Vancouver · Melbourne

The New World Order

Unless otherwise noted, Scripture quotations are from the New King James Version. Copyright © 1979, 1980, 1982, Thomas Nelson, Inc., Publisher.

Robertson, Pat.
    The new world order / Pat Robertson.
        p.   cm.
    Includes bibliographical references and index.
    ISBN 0–8499–0915–5
    ISBN 0–8499–3394–3 (pbk.)
    1. World politics—1989–   . 2. Civilization, Modern—1950–
I. Title.
D860 . R64   1991
909 . 82—dc20   91–32023
                                                          CIP

    6 7 8 9 9 AGF 9 8

Printed in the United States of America

Then the devil, taking Him up on a high mountain, showed Him all the kingdoms of the world in a moment of time.

And the devil said to Him, "All this authority I will give You, and their glory; for this has been delivered to me, and I give it to whomever I wish.

"Therefore, if You will worship before me, all will be Yours."

And Jesus answered and said to him, "Get behind Me, Satan! For it is written, 'You shall worship the Lord your God, and Him only you shall serve.'"

Luke 4:5–8

Contents

Preface to the Paperback Edition

Since the hardcover edition of this book was first published in September 1991, much has changed in our world. The collapse of European communism, the dissolution of the Soviet regime, the departure of Mikhail Gorbachev, and the rise of Boris Yeltsin as president of the Russian Republic are all stunning changes. It is striking how much these changes underscore the perspective of this book and support its conclusions.

The new world order promised by President George Bush at the outset of the Persian Gulf War in 1990 was no mere rhetoric. We can see that even more clearly now. The evidence is all around us, in the headlines and on the nightly news.

This vision of a "global community of nations" is a precise, systematic, and rigorously planned mechanism to manage people and nations collectively by proxy and by global authority. It is a program to ensure that principles of geographical and racial "balance" are scrupulously applied, regardless of the outcome. That authority is no longer a futurist dream—it is a fact.

When Boutrous Boutros-Ghali of Egypt assumed the office of Secretary-General of the United Nations on New Year's Day 1992, the UN's military apparatus was already in the process of dispatching a "peacekeeping" force of some ten thousand men and women to war-torn Yugoslavia. This was in addition to the tens of thousands of UN forces and observers currently in Latin America, Cyprus, India, Pakistan, Iraq, Lebanon, Israel, Angola, the Western Sahara, and other strategic locations. Twenty thousand UN personnel also stood in control of the government of Cambodia, awaiting national elections to be held sometime in 1993.

In its February 3, 1992 issue, *Time* magazine quoted the Ford Foundation resident scholar, Sir Brian Urquhart, a forty-year UN veteran, who said: "We've got to stop looking at the UN only in terms of day-to-day emergencies and start seeing it as the only organization that can foster institutions for a global society."

That, indeed, is the vision of the new world order. A global society, managed by an elite central government that exercises supervision and control by means of its massive army of so-called peacekeeping forces. If the pace of global re-ordering seems modest—a few skirmishes here, a few trouble spots there—the ultimate goal is nevertheless a one-world government under a centralized authority.

As we observe the Republican and Democratic presidential contenders sparring in our own public arena during this election year, we should know that the philosophies being debated are not simply issues of local or regional consequence, but issues that will determine the very fate and future of our world. The stakes are immeasurably greater than just a year ago.

The Publisher

Foreword

My work on the manuscript of *The New World Order* was completed, the final proofs had been checked, and the book was essentially on the presses when the first satellite reports flashed on the monitors in our CBN broadcast center with the news that Soviet President Mikhail Gorbachev had been overthrown in a coup led by the KGB, the Soviet Army, and the secret police. His hand-picked vice-president, Gennady Yanayev, had been named by the hard-liners to head their revolutionary government.

But as suddenly as it all happened, this action was not entirely unexpected. Despite his popularity abroad, Gorbachev had been becoming increasingly unpopular at home. Some said he had walked too long on the razor's edge of compromise, but there were other possibilities.

The "coup" began on Monday, August 19, 1991. By Wednesday, August 21, it had collapsed. Boris Yeltsin, the charismatic president of the Russian Federation, emerged as the leader who had defeated the gang of eight. At his side was none other than Gorbachev's longtime ally, Eduard Shevardnadze, the former Soviet foreign minister and a former head of the interior ministry, the body which controls the secret police. Shortly thereafter, word came that Gorbachev was returning to Moscow as the "constitutionally elected" head of a "Democratic Soviet Union." Only time will tell what sort of structure will actually emerge.

From President George Bush's vacation home in Kennebunkport, Maine, on Wednesday, August 21, the day it became clear that the coup had failed, came the startling observation of CNN reporter Mary Tillotson that the president's *"new world order* is back on track, now stronger than ever." And suddenly the perspective becomes clearer.

On pages 83 through 89 of this book, I quote from Anatoliy Golitsyn's book, *New Lies for Old*, written in 1984, which gives a startling and detailed account of the KGB plan that was actually played out in 1989 to lull the West with false "liberalization." On page 81 I quote headlines from the *New York Times* which reveal a virtually identical program carried out by Nikolai Lenin in 1921, a program he called *glasnost*. Such precedents for deception should jolt the public conscience, but memories are short.

As I kept track of events—actually the remarkable lack of them—during the August "coup," it became all too clear that many facts just did not add up, except as an attempt to make the Soviet Union more palatable as a partner for the United States in the coming new world order. Consider the following.

The eight "coup" leaders were all part of the group that had engineered the rise of Mikhail Gorbachev to power. KGB Chief Vladimir Kryuchkov, Defense Minister Dmitri Yazov, Deputy Defense Chairman Oleg Baklanov, Prime Minister Valentin Pavlov, Farmer's Union Chairman Vasily Starodubtsev, Interior Minister Boris Pugo, Industrial Chairman A. I. Tizyakov, and Vice-President Gennady Yanayev were all placed in power relatively recently by Gorbachev himself. The first question to ask is why these members of Gorbachev's hand-picked team would turn against the man who not only placed them in power but was effectively keeping them there?

Another very odd fact, duly noted by several network analysts, was the failure to cut outside communications. That is the first thing any revolution would do. I was in Greece right after the so-called Colonel's Coup of 1974. When that revolution occurred, both domestic and overseas phone lines were cut; all radio, television, and press were silenced immediately; and all potential opponents were jailed. Neither the Greek citizens nor the world press knew what had happened until the revolutionary council was firmly in control and unassailable.

In the Soviet Union, the leaders of the August "coup" controlled the army, the secret police, and the KGB. They were all highly trained and experienced in espionage, military tactics, and propaganda. Furthermore, they were cautious older men, not impetuous youths given to reckless adventurism. Yet their "coup" seemed reckless, ill-conceived, half-hearted, and incredibly inept.

All the Soviet airports remained open. Domestic and long-distance telephone service was uninterrupted. Opposition newspapers were allowed to publish. Boris Yeltsin was permitted access to national television and even had the opportunity to address the world from the podium of the Russian Parliament. No arrests were made of any leaders or potential leaders of any group that would naturally rise to oppose the "coup."

Even more striking, the entire spectacle was allowed to play itself out before the television cameras and the press of the free world. Instead of the obligatory press shut down, it was as if those planning the "coup" actually wanted the entire world to see what was taking place—a move that by itself would virtually guarantee the failure of their undertaking.

In short, this "coup" was programmed from the beginning to fail. So, if that is the case, why did it take place at all?

The reason is obvious. Any careful observer of recent Soviet history must realize that Gorbachev was the hand-picked protégé of Yuri Andropov, the late Soviet premier and the head of the KGB. People were suspicious that Gorbachev's reforms were merely cosmetic, not genuine, and that lurking around him were hard-line Stalinists and Marxists eager to revive the military confrontation with the United States.

I noticed that a number of Soviet commentators used an American phrase to describe the source of the "coup" as the Soviet "military-industrial complex." Boris Yeltsin said that, if allowed to succeed, the "coup" would mean an end of freedom in the Soviet Union and a return to the military confrontation of the Cold War.

Now Gorbachev, Yeltsin, and Shevardnadze can proclaim that democracy has triumphed in the Soviet Union, that the reforms of the past are permanent, and that the hard-line, reactionary communist elements of the "military-industrial complex" have been banished from the land forever. Therefore, it must follow that the Western democracies can make massive reductions in their military arsenals without risk while they, in turn, pump billions of dollars into the Soviet economy to "keep democracy alive."

Are we so gullible as to believe that all this could be accomplished by a silly little three-day adventure during which four people were killed and one armored vehicle was set on fire? If the Stock Market is any barometer of public opinion, the answer is yes. We are that gullible. We want so desperately to live in a peaceful world that we will accept virtually any fraud which offers that hope.

Whatever happens in the days and months following the "coup," I do not believe that the global design for a new world order will be hampered by this kind of acceleration. Those who favor the globalist vision of world order will quickly find the necessary rhetoric to glorify the implications of the August "coup" and then to whitewash the rest.

For me, the "August Surprise" of 1991 is not unlike the similar surprise we received in the early morning hours of August 2, 1990, when we saw the first reports of the impending Persian Gulf crisis. At that time, I had just completed work on my book, *The New Millennium*, when the satellites began beaming the news of Saddam Hussein's incursion into Kuwait.

As the day unfolded, the CBN newsroom was on constant alert to see what, if anything, would transpire and how this latest flareup in the Middle East would affect world events. At the same time, I was anxious to know how the crisis would affect my work of the past several months on the book.

When it became clear what was happening, and that a military showdown of some kind was indeed very likely, I quickly updated the manuscript, and the book was released shortly thereafter. Now the manuscript of this book, *The New World Order*, has been updated in much the same way, to take into account this latest development in world history.

The ramifications of that historic week in 1990 have not yet been fully absorbed. Operation Desert Storm, the One-Hundred-Hour War, the March 1st "cease-fire," and the proclamations of a "new world order" that came out of the crisis in the Persian Gulf have added a new dimension to our lives. If there is greater hope in the world, there is also greater anxiety, and as we move ever closer to the coming *new millennium,* we can hardly doubt that other and more auspicious dramas lie just ahead.

It is clear now that this book, *The New World Order,* is actually a continuation of the last one. Today we can see more clearly than ever that the coming decade will be a time of turmoil, of controversy, and of even greater political and spiritual unrest. I believe that the issues I have addressed in these pages are proof of the depth and complexity of the problems.

While I have tried to challenge each reader to take them seriously—as life-and-death issues—I have an undeniable sense that we are witnessing the unfolding of a historic age, "a time of troubles," if you will, of biblical proportions, and the end of the age will truly bring the revelation of a new world order to justify the hopes and dreams of all mankind and the divine will of God. That, in essence, is the perspective I have tried to bring to this narrative.

For their assistance in preparing this work, I would like to express my gratitude to all the people who have helped with the research, analysis, and information gathering. Thanks to Dr. Jim Black for his able assistance in the organization and preparation of the work; to CBN News Director Drew Parkhill, whose professional research and fact checking have been invaluable. And special thanks to Beverly Milner from my staff for her long hours deciphering my handwritten notes and preparing the manuscript.

I would also like to thank Word Publishing executives Kip Jordon and Joey Paul for their ongoing stimulation and support and for their commitment to publishing the truth in these troubled times. And I would especially like to thank my wife, Dede, for her faithful support and encouragement, for reading and critiquing the work in progress, and for her patience throughout the months of reading, writing, and seemingly endless revision.

And finally, I would like to thank you, the readers, for your participation in this adventure, for you are the ones who, in the long run, will make the real difference. It is you who must exercise the rights and responsibilities of your citizenship, to make appropriate demands on your elected representatives, and ultimately to hold accountable all those who offer a vision of a new world order.

Pat Robertson
Virginia Beach, Virginia

PART 1

---

*Perspectives on
World Order*

1

The World Order Agenda

IN THE FALL AND WINTER OF 1989, communism collapsed in Eastern Europe. By mid-1990, the once-mighty Soviet Union was in economic and political ruin. In the late summer of 1990, war erupted between Iraq and Kuwait, and the following spring America and her allies—on the strength of superior technology and dynamic leadership—crushed Iraq's military force in a lightning-fast, one-hundred-hour war that was witnessed, via satellite, by virtually the entire world.

In 1992 the European community will emerge as the possible forerunner of the United States of Europe. And just eight years from the first publication of this book, the world will conclude the second millennium of its existence since the birth of Jesus Christ, and will begin the third millennium, A.D.

Against this backdrop of history, from the podium of the legislative chamber of the United States House of Representatives, the elected president of the United States of America has announced the beginning of a *New World Order*.

It was a deliberate and significant announcement, but what does this promise of a new regime mean to you, to me, and to our families? What kind of world will this new world order bring us? For the first time in their lives, many people have the undeniable sensation that they are living in a time when history is being made—when events are taking place in the world that will have a profound effect on their future lives.

In preparation for a television special entitled, "Don't Ask Me, Ask God," which was to become, we believe, the top-rated religious television special in American history, the Christian Broadcasting Network commissioned the Gallup Poll to survey a representative cross section of the American people to discover the answer to this proposition, "If you could ask God one question, what would it be?"

We tabulated the top ten concerns of the American people and then enlisted the aid of such well-known personalities as Steve Allen, Ned Beatty, Ruth Buzzi, Tony Danza, Norman Fell, Michael J. Fox, Anita Gillette, Dean Jones, Marvin Kaplan, Doug McClure, Jayne Meadows, Vincent Price, Ben Vereen, and many others to dramatize the top five questions that were on the hearts and minds of the American people.

Those who advocate a new world order are trying to answer these crucial questions by political means:

1. Why is there suffering in the world?
2. Why is there evil in the world?
3. Will there ever be lasting world peace?
4. Will man ever love his fellow man?
5. What does the future hold for me and my family?

An Impossible Dream

To some the new world order will usher in an era of unprecedented peace, harmony, justice, and prosperity. In one chapter of this book I will address the utopian dreamers and their plans through the ages. Typical of their thinking is the musing of the late megastar John Lennon, whose song "Imagine" has been sung without true comprehension by hundreds of millions of misty-eyed teenagers and young adults worldwide.

Lennon asked those listening to his song to imagine a time when there were "no countries," "no religion," "no heaven," "no hell," "no possessions," everyone "living for today," and the world "as one."

The former Beatle's dream world would be a world of hedonism—without religious faith, without national pride or sovereignty, without "anything to fight for," without any private property—but with a one-world government and communal property. Of course, if a one-world government had taken away all our property, our values, our faith, and our freedom, there indeed would be nothing left worth fighting for—unless we decided, like the people under the slavery of communism, that our precious freedom was worth fighting and dying to get back.

Some of his most ardent fans apparently have failed to recognize one glaring and essentially hypocritical inconsistency between the words and the life of this much-acclaimed troubadour. Lennon, who sang about a new world with no private property, left to his Japanese widow an estate valued at a staggering $250 million. In fact, in almost every world utopian scheme, from Karl Marx on, there is a chasm between the lyrical rhetoric meant to ensnare the masses and the personal lifestyles of the expositors and leaders of the planned utopia.

George Bush and John Lennon are not alone in championing a new world order. Consider the following words that have spanned decades, even centuries of history:

> The Colonel's [Colonel Edward Mandell House, aide to Woodrow Wilson] sole justification for preparing such a bath of blood for his countrymen was his hope of establishing a new world order of peace and security as a result.
>
> Walter Millis, *Road to War: America, 1914–1917*

> In an address to the International Platform Association at the Sheraton-Park Hotel, [New York Governor Nelson] Rockefeller called for the creation of a "new world order."
>
> *New York Times*, July 26, 1968

> National socialism will use its own revolution for the establishing of 'a new world order.'
>
> Adolf Hitler, cited in
> *The Occult and the Third Reich*

In short, the 'house of world order' will have to be built from the bottom up rather than from the top down. . . .

An end run around national sovereignty, eroding it piece by piece, will accomplish much more than the old fashioned assault.

> Richard N. Gardner, former deputy assistant secretary of state for international organizations under Presidents John F. Kennedy and Lyndon B. Johnson, in *Foreign Affairs,* April 1974

We must replace balance of power politics with world order politics.

> Jimmy Carter
> Democratic presidential candidate, 1976

It is necessary to establish a universal regime and empire over the whole world.

> Writings of the Illuminati, ca. 1780

We deplore the division of humankind on nationalistic grounds. We have reached a turning point in human history where the best option is to transcend the limits of national sovereignty and to move toward the building of a world community . . . a system of world law and world order based upon transnational federal government.

> *The Humanist Manifesto II* (1973)

Implacable Realities

A single thread runs from the White House to the State Department to the Council on Foreign Relations to the Trilateral Commission to secret societies to extreme New Agers. There must be a new world order. It must eliminate national sovereignty. There must be world government, a world police force, world courts, world banking and currency, and a world elite in charge of it all. To some there must be a complete redistribution of wealth; to others there must be an elimination of Christianity; to some extreme New Agers there must be the deaths of two or three billion people in the Third World by the end of this decade.

In an article on the new world order in the Summer 1991 edition of *SCP Journal,* Tal Brooke quotes Brock Chisolm, director of the United Nations World Health Organization, as making the following appalling conclusions:

> To achieve world government, it is necessary to remove from the minds of men their individualism, loyalty to family traditions, national patriotism, and religious dogmas.

Whatever fringe groups might say or believe, the core premise of a new world order is aptly summarized in the Rothschild publication, *The Economist,* in its cover story of June 28, 1991, entitled, "The World Order Changeth," which says:

> There should, however, be no illusion that a global police force run by a global democracy is feasible. Those who have carried the winning ideas to the top of the mountain, and now wish to spread them, will not allow this process to be vetoed by the semi-converted or by plain toughs. . . .
>
> And if that sounds painless, it is not. The mountaintop is thick with those who would rather not see trade that is liberal, aid that is too principled, or arms control that is too self denying. And America needs to remember that a willingness to involve others is not enough to make a collective world order work. *There must also be readiness to submit to it. If America really wants such an order, it will have to be ready to take its complaints to the GATT, finance the multilateral aid agencies, submit itself to the International Court, bow to some system to monitor arms exports, and make a habit of consulting the U.N.* (Emphasis added.)

But do Americans want the government of the United States to defer to the United Nations General Assembly before initiating an action it considers in this nation's best interest? Do they want to be taxed to support an international assistance agency? Do they want cases involving themselves or their families to be tried by world courts? Do they want to be citizens of the world instead of citizens of the United States?

Conversely, are Americans willing to be bound by the actions of the United Nations to condemn a nation, such as Israel, that might not be following the dictates of the new world order? For that matter, would they be willing to be drafted into an army by United Nations mandate to fight a war of its choosing?

Will the new world order usher in a glorious era of peace, or is it the beginning of a dictatorial world nightmare? This book will raise the troubling questions and, where possible, give some answers to those questions.

The Invisible Cord

As a broadcaster, an author, and a longtime follower of and participant in the political process, I have been an observer of world events for several decades and have known personally a considerable number of this nation's political and industrial leaders. It is clear to me, beyond a shadow of a doubt, that for decades there has been a continuity of policy and leadership in the United States that operates the same regardless of which nominee of the major political parties gains access to the White House.

It is relatively easy to trace the continuity of thought and purpose of our policy elites from Cecil Rhodes, whose fortune rested on African gold and diamonds; to the Federal Reserve Board; to Colonel E. M. House, the éminence grise of the Woodrow Wilson presidency; to the English Round Table; to the J. P. Morgan bank; to the Rockefellers and the Council on Foreign Relations in New York; to the powerful Carnegie, Rockefeller, and Ford Foundations; to the United Nations; to Henry Kissinger; to the Trilateral Commission; to Jimmy Carter; and finally to George Bush.

What is not easy to explain is why the concept of a new world order, taking as it does so many overtones from secret societies and the occult, could have been handed down and then carried forward in a purely natural progression for such an extended period of time.

Wealth does not explain it, for the people behind the concept have gained wealth beyond the dreams of avarice. Political power does not explain it, for all these players have reached the very pinnacles of power. Monopolistic capitalism does not explain it, because although one man or group of men may be seized with megalomania, the heirs and successors to the business soon forget the dreams of empire held by their ancestors and predecessors in order to enjoy the possessions at hand.

No, there has to be something more. There has to be some other power at work which has succeeded in molding and shaping United States public policy toward one clear goal—world government—from generation to successive generation. Some authors and researchers have pointed to the influence of the eighteenth-century elite group, the Illuminati. Others have pointed to the demonic "ascended masters" of the New Age religion—and still others have pointed to the world designs of a well-known but secret fraternal order. Some point to the greed of international banks, multinational corporations, and the vested aristocracy of the old and new world.

There are many suspects, but little consensus. Whichever is correct, it is my firm belief that the events of public policy are not the accidents and coincidences we are generally led to believe. They are planned. Further, I do not believe that normal men and women, if left to themselves, would spend a lifetime to form the world into a unified whole in order to control it after it had been so unified. No, impulses of that sort do not spring from the human heart, or for that matter from God's heart. They spring, instead, from the depth of something that is evil, neither well intentioned nor benevolent.

The Gulf Connection

As it happens, the recent war in the Persian Gulf served as the convenient backdrop for the most recent announcement of the arrival of a new world order. Despite the brilliant victory, there are troubling facts that raise very serious questions about the integrity of the origins of that war and its ultimate conclusions. Is it possible that the Gulf War was, in fact, a setup? Consider carefully the following irrefutable facts.

On August 2, 1990, Iraqi tanks and armored personnel carriers poured across the border into tiny Kuwait. The Iraqis then proceeded to kill, rape, burn, loot, and pillage the people and property of that hapless land.

The game begun in Kuwait by the ruthless dictator, Saddam Hussein, had been played out for centuries in the Middle East. The strong have always preyed on the weak. Had not the forces of Syria's Hafez Al Assad ruthlessly butchered twenty thousand members of the Muslim Brotherhood in the Syrian city of Hama? Didn't Assad launch a murderous tank and artillery battle against the predominantly Christian Lebanese city of two hundred thousand inhabitants called Zahle?

Didn't the streets of Beirut, once known as the "Paris of the Middle East," flow red with blood when shells launched by invading Syrian forces ripped into buildings, maiming and killing innocent women and children? Wasn't it true in Lebanon that Palestinians killed Christians and Christians killed Palestinians? Druses shelled both Christians and Palestinians, and Christians and Palestinians shelled Druses, and Syrian gunners indiscriminately shelled them all.

Indeed modern Saudi Arabia was formed as a nation only after the brutal military conquest of smaller sheikdoms by King Abdul Assiz Ibn Saud. Ibn Saud was feted by the world's leaders, not condemned by them. Was it not true that the great powers had all but ignored Iraq's territorial grab against Iran that set off the carnage that lasted for eight years and cost more than one million lives?

So why would Iraqi aggression against neighboring Kuwait be treated any differently by the world powers? In fact was it not true that April Glaspie, the United States ambassador to Iraq, had assured Saddam Hussein that Kuwait enjoyed no special defense treaty with the United States? Hussein must have taken note that on July 31, 1990, in testimony before a House Foreign Affairs Subcommittee on the Near East, Assistant Secretary of State John Kelly made it clear that there was no mutual defense treaty between the United States and Kuwait. His words were echoed in precise detail by Margaret Tutwiler, an official spokeswoman of the United States State Department, who assured a press conference that the United States had no special obligation to come to the defense of Kuwait. Washington sources told CBN News that in April 1990, John Kelly and another individual spoke with Secretary of State James Baker to warn him that America needed to send Saddam a strong warning, even accompanied by economic sanctions. Baker apparently agreed, but somehow the concept died.

Saddam Hussein knew that United States satellite reconnaissance had charted precisely the formations of Iraqi troops and armor on the Kuwaiti border, obviously in preparation for war. He calculated that if the United States objected to what he was planning, it had plenty of ways to communicate its displeasure. It used none of them! By words and by silence, the United States flashed Saddam Hussein a green light.

Soviet Involvement

But what of the other superpower, the Soviet Union? At least thirty-five hundred key Soviet military advisers were stationed in Iraq under the command of a high-ranking Soviet general officer, training Saddam's troops. Saddam was armed with Soviet weapons, from Scud missiles to MiG fighters. Iraq was a Soviet client state.

By invading Kuwait, Saddam was putting billions of dollars into the Soviet economy. The Soviet Union is the second-largest oil producer in the world, with an annual output of 10.5 million barrels per day. Kuwait in 1990 was producing 4 percent of the world's oil and had been fudging on the OPEC cartel's production and pricing guidelines. Saddam and the Soviets wanted a price of $22 per barrel, not the $16 to $18 price per barrel that had resulted from a worldwide glut of crude oil.

This uptick in the price of oil would be worth as much as $20 billion annually to the cash-starved Soviets. The invasion of Kuwait by Iraq would have given the Soviets fabulous gains at no risk. Can any thinking person believe that Saddam's Soviet advisers did not encourage him to invade Kuwait and raise oil prices?

By invading Kuwait, Saddam could wipe out $10 billion of Iraq's debt incurred during his war with Iran, steal Kuwait's gold reserves, control the vast Kuwaiti oil fields, and raise the price of each barrel of Iraq's oil production at the same time.

He would also dominate almost one-quarter of the world's oil production with which he could have held hostage the economy of the entire world. Given this dictator's overwhelming military superiority in the Gulf, he then could either invade Saudi Arabia and the other oil-producing nations in the Gulf, or he could bend them to do his bidding.

Saddam Hussein, therefore, was clearly not just one more in a long line of Arab bullies trying to pick up some fast booty. Any junior analyst at the CIA, the Defense Department, or the State Department could have seen the threat that an invasion of Kuwait by Iraq posed to the economic security of the Free World.

The prospect of a single madman controlling commodity prices, energy prices, manufacturing costs, inflation, deflation, unemployment, in fact, the economic and political well-being of every human being on this planet is, frankly, too horrible to contemplate. On the face of it, that was the certain outcome of an undisputed, successful military takeover of Kuwait by Iraq.

Why then did the United States government not warn Saddam away from his course of folly? Why on three occasions did we encourage him? Why did we not send a clear message to the Soviets that any attempt to manipulate world oil prices through Iraqi military force in the Persian Gulf would be viewed as an act of hostility against the United States? Why did the admirals, the generals, the scientists, the economists, the politicians, and the spies working for the entire United States government not take any action to head off a military adventure that could have destabilized the world?

Why, in essence, did our government treat the entire incident as if it involved just one more desert bandit attacking a wealthy merchant's camel caravan?

Hidden Motives

Could it have been that the wrong signals were sent to Saddam because powerful people wanted a situation that was so obviously dangerous to the entire world that all nations would join together to deal with it? A situation, indeed, that would cause the nations of the world to forget for a time their own claims of sovereignty in order to submerge their interests into that of a worldwide authority such as the United Nations? A situation which seemed on its face very ominous, yet which was certain of military victory by the massed armed forces of the world?

However formidable Iraq could have become with nuclear weapons and the world's oil wealth, it certainly was not that formidable on August 2, 1990, when the invasion of Kuwait began. There was a limited Iraqi navy, no Iraqi submarines, few modern aircraft in the Iraqi air force, no Iraqi spy satellites, no Iraqi AWACS spy planes, no Iraqi nuclear weapons, few Iraqi high-tech communications, and few truly motivated fighting men in Iraq's battalions. The United Nations forces had a leisurely six months to assemble a vast array of the most sophisticated battle gear on earth without any real threat of naval or air bombardment. Without in any way denigrating the brilliant leadership of our forces or their discipline and courage, the "One-Hundred-Hour War" in the desert was a clearly predictable turkey shoot.

Why then was Saddam Hussein given a green light by the United States to begin a war during which his forces would be demolished? Why permit a war to begin which cost over $50 billion and risked the lives of our fighting men and women, when a clear warning and a show of force probably would have kept the entire thing from starting?

Perhaps the leaders of America were preoccupied with other, more pressing matters. Perhaps they truly did not understand the geopolitical significance of Middle Eastern oil. Perhaps key data were kept from them. Or perhaps some very powerful being or some very powerful group, somewhere, wanted it all to happen just the way it did to set the stage for something that indeed transcended Saddam Hussein, or Iraq, or Kuwait, or even Middle East oil.

For out of the War in the Gulf emerged, full blown, what President George Bush and General Brent Scowcroft, his national security adviser, have proudly proclaimed as the new world order. In fact, our president has said publicly that the fate of Kuwait was not the main issue. Launching the new world order *was* the main thing.

He told the Congress and the nation on January 29, 1991:

> What is at stake is more than one small country, it is a big idea—a new world order, where diverse nations are drawn together in common cause to achieve the universal aspirations of mankind: peace and security, freedom, and the rule of law. Such is a world worthy of our struggle, and worthy of our children's future!

The Coming Journey

This book is written in an attempt to explain to each reader what this new world order is all about, how it came to be, who its advocates are, and, most important of all, what the meaning of the new world order will be to you and your family. Especially, I will show how the new world order, if allowed to proceed as planned, will radically alter the life you lead and the freedoms you now enjoy.

Finally, this book will place the origin, meaning, and ultimate destiny of the new world order within the clear purview of Bible prophecy, so that you can understand what God has to say about the one-world government that from 1990 onward may trace its public and official debut back to the Tigris-Euphrates Valley, where the first known civilization was born and from whence mankind was scattered because it had rebelled against God, and into which was born Abraham—the man whose seed was appointed by God to redeem the world.

That is the journey we are now set upon.

2

The Cry for Change

In 1984 and 1985, our television screens were filled with images of emaciated Ethiopian men, women, and children, near comatose from starvation, flies crawling over their faces, and their eyes staring blankly from skeleton-like sockets. The world was shocked into action to send relief. Hollywood megastars donated their time for the record "We Are the World," and a huge world satellite rock music festival called "LiveAid" raised tens of millions of dollars for emergency relief to Ethiopia.

Six years later, almost 6 million people in Ethiopia face imminent starvation, and most of the world no longer cares.

But the starvation has spread to Sudan and into Somalia, where a vicious civil war—as was the case in Ethiopia—has prevented the shipment of food to the people. A recent report in Congress declared that a disaster of "biblical proportions" was taking place in the Horn of Africa. Yet the rival factions fight on, the people are suffering unimagined agony, and the world looks away—uncomfortable at being reminded of the tragedy.

Simultaneously with the famine in Africa, a killer typhoon struck Bangladesh, that poverty-stricken country carved out of India and

15

Pakistan, in the spring of 1991. Flooding was so bad that a hundred thousand people lost their lives, a million were rendered homeless, and the entire population, where the per capita income is barely $179 per year, was pushed deeper into grinding poverty.

Surely the hearts of those who suffer in what is known as the "Third World" and the hearts of those in affluent countries who care must cry out for change. Something—anything—to make life more bearable. In fact, some urgent change is needed just to let them live.

As we look at the world around us, we see such an enormous disparity between the quality of life in the northern and southern nations. On the one hand, we see nations like the United States, Europe, and certain Asian nations in the Northern Hemisphere enjoying a high standard of wealth and prosperity; on the other hand, we see grinding poverty in Africa, Central and South America, India, and other nations in the Southern Hemisphere and the tropical regions.

While one segment of the world's population enjoys an incredible abundance, and the very rich among us enjoy extravagant excess, an equal or greater segment is living in absolute squalor with famine, political chaos, civil unrest, personal cruelty, and environmental disaster.

The Specter of Death

From the Sudan and Ethiopia in the Southern Sahara, and from Northern Mexico to Argentina, we see the darkest images of human suffering. With the exception of South Africa and nations such as Tunisia on the Mediterranean Coast, there isn't a single politically stable and fiscally solvent nation on the entire continent of Africa. In fact, the entire economic output of all 450 million people in sub-Saharan Africa barely equals that of tiny Belgium.

In Latin America and the Caribbean, we find nations such as Nicaragua and Haiti where the per capita income is at a misery level of $330 a year. In Guatemala, which has had its share of revolution and trouble, I saw people living on garbage dumps, competing with the vultures to get to the refuse.

In Guatemala City, I was personally giving out relief supplies to some of the eight thousand people who stood in line for hours in the broiling hot sun at the city dump just to get a bag of rice and beans which CBN's Operation Blessing was giving to each of them. This is life well below the subsistence level. The mayor of Guatemala City told me later that if his citizens could just move from "misery to poverty" it would be a great improvement.

Most of us cannot even imagine this kind of degradation. It is impossible for even the poorest American to conceive of the near-subsistence poverty that exists in nations like this all around the globe. Tens of millions of people of every race and culture are living in stark, dehumanizing poverty. They are not on strike; they will do anything for work. They're not screaming political slogans and ideological rhetoric; their lives are much too hard for theories and dreams. Ideologies are the luxuries of the privileged classes.

All the extreme political ideologies in the world—whether they come from the extreme right or the extreme left—have come from the privileged classes. Those who want to determine how the poor should live have never endured or even seen real poverty. Socialism in Britain was a creature of the aristocracy. Communism was the brainchild of German-Jewish intellectuals. Grand ideas don't come from the slums, they come from idealists and dreamers.

The poor in Africa, Asia, and Latin America are so beaten down they don't have time for idealistic theories. When the poor rise up it's because there's an upper-class reformer somewhere stirring them up.

The Poor of This World

Peru and other South American nations are being savaged by cholera at this very moment. Cholera is called the disease of the poor. The people contract it by eating fish from polluted waters and by washing their clothes and drawing their drinking water from garbage-laden rivers and streams.

In most of these places, people are pouring raw, untreated sewage into the streams and into the oceans, and disease breeds there.

That is precisely how the Black Death started in Europe in the fourteenth century. There is hardly a single place in all of South America where the water is safe to drink.

In Egypt, halfway around the globe, the water is absolutely filthy, full of liver flukes and amoebas. People are wasted by intestinal disease and dysentery. This and the other diseases that breed in the rivers and streams and dumpsites spread contagion throughout the land and just sap the life out of the people. Ironically, natives who have developed some tolerance to the conditions may live for years with these diseases, while infected foreigners often die within days.

Nevertheless, the mortality rate is very high, especially among the children in these countries. The children succumb quickly to dysentery, and they are totally dehydrated by it. I have been told that just a little sugar water from a pure source can keep a child alive, but the natives have been told to give the children formula mixed with the local drinking water, and the water is so bad it is killing the little children in the hundreds.

Hopeless poverty combines with crushing monetary debt in these Third World nations, and this is compounded by ongoing environmental rape. The most critical environmental problem in tropical countries today is desertification, which comes from cutting down the forests. The rain forests are being decimated in Brazil; the beautiful hardwood forests of Southeast Asia are being systematically plundered. The ominous growth of the Sahel region in Africa is gradually turning the entire northern half of that continent into desert at the rate of eight or nine miles a year.

It is a vicious cycle. The poor need fuel to cook and to provide warmth. They cut down trees because trees don't cost them anything. Some years ago I visited an Afghan refugee camp in an area of Pakistan called Baluchistan. The entire landscape was so pockmarked that it resembled the surface of the moon. My guide informed me that the refugees cut down all the trees and shrubs for fire and shelter, then they dug up all the roots and burned them as well.

The Unending Cycle

Of course the poor neither know nor care about ecology. When the trees go, the topsoil also goes. When the topsoil goes, not only does the food supply drop sharply, but mud slides wipe out houses, silt up rivers, and damage the water. Then, without trees, the ambient temperature rises, and natural wildlife and plant life disappear. So the people, now facing starvation, move on to start the cycle again.

I lunched several years ago in Jerusalem with the assistant minister of commerce of Israel. He was an ardent scuba diver. After Israel took over the Sinai Peninsula, he used to go down to the Red Sea where he took great pleasure in exploring the exotic plant and animal life in those waters. He told me how the Israeli Ministry of the Interior had done everything it could during the occupation of the Sinai to preserve the natural habitat of the coral and the various tropical fish in the Red Sea.

But when the Israeli government gave back the Sinai, he said, the unlettered Egyptian fishermen in the Red Sea would position their boats over schools of fish and toss sticks of dynamite into the water. The edible fish that floated to the top after the resulting explosions would be sold. Everything else was wasted. As anyone knows, that is the most destructive thing they could have done. The explosions destroyed the coral, decimated entire species of tropical fish, and demolished the food chain and the environment of all the closely interdependent aquatic life in that area for generations. And all the delicate and precarious natural environment of that ancient body of water has been changed forever.

Gorgeous, priceless species of fish—which, incidentally, are totally inedible—and the beautiful natural paradise that existed there were devastated by these thoughtless marauders. Why? Because they were ignorant of the repercussions of what they were doing. They had no respect for the environment or the importance of preserving their natural heritage. They had no idea what the effects of pollution and man-made destruction of these natural treasures would be.

But like the ignorant woodcutters, these "fishermen" were pushing their nation further into poverty. Not only were they ruining the food chain and destroying the breeding grounds of edible species of fish, they were destroying a major source of hard currency for their economy.

The Red Sea waters were a mecca for European and American tourists because they offered probably the finest scuba diving environment in the world. As is the case of the Red Sea fishermen, the poachers of Africa injured long-range tourism by their slaughter of elephants and rhinos for ivory. Such short-term thinking, ignorance, and selfish greed have effectively sealed the economic fate of millions of innocent people in the Third World.

But are such men who poach and pillage the only ones guilty of wanton destruction? Certainly not. Things just as ignorant and destructive are taking place in this country right now. And this concerns not just the destruction of wildlife, but also human life.

For example, it is absolutely incredible to me that United States tobacco companies are exporting cigarettes to these same Third World countries by the ton. In this country we're learning about the dangers of tobacco, about lung cancer and emphysema. Every day thousands of people are quitting this deadly habit. But we export millions of tons of tobacco products to poverty-stricken nations, guaranteeing more death, disease, and suffering. The trade in tobacco is every bit as bad as the opium trade in China at the turn of the century, and, ultimately, I suspect, no less costly in terms of human life.

Who's to Blame?

Beyond the threat of environmental rape, we have also had nuclear terror hanging over our heads ever since World War II. When will some superpower confrontation take place? And if not a superpower, when will some madman like Mohamar Qaddafi steal a portable device; or when will a dictator like Saddam Hussein succeed in building his own nuclear arsenal with which he can hold the rest of the world hostage?

Already we have had wars and revolutions on every continent. There have been communist-inspired revolutions in Asia, Africa, and Latin America virtually continuously since 1945. There have been military coups and countercoups in the Sudan, Uganda, Ghana, Liberia, Zimbabwe (Rhodesia), Mozambique, and Angola, along with socialist-type takeovers in places like Tanzania. We have a silent war going on now in North Africa, carried out by Qaddafi against the nation of Chad on his southern border. Obviously the racial strife of white versus black and Zulu verses ANC is not over in South Africa. And you can project a rising level of violence all around the world.

Consider Southeast Asia and the terrible struggles that have been going on there during the last thirty years. First in Vietnam, then in Laos and Cambodia, and then along the Cambodian border with Thailand. There have been revolutions and counter-revolutions in Burma, and continuous political instability throughout the region.

There have been problems of equal or greater magnitude in Central and South America with communist-led revolutions in Cuba, Chile, and Peru. Most recently we have witnessed the bloodbaths in Nicaragua and El Salvador. Sometimes it seems our world is bleeding to death, and everywhere people are crying out for solutions to the problem of war.

Who'll Stop the Rain?

How do we stop terrorism? How do we stop the killing of innocent civilians? How do we stop the Arab-Israeli conflict that has been so bloody in the Middle East, or the factional killing in Lebanon? The Iraqis have been fighting the Iranians. The Soviets have been fighting the Afghans. Armed conflict is breaking out in Yugoslavia between Croats, Slovenes, and Serbs. Tension is building between Czechs and Slovaks, and between Rumanians and their Hungarian minority.

More ominous for us all are the heightened tensions and conflicts in the Soviet Union between the central government and the republics of Latvia, Estonia, and Lithuania. There is a growing protest for secession in Russia, the Ukraine, and the Muslim republics. Will the Soviet Union disintegrate in the next couple of years, or will the forces of reaction and repression begin a crackdown that will bring back memories of the terror last known under Joseph Stalin?

Consider the age-old tensions between India and Pakistan, the internal warfare between the traditional Hindu ruling caste in India and the Sikhs, Tamils, and Sinhalese, all fighting on separate fronts for autonomy and independence. In the last decade the world has witnessed the deaths of three key political leaders in that country, including the plane crash that killed Rajid Gandhi, being groomed at that time for political office, the assassination of Mrs. Indira Gandhi, and the recent assassination of Rajiv Gandhi, Mrs. Gandhi's youngest son, in May 1991.

Further north, we have seen the rape of Nepal and Tibet by Communist China. The world is being torn apart by war and confusion and repression. Some 2 billion people have been under the heel of communism. We have seen the unstoppable ravages of poverty, war, and pestilence.

We have seen typhoons, cyclones, tornadoes, hurricanes, floods, and earthquakes in every corner of the globe. Of course there were terrible civil wars in Bangladesh, Biafra, and Nigeria. For forty years there has been carnage and destruction, both man-made and natural.

The cry rings out from every nation in a single voice, "Isn't there a better way?" Isn't there some way we can ensure justice, peace, law and order, an orderly approach to the environment, and greater equity between the wealth of rich and poor nations?

When we see such agony, is there any wonder that people applaud the concept of world order? It seems there has to be some forum for universal justice. There must be something we can do. The world tried after World War I with the League of Nations, which was shunned by the United States. Then we finally established the United Nations in 1945, in the wake of World War II, but that organization has been notoriously ineffective.

Now in the 1990s our leaders are telling us that the better way has already begun. But has it really?

Feeding on the Poor

Unfortunately, in these Third World countries there are not only unavoidable problems, but overt oppression of the people by their own leaders. A close look reveals people like Lopez Portillo, the former president of Mexico, who reportedly enriched himself by as much as $3 billion. Ferdinand Marcos of the Philippines may have looted as much as $2 billion from the treasury of his country. The leaders of African nations have reputedly looted billions, and we have recently read that Saddam Hussein and his family may already have helped themselves to as much as $10 billion from the beleaguered people of Iraq.

Despite incredible poverty, Third World leaders continue to enrich themselves at the expense of the poor. In Mexico, upwards of 60 percent of the nation's foreign debt under previous administrations went back out of the country in so-called expatriate remittances. The same is true of Argentina and Brazil. Money that has been given in aid to the poor has been put into the hands of the wealthy few and passed right back out to the international banks in Switzerland, the United States, the Cayman Islands, or pumped into real estate in South Florida.

The amounts of these "expatriate remittances" are huge. The United States ambassador to Argentina told me when I met with him in Buenos Aires that the figure of "flight capital" in Argentina was $27 billion. In Guatemala I learned that under the administration of President Lopez Garcia, 30 percent of the price of every public works project went directly to the president and his cronies. In the Philippines, I was told by a Chinese property developer in Manila that a surcharge of 10 percent of the cost of every major private building project had to be paid as a bribe to a relative of Imelda Marcos, the wife of then President Ferdinand Marcos.

Third World debt stands at some $1 trillion, and it is a dagger pointing at the financial heart of the Western banking system. Most of these loans are a joke. The attitude of the newly enriched leaders is simple, "If you were stupid enough to loan us the money, why do you think we are stupid enough to pay it back?"

In Indonesia there was a terrible scandal involving the Pertamina Oil Company concerning bribery, looting, graft, and the loss of billions of dollars. In state-run companies in the Third World, the damage from gross mismanagement and overstaffing probably exceeds the damage from venality and looting. These problems are reaching epidemic proportions all over the world; so the poor stay poor and the rich grow even richer. And when you add to that the fallout of the 1973 oil crisis, it means that the people of the poor nations have had the blood sucked out of them for the better part of the past two decades, and most of the time by their own selfish and incompetent leaders.

These poor nations cannot pay these escalating debt charges, so they go deeper and deeper into debt to the international banks. At times debt service on their loans may equal their entire revenue from external trade. Now because of their misuse of previous credit, no new credit is available to them. There seems to be no way out of it for most of them. At least to human eyes they appear to be hopeless. They are caught in a constant cycle of runaway inflation, degradation, despair, and rapidly compounding debt. Something needs to come along to clean the slate.

The Situation in Zaire

I visited the nation of Zaire in July 1991 at the invitation of its president, Mobutu Sese Seko. Zaire, formerly known as the Belgian Congo, occupies a strategic area of Central Africa three times the size of Texas. With 35 million inhabitants barely existing on a per capita annual income of $150, Zaire is a microcosm of the troubles facing the entire Third World.

The Congo, once the private possession of King Leopold of Belgium, was granted independence from Belgium on June 30, 1960. Parliamentary elections were held in April 1960, and a pro-communist, Patrice Lumumba, was named prime minister.

Peace lasted just one week. On July 5, 1960, the army mutinied, and political authority broke down. Belgium intervened on July 10, and on July 11, Moise Tshombe set up a separate government in the mineral-rich Shaba district, then called Katanga.

When Patrice Lumumba turned to the Soviets for help, the United States CIA chose an army colonel, Joseph Mobutu, to take over the government, expel all Soviet diplomats, and imprison Lumumba. Lumumba later died under mysterious circumstances and was proclaimed an honored martyr by the Soviets.

Mobutu then returned the government to civilian hands, but from February 1961 until 1965 the nation was racked by a violent civil war that seriously damaged its economic infrastructure. The former colonel (now lieutenant general), Joseph Mobutu once again took control of the government and declared himself Mobutu Sese Seko, the "Guide."

Since that time Zaire has had one party in power, one national leader, and except for a murderous rebellion in Katanga in 1977, relative peace and security. Mobutu, for all practical purposes, is the supreme leader of the nation—enjoying a parliament from his own party, choosing the cabinet, choosing judges, ruling by decree if parliament is not in session, and leading the army.

Mobutu Sese Seko rules as an African chief, regarding the people somewhat like his family and the wealth of the nation as his own, to keep or disperse to friends at his pleasure. Published reports place his accumulated personal wealth at $5 billion—equal to the annual gross national product of the nation of Zaire. He admits to a more modest $50 million, but his lifestyle is much grander than a mere $50 million would permit.

During the past twenty-five years, almost all European or other white technicians and managers have been expelled or have left the country voluntarily. Since only a handful of college-trained specialists remain, the infrastructure, services, agriculture, and goods-producing sectors are in shambles.

The nation owes $8 billion and has defaulted once again on its latest attempt at debt restructuring organized by the International Monetary Fund (IMF). Inflation is running at 1,000 percent. There is not enough food. Telephone communication with the outside world is almost impossible. There are only a hundred thousand automobiles for 35 million inhabitants. Health care and education are in a state of crisis.

The city streets are pockmarked and filthy. In the countryside the eighty-three thousand miles of roads left by the Belgian colonial government have deteriorated to a sparse twelve thousand miles. Farmers in the interior have no way to transport their crops to the cities, which are experiencing critical food shortages.

A Collapsing System

Before independence, Zaire was an agricultural powerhouse—a net exporter of rice, corn, sugar, cocoa, palm oil, cotton, and coffee. Now it must import large quantities of rice, corn, soybeans, and other food to feed its people.

I visited one agricultural complex that had originally been managed by some Israelis. Well-built and well-equipped chicken houses were standing in neat rows, completely empty, without evidence of a single chicken. Eighteen years before they had housed at a single time 270,000 chickens and had sent up to a million chickens each year for domestic consumption into the capital city. Then, for political reasons, the Israeli managers were deported. There was no one to take their place. Now Zaire imports most of its edible chickens from faraway Belgium, and domestic poultry production is virtually nonexistent.

I visited an inefficient canning factory turning out tiny cans of tomato paste. We were told that the tomatoes used by this small operation had to be imported from Italy. We visited an egg production operation where the chickens were falling ill because of guano disease. The reason? No one could fix or replace a one-half horsepower motor that was there to drain the chicken droppings into septic tanks outside the building where the chickens were located. The manager of the complex told me he had to haul water for the chickens in a small trailer. Since the facility was located adjoining a river, I asked the obvious question, "Why don't you drill a well for your water?" His answer reveals the essence of Zaire's problems, "No one has come to dig a well for us."

Prior to 1960, this nation had one of the most highly developed and diversified economies in sub-Saharan Africa. It was, and is, unbelievably rich in national resources. It has fertile soil and multiple growing seasons. Sixty-seven types of tropical fruit grow in the country. Delicious mangoes and papayas grow wild throughout the land. Virtually every known edible variety of vegetable can be grown somewhere between Zaire's lowlands and the inland mountain ranges.

The nation has abundant deposits of iron, copper, nickel, tin, cobalt, gold, diamonds, rare earths, and oil. It has between 40 and 50 percent of all the hardwoods in Africa. It has 13 percent of all the hydroelectric capacity in the entire world. Yet with all that wealth, there is a budget out of balance, a $400 million balance-of-payments deficit, and a defaulted debt of $8 billion.

Keeping Up Standards

When someone discovers the answer to how Zaire got to where it is today, they will also find the answer to the riddle of poverty in the Third World.

First, we must remember that during colonialism the wealth of the colonies was used for the benefit of the mother country, the white plantation owners, and the white traders and business men. To be sure, there were roads and communication and clinics and law and order. But the native populations were often not given opportunities for the university educations and practical apprenticeships needed to develop business managers, civil servants, health professionals, agricultural specialists, mining engineers, finance specialists, marketing experts, and the host of other skills that a complex society demands.

In the United States there are in excess of 14 million students in colleges and universities, and at least 70 million Americans have some college training. Out of Zaire's population of 35 million, only a relative handful have university training. (There are now eight thousand

Zairians who have graduated from American colleges and universities.) The technical base below the top levels is woefully inadequate.

Emerging nations, like Zaire, have been racked by bitter warfare between rival tribes, or communist insurgences, or liberation movements against communists, or army-led coups, or uprisings against colonial structures, or strife between religious groups. Each civil war or insurgency is devastating to the material well-being of the nation involved and often those nations that adjoin it as well.

But war and the lack of education are not the only problems. There is a fierce desire for racial independence that seeks to rid the nation of every vestige of those perceived as oppressors. Too soon they learn the truth of Shakespeare's words, "The fault, dear Brutus, is not in the stars but in ourselves." Or in the words of Pogo, the sage of the swamps, "We have met the enemy and he is us."

In 1973, President Mobutu announced measures to place all firms in the hands of Zairians. Bigger firms were nationalized. Following the decree, commerce was devastated. Although the decree was rescinded in 1976 to restore ownership as before, the damage had been done. Many businesses were either in poor condition or had closed. But there were other assaults inflicted by the government of Zaire on its own economy.

Following the course of many Third World nations, the government of Zaire tried to appease its rapidly growing urban population by placing price controls on agricultural products. Price controls on food had an opposite effect from that intended. Farmers stopped growing crops and moved to the cities, which meant more demand, less food, and higher market prices than before.

The devastation that nationalization, socialism, and economic mismanagement has brought about in Africa was summed up in this candid admission by the former socialist leader of Tanzania, Julius Nyerere, "We have ruined the plantations so badly that their former owners would not want them if we gave them back to them at no charge."

The unlettered and untrained leaders of Zaire, like those of other Third World countries, appeared to the salesmen from more developed nations like pigeons waiting to be plucked. They came with a bagful of monumental development projects, ill-conceived public works, and sophisticated weapons. By the salesmen's sides were government banks, private banks, regional banks, and world banks willing to shovel billions of dollars into projects of questionable value and lacking in fiscal controls.

Financial Ruin

The magnitude of the projects and the lax fiscal controls of the leaders were a breeding ground for fraud. Who could blame an official with a wretched salary and little business sophistication for occasionally dipping into the torrent of money passing before him?

But once the deals were done, the commissions and bribes paid, the buildings built, and the machinery in place, no one stayed around to show the people how to make everything operate well or profitably.

From then on they were to depend on the vagaries of the world commodities markets to service huge debts and operate their governments. From that point there quickly followed disappointing earnings and frequently defaulted loans. Then there was no credit for repairs, replacement parts, and other necessary services.

With its back to the wall because of a deteriorating situation that was primarily of its own making, the government of Zaire decided to print the money it needed. They did this to such an extent that during my visit I learned that the local currency on the black market had depreciated about eight thousand times against the dollar. A modest lunch for two that used to cost about Z29 now cost Z235,000. It goes without saying that the soaring price of food and the other necessities of life brought the population to riots, demonstrations, and possible revolt.

A new program of participatory democracy and privatization is being put into place in Zaire. Religious expression is encouraged by the government. Foreign investors are being offered undreamed of concessions. It is much too early to tell whether gradual reform will succeed, or whether the country will disintegrate into warring factions. It seemed to me that only a spiritual revival and leadership by a strong economic Czar working under a powerful transitional head of state (like General August Pinochet of Chile) would restore the economy sufficiently for democracy to take root and flourish. If not, with no strong, reliable center, the entire nation will fall apart. Only time will tell what the ultimate outcome will be in Zaire. Anyone who visits that potentially wonderful land comes away with a clear conviction—something must be done to give these people hope.

One World Currency

Two things relating to the main subject of this book surfaced while our group was visiting Zaire. Although there were no phone lines or telefax links between Zaire and the rest of the world, when the group vice-president of CBN's international division, Michael Little, presented an American Express card to guarantee our hotel bill, an amazing thing happened.

The hotel clerk in Kinshasa, Zaire, inserted Michael's credit card into a standard verification machine that requested a search of a databank in Brussels, which in turn searched data records in New York. Within two minutes from the initiation of the process, the credit verification and credit limits had been received back in Kinshasa from New York.

If plastic money can be accepted or rejected within two minutes from New York to a broken-down city in Central Africa, can any of us doubt the truth expressed in the Book of Revelation that all credit could one day be controlled by a central one-world financial authority and that no one could buy or sell without its approval. As we will discuss in later chapters, it is abundantly clear that a one-world credit system, a one-world currency, and a one-world central bank has been the centerpiece of all significant planning for the new world order.

Of lesser significance was the seeming unwillingness of United States AID officials to address solutions to Zaire's most obvious and pressing economic problem, agricultural self-sufficiency. The United States government, on the other hand, is more than willing to loan money at interest to Zaire to purchase, under what is called Public Law 480, the surplus corn, rice, and soybeans grown by American farmers.

Belgium not only does not help Zaire become self-sufficient in poultry production, it actually dumps chickens on the market in Zaire at prices cheaper than what it costs the farmers of Zaire to raise chickens inside their own country.

It is obviously dangerous to generalize from fragmentary information, but I believe that neither Europe nor the United States is anxious to have Zaire become a net exporter of agricultural products in competition with their own farmers. Even widespread sales of American grain on credit at low prices, while appearing to be a humanitarian gesture, actually tend to depress agricultural productivity in a Third World country.

Maybe the troubles of Africa, the Soviet Union, and other Third World countries happened because of ignorance, corruption, and socialism. But it is also fair, I believe, for us to ask ourselves whether, in order to prepare for the new world order, powerful international economic interests have pushed the nations of Africa prematurely into freedom so that their faltering steps into socialism would in turn ruin their agriculture to such a degree that they would not be able to challenge the agriculture of the world's leaders, and in turn their vast mineral riches could one day be had for a song.

And we also must ask why, with all of sub-Saharan Africa in economic shambles, has the political left mounted such an unremitting campaign to bring about the same chaos in the only vibrantly healthy economy on the African continent—South Africa? In fact, is there not a possibility that the Wall Street bankers, who have so enthusiastically financed Bolshevism in the Soviet Union since 1917, did so not for the purpose of promoting world communism but for the purpose of saddling the potentially rich Soviet Union with a totally wasteful and inefficient system that in turn would force the Soviet government to be dependent on Western bankers for its survival?

Will indeed the new world order be a mechanism to enslave, control, and loot vast portions of the world's populations, rather than a mechanism to give them economic self-sufficiency and freedom?

Who's Paying the Bills?

From a different perspective, there are also some who wonder how the biggest banks in the United States, in concert with our government, could have poured out billions upon billions of dollars to failing communist governments and crooked Third World dictators who had no intention of paying us back. Surely we knew that hundreds of billions of that loan money was leaving those nations and that the loan proceeds would never be used for their intended purpose.

Now that it has been done, will the American taxpayers be asked to make the banks financially whole? Only a few Americans are aware that under the Monetary Control Act of 1980, the Federal Reserve Board of the United States has the authority to issue United States dollars in exchange for the debt securities of any nation for any purpose, including, of course, repaying United States banks.

Was the debt problem of Third World countries something that happened accidentally as part of the long wave economic cycle? Was it an attempt by the lenders to dominate and control these people? Or has there been a deliberate attempt to weaken America's financial strength by improvident lending so that it would enter meekly into the one-world government of the new world order?

Whatever the economic causes, we see a world that is bleeding, crying out for relief, for justice, for a chance for normal human existence. We all want a better world.

But like the line in the popular song of a few years ago, "Looking for Love in All the Wrong Places," are we looking for something that is too good to be true, or for that matter, something that could turn out to be false and dangerous? Are we looking in all the wrong places for the answers to the world's dilemmas?

Particularly, we must ask ourselves if the internationalists, the banking and industrial complex, the European socialists, and their allies are truly desirous of establishing a world order to help the poor, to end wars, to balance budgets, and to give the little guy a better world for himself and his children. Or are these advocates of the new world order really seeking global control of the world's money, natural resources, and military power so that they can establish themselves, whether the people like it or not, as the dominant elite to determine the type of world in which we all will live?

The moving spirit of the Trilateral Commission, the mentor of former President Jimmy Carter (later his national security adviser) and the leading advocate of a new world order, Zbigniew Brezinski, had this to say in his book, *Between Two Ages*, written in 1970, about his vision of the new society:

> [T]he gradual shaping of a community of the developed nations would be a realistic expression of our emerging global consciousness; concentration on disseminating scientific and technological information would reflect a more functional approach to man's problems; both the foregoing would help to encourage the spread of a more personalized rational humanist outlook that would gradually replace the institutionalized religious, ideological, and intensely national perspectives that have dominated modern history.

This does not sound to me like a concept for democratic freedom to meet the needs of the poor and downtrodden. It sounds much more like the command society of socialism or communism. Since the Council on Foreign Relations and the Trilateral Commission are the dominant force espousing a new world order, and since President George Bush has not only been a member of both organizations, but has surrounded himself with many of their members, it will be appropriate in a later chapter to focus on what the Council on Foreign Relations is, what its vision of the world order is, and what it means to you.

In the following chapters I would like to put some perspective on these issues by briefly reviewing the historical record. In order to judge the events of the past half century with any clarity of vision, it will be important to see how the map of the world was laid out and how it has changed over time. In that light, then, we will be prepared to examine the political and economic challenges of our own time in the context of the old world order, the age of transition, and the utopian dreams that have led us to this moment.

3

The Old World Order

P RINTED ON THE REVERSE SIDE OF EVERY United States one-dollar bill is what is called the Great Seal of the United States. This seal was adopted by Congress in 1782.

Both faces of the seal are printed on the currency. One shows the American eagle with an olive branch of peace in one claw and thirteen arrows of war in the other. The second face of the seal depicts an unfinished pyramid, above which is an eye set in a blaze of glory. At the base of the pyramid are inscribed the Roman numerals MDCCLXXVI, or 1776. Overarching the pyramid are the Latin words "Annuit Coeptis," loosely translated as "He looks favorably on our endeavor," and below the pyramid is the Latin phrase, "Novus Ordo Seclorum," a line by the poet Virgil, meaning a "new order of the ages," or *a new world order.*

The designer of the great seal was Charles Thompson, a member of the Masonic order who served as secretary to the Continental Congress. This pyramid has special meaning for Masons, even as crystals and "pyramid power" today hold occultic significance for followers of the so-called New Age movement.

To some, the "all-seeing eye" represents divine providence. To others it does not represent the God of the Bible, as some think, but the eye of an ancient Egyptian deity, Osiris, who is revered in the secret high ceremonies and sacred rites of the Masonic Order. I will review some of these beliefs and practices of high-degree Masons and how their "mystery cult" figures into the new world order in a later chapter.

However, the pyramid shown on the seal is not complete, thus indicating that the task of nation building had not been accomplished. Thus, the implication for Thompson and others was that under the watchful eye of Osiris, the endeavor begun in 1776 would, according to their secret Masonic rituals, bring forth a new world order.

But a "new order of the ages" in relation to which old world order? Was it to be *new* in relation to the old monarchies of the time, or in regard to the old aristocratic ideas of nobility? Was it new in regard to human rights and freedom? Was it new in relation to the old idea of private ownership of property? Or did the "new order of the ages" have a double meaning?

Is it possible that a select few had a plan, revealed in the great seal adopted at the founding of the United States, to bring forth, not the nation that our founders and champions of liberty desired, but a totally different world order under a mystery religion designed to replace the old Christian world order of Europe and America?

The More Things Change

From 1782 to the present day, the call for a new world order continued against a backdrop of radically different times and places. The agricultural society of 1782 was obviously different from that of 1848, when the Industrial Revolution blossomed, yet Karl Marx published his *Communist Manifesto* and called for his own version of a new world order in that year.

The world of 1917 differed from both 1782 and 1848, yet Colonel Edward House and Woodrow Wilson called for a new world order in 1917. The world in 1938 differed from that of 1917, yet Adolf

Hitler called for his new world order in 1938. And the world in 1968 differed from the world of 1938, yet Nelson Rockefeller called for his new world order in 1968.

Indeed the world has changed many times during two hundred years. The forms of government are different. The quantity and distribution of wealth and privilege are different. The power of individual nations and alliances of nations is different. Communications are vastly different among people, and, if in scientific achievement our world is light-years ahead of the world of just fifty years ago, how much more scientifically advanced is it than the world of two hundred years ago?

Every generation represents a new world order. The life and customs and mores of the world are constantly undergoing change. Old things die; new things are born. This common-sense observation may explain in part why the noninitiated among us are somewhat baffled when certain elites tell us that they are bringing us a new world order.

But given the clearly observable reality of change and renewal, how can we account for the fact that for over two hundred years a small group, their spiritual successors, and their converts have labored ceaselessly to bring us what we thought we already had—a renewed world order?

Can it be that the phrase *the new world order* means something entirely different to the inner circle of a secret society than it does to the ordinary person? In fact my research leads me to believe that within the very organizations promoting the new world order, the term has one meaning to the general membership and an entirely different meaning to the small inner circle of leadership.

Indeed, it may well be that men of goodwill like Woodrow Wilson, Jimmy Carter, and George Bush, who sincerely want a larger community of nations living at peace in our world, are in reality unknowingly and unwittingly carrying out the mission and mouthing the phrases of a tightly knit cabal whose goal is nothing less than a new order for the human race under the domination of Lucifer and his followers.

The Kinder, Gentler World

Laying aside until a later chapter the thoughts of such a possibility, just what does President George Bush have in mind when he and his aides speak of the new world order?

When the president declared in early 1991 that the end of the Cold War had helped to usher in a new world order, it seemed to be his contention that the law of the jungle was on the way out, along with all the old rules of strife and discord. The "kinder, gentler world" the president first promised in his 1988 campaign would be a place where tyranny could not (or at least should not) prevail.

The very words, *new world order,* have a utopian flavor to them. Nations within this new system are to be governed by the democratic principles of consent and agreement—the paving stones of the president's "kinder, gentler world."

But to most of us the term *new world order* is uncertain and imprecise—apparently more fantasy than fact, more rhetoric than reality. It is a vision of global peace submerged in a sea of political theory dating in modern times back at least to the time of Woodrow Wilson and the League of Nations. It seems to be little more than an elegant image for a somewhat ambiguous agenda for order that has made its way from the think tanks of Washington, D.C., to the nightly news in millions of American homes.

Fred Barnes wrote in *The New Republic* that the idea of a new world order has been tossed around in private conversations at the White House for a long time, although the exact meaning of the term was always uncertain and imprecise. "Whatever cropped up post-cold war, that was the new world order."

In an interview on CNN at the height of the Persian Gulf Crisis, General Brent Scowcroft, the current national security adviser, former aide to Henry Kissinger, and a one-time director of the Council on Foreign Relations, said he had doubts about the significance of Middle Eastern objectives concerning global policy. When asked, "Does that mean you don't believe in the new world order?" Scowcroft snapped back, "Oh, I believe in it. But our definition, not theirs!"

President Bush used the phrase in a speech at a San Francisco fund-raiser in February 1990, saying, "Time and again in this century, the political map of the world was transformed. And in each instance, a new world order came about through the advent of a new tyrant or the outbreak of a bloody global war, or its end."

Soon the president was speaking of "collective security," describing it as virtually synonymous with the new world order. Later his speeches were sprinkled with terms such as "collective resistance" and "collective defense," and the escalation of the Persian Gulf crisis as "a test" of the theory.

In any event, Bush was determined to test the idea on the American people, and it soon became a feature of every public address. In his September 11, 1990, televised address to Congress, he said, in part:

> A new partnership of nations has begun. We stand today at a unique and extraordinary moment. The crisis in the Persian Gulf, as grave as it is, also offers a rare opportunity to move toward an historic period of cooperation. Out of these troubled times, our fifth objective—a new world order—can emerge: a new era, freer from the threat of terror, stronger in the pursuit of justice, and more secure in the quest for peace. An era in which the nations of the world, east and west, north and south, can prosper in harmony.
>
> A hundred generations have searched for this elusive path to peace, while a thousand wars raged across the span of human endeavor. Today that new world is struggling to be born. A world quite different from the one we've known. A world in which the rule of law supplants the rule of the jungle.

Later, the president added:

> When we are successful, and we will be, we have a real chance at this new world order, an order in which a credible United Nations can use its peacekeeping role to fulfill the promise and vision of the United Nations' founders.

On October 30, 1990, Bush commended the role of the United Nations Security Council and suggested that the United Nations could help create "a new world order and a long era of peace." In his address to the people of Prague on November 17, 1990, the president said the situation in the Persian Gulf provided "an opportunity to draw upon the great and growing strength of the commonwealth of freedom and forge for all nations a new world order far more stable and secure than any we have known."

On January 29, 1991, during his State of the Union address, President Bush said that the military response to Iraq's invasion of Kuwait was meant to be a bold statement of international purpose. "What is at stake is more than one small country," he said, "it is a big idea—a new world order, where diverse nations are drawn together in common cause to achieve the universal aspirations of mankind: peace and security, freedom, and the rule of law. Such is a world worthy of our struggle, and worthy of our children's future."

A Framework for Peace

The central issue, President Bush said, was the "long-held promise of a new world order," a promise which maintains that "brutality will go unrewarded and aggression will meet collective resistance."

During his whirlwind tour of military bases, the president spoke to families of servicemen at Fort Gordon, Georgia, on February 1, 1991, saying, "When we win, and we will, we will have taught a dangerous dictator, and any tyrant tempted to follow in his footsteps, that the United States has a new credibility and that what we say goes, and that there is no place for lawless aggression in the Persian Gulf and in this new world order that we seek to create." Bush used the phrase *new world order* three times that day alone.

Fred Barnes observed that the term has found a new currency since the conclusion of the Gulf War. "At the White House the phrase 'new world order' has all but become holy writ," he says. "Speechwriters now routinely include it in every military or foreign policy speech by the president."

Reportedly National Security Adviser Scowcroft was the first White House executive to use the phrase, but he has now grown tired of it. The president's press secretary, Marlin Fitzwater, thinks some new expression will come along to replace it, while others find the phrase uncomfortably close to Hitler's phrase, "the new order." Barnes suggests, "They fear it sounds too fuzzy-minded and one-worldish."

Nevertheless, in his March 6, 1991, address to Congress, commemorating the successful conclusion of the Gulf War—the speech subtitled "A Framework for Peace"—Bush said,

> Until now, the world we've known has been a world divided—a world of barbed wire and concrete block, conflict and cold war. Now, we can see a new world coming into view. A world in which there is the very real prospect of a new world order. In the words of Winston Churchill, a "world order" in which "the principles of justice and fair play . . . protect the weak against the strong." A world where the United Nations, freed from cold war stalemate, is poised to fulfill the historic vision of its founders. A world in which freedom and respect for human rights find a home among all nations.

He added, "Our success in the gulf will shape not only the new world order we seek but our mission here at home."

In reality it is clear that the United States foreign policy establishment used the United Nations mandate as a pretext for the Gulf War. Even as the administration said, "This action was mandated by the United Nations," the president called it "a test" of the new world order apparatus.

We were told that our involvement was at the urgent request of the United Nations Security Council, but in days gone by anyone in his right mind would have said, "Who cares?!" We would never have considered following the dictates of the United Nations unless it was something America already wanted.

Then when the dictator of Iraq lashed out against people in his own country who supported the allies, suddenly America refused to intervene. We cannot support the Kurds, we were told, because it was not part of the United Nations "mandate." In the past it was, "What's best for America? What's the right thing to do?"

At the end of all this, will we find that we have handed over our long-range foreign policy to an international body that is not concerned with our internal problems—such as genocide? Many fear that has already been done—*fait accompli.* So, the next time an American president says, "I think we should send troops into Lebanon, or some other hot spot," his advisers will say, "Sorry, Mr. President. The precedent was set in the Gulf War. If you don't get a United Nations resolution you can't send troops anywhere!"

A *Washington Times* editorial recently expressed the attitude of a lot of people: "Are we hearing this right? For twenty-five years the United Nations has been little more than a joke, and now you're telling us they're going to run the world? Is that what you're saying?"

Whatever he means by it, one thing is certain. The president of the United States has become the key player to prepare the world for the introduction of a new world order which may one day resemble an order defined by someone else, not him.

Since its inception the United Nations has been an example of bureaucracy run amok. It is rife with fraud, pointless debates, internal mismanagement, and ludicrous behavior. Nikita Kruschev's shoe-pounding tirades were only one early example. Jeanne Kirkpatrick, who was our ambassador to the United Nations from 1981 to 1985, blasted the organization over and over again. But how can such an organization ever hope to be effective? Tiny, unsophisticated nations which hold 80 percent of the voting power pay less than 1 percent of the budget, and the people paying 99 percent have only a minority voice.

The attitude of the United Nations member nations hardly suggests a realistic forum for world order. They wholeheartedly applauded the tyrant of Uganda, Idi Amin; 80 percent of them vote with the Soviet Union and against the United States on virtually every issue. Are we to believe that somehow this organization has suddenly been transformed by the action in the Persian Gulf? These distinguished people will lead us to world peace?

The New Paradigm

The rhetoric of President Bush's public statements is strikingly similar to statements being made by other officials throughout the administration. The same words and phrases appear again and again. In his address entitled "Building a Framework for the Rule of Law," presented at a judicial conference in July 1990, CIA Director William Webster commented that,

> A new European order of stable, prosperous and just democracies is still a long way off. It will require a new framework of political and economic systems. It will demand transitions—from rule by individuals to the rule of law. And finally, a new order will be meaningful only if there is trust—trust in the leaders and in the institutions of government.

The ideas and the expressions have become commonplace. Earlier, in an April 1990 address to the Reason Foundation in Los Angeles, another White House official, James Pinkerton, deputy assistant for policy planning, said, "If the last decade will be remembered as the time when the New Deal model broke down, I believe this decade will be remembered as the time when a new order for the age was established, not only in the U.S., but around the world."

Pinkerton also remarked—prematurely as it turned out—that, "In defiance of received opinion, the president has kept his campaign promises of a Kinder, Gentler Nation, and No New Taxes. Because of his policies, America stands at the horizon, ready for the dawning of the New Paradigm around the world." Bush had originally used the term "new paradigm" in his inaugural address, but he now apparently prefers the phrase *new world order*. At any rate, less than nine months after Pinkerton's comments in Los Angeles, the president had broken his tax pledge and immediately ordered American troops into combat in Kuwait.

Pinkerton credited his use of the term *new paradigm* to Thomas Kuhn's *The Structure of Scientific Revolutions*—which chronicles historical readjustments of scientific thinking about the world. He then listed five principles of the new paradigm which the Bush administration is following. Perhaps these principles will offer some insight into the objectives of the new world order.

First, Pinkerton said, the new paradigm recognizes a greater influence of market forces upon government than ever before; second, there will be increasing individual choice (especially in education); third, there is empowerment of the people to choose for themselves; fourth, there is greater decentralization of authority; and fifth, there is great emphasis on results rather than on theories.

The emphasis on business is not surprising, and the focus on the individual is consoling, but it is hard for most of us to see the reality in such statements. And even if the administration's vision of world order still seems to be more wishful thinking than practical reality, it is nevertheless an idea that has touched the public imagination and raised many new questions. Even the most passive observer must wonder what the president has in mind. Certainly the world took notice when, in announcing the siege of Iraq on January 17, 1991, Bush took such pains to promise this new vision of unity to the world.

Birthing a Global Vision

For all its vagaries, the phrase *new world order* was anything but concrete earlier this century when it first began to appear in the conversations of scholars and policy gurus meeting at Pratt House, at Sixty-Eighth and Park in New York City. It was only an idea, a catch phrase, but it offered an apt expression for Woodrow Wilson's premature vision of world unity which sparked his Fourteen-Point Plan and his ill-fated hopes for a League of Nations.

To members of the Council on Foreign Relations (CFR)—the nongovernmental body that has advised presidents and politicians since Wilson's time—the concept of a *new world order* became a useful paradigm for expressing the image of a managed global economy where reason and order supplanted the shifty and uncertain machinations of public policy debates. It was an idea that offered a grander vision of the art of statecraft and the rightful business of nations.

Harvard Professor Stanley Hoffman, writing in *Foreign Affairs,* the journal of the CFR, claims we are in "a new phase of history." This scholar certainly speaks for the consensus of CFR analysts when he says, "The world after the Cold War will not resemble any world of the past." This belief has been a central tenet of CFR policy for so long, Hoffman could hardly come to any other conclusion.

Then he adds another observation that is central to the idea of the new world order. He says:

> The fate of this new world will depend on the ability of the [sources of military, economic, and demographic power] to cooperate enough in order to prevent or moderate conflicts, including regional ones, and to correct those imbalances of the world economy that would otherwise induce some states, or their publics, to pull away from or to disrupt the momentum of interdependence.

Interdependence is a key concept of the globalist vision. Whether it would be called the League of Nations, the United Nations, or the new world order, the idea of a world organization to monitor world peace and foster interdependence has had many vocal supporters, both friend and foe. In 1937 Winston Churchill urged the English Parliament to proclaim its allegiance to the League of Nations, saying, "What is there ridiculous about collective security? The only thing that is ridiculous about it is that we haven't got it." The idea of collective security depends entirely upon the interdependence of nations.

Recently, conservative author George Weigel, director of the Ethics and Public Policy Center in Washington, D.C., said, "If the United States does not unashamedly lay down the rules of world order and enforce them—in both instances, the allies if possible, but unilaterally if necessary—then there is little reason to think that peace, security, freedom or prosperity will be served."

In an article for *World* magazine's special issue on the new world order, Mark Amstutz pointed out that the foundational principles of the new world order are outlined in the mandate of the United Nations peacekeeping apparatus. These principles are:

(1) the integrity of territorial boundaries and the political independence of nation-states; (2) the legitimacy of force in repelling aggression; and (3) the legitimacy of collective defense and punishment of aggression.

The real teeth of this concept of interdependence were exposed in United Nations Resolution 678, which authorized the deployment of combined allied forces in the Persian Gulf area if Iraq did not voluntarily withdraw from Kuwait by the January 15, 1991, deadline set by the Security Council. It also provided the justification for war.

A Time for Change

Today the idea of a new world order is a part of the currency of contemporary foreign affairs ideology. The editors of the journal *New Perspectives Quarterly,* published by the Center for the Study of Democratic Institutions, a liberal think tank, commented in their special issue on the new world order that "The opening months of 1990 will be remembered as the time when the founding assumptions of postwar power alignments crumbled, bringing into view the outlines of a new world order."

Political events that began unfolding in the closing months of the last decade have indeed shaken everyone's image of the global political structure. The end of the Cold War has changed not only the hypotheses of the old world order but the creative tensions upon which our understanding of the world once depended.

In less than eighteen months, literally hundreds of scholarly texts were invalidated, along with innumerable social theories. And the shock waves of political and economic change—particularly within the Soviet Empire and the Eastern Bloc—continue to rumble and reverberate through the halls of power.

Mikhail Gorbachev has been a spectral figure throughout these events, and much of the current debate focuses on him. But there are many dimensions to the emerging vision of the coming new world order. There are political, demographic, geographic, and economic dimensions, but there are also philosophical and spiritual ones.

Jacques Attali, French President François Mitterand's top aide, made a particularly striking observation in a *New Perspectives* article when he wrote:

> Like Luther and Muhammed before him, Gorbachev is bending history. And he is doing it at such a speed that it is impossible to know the results. The world, it seems, will change more in the next ten years than in any other period of history. What was beyond the grasp of imagination yesterday is already happening today.

As the world approaches the beginning of a new millennium, Attali believes the superpowers of the old millennium, the United States and the Soviet Union, are "slouching toward relative, if not absolute, decline." Military might is no longer the token of power in the world. The new order, he says, will be the "Order of Money," and in that light the big money players—the Pacific Rim nations and the European Community—will lead the way to a new age of "hyper-individualism" and unprecedented materialism.

Nobel laureate and political leader Willy Brandt of Germany wrote, "The logic of reform has already taken Gorbachev far beyond where he originally intended to go." And today, Brandt believes, "the trend is irreversible." At first glance, Brandt's vision seems prophetic. But we have to wonder how much Gorbachev may have known about the August 1991 "coup" beforehand, since his agenda for a new world order has suddenly gained such incredible momentum.

The View from the Top

Henry Kissinger, a member and the former director of the Council on Foreign Relations and foreign policy adviser to two presidents, wrote in the January 28, 1991, issue of *Newsweek* magazine that America's biggest challenge in the coming decade will be to preserve "the new balance of power" that is emerging from the Persian Gulf conflict. He says:

> Today, it translates into the notion of "a new world order," which would emerge from a set of legal arrangements and be safeguarded by collective security. The problem with such an approach is that it assumes that every nation perceives every challenge to the international order in the same way, and is prepared to run the same risks to preserve it. In fact, the new international order will see many centers of power, both within regions and between them. These power centers reflect different histories and perceptions. In such a world, peace can be maintained in only one of two ways: by domination or by equilibrium. The United States neither wants to dominate, nor is it any longer able to do so. Therefore, we need to rely on a balance of power, globally as well as regionally.

This is a peculiar statement, since the balance-of-power strategy was one of the things rendered useless by the end of the Cold War and the birth of the new world order. But most notably, Kissinger observes that the clash of arms in the Middle East is part of an ancient historical problem at the epicenter and birthplace of three world religions.

He says, "In several thousand years of recorded history, the Middle East has produced more conflicts than any other region. As the source of three great religions, it has always inspired great passions." The stalemate between Arabs and Jews, Arabs and the West, and the Jews and "world opinion," he says, has kept tensions at fever pitch in the region for the last half century. But in his summation, the elder statesman writes, "Victory in the gulf will create a historic opportunity to alter that particular equation—and it should be seized."

But it is not just the Middle East that has inspired the passion of war. General William Westmoreland, the former commander of all U.S. forces in Vietnam, once told me that in the history of the world there had been over forty-one hundred wars. The old world order has never known lasting peace.

Listen to the sounds of twenty centuries of war. Hear the ominous thunder of armed legions marching on foot, the relentless clatter of chariots over ancient cobblestones. Listen to the clash of steel on steel, the roar of fires ravaging entire cities, and the sound of buildings crashing to earth in ruins. Hear the panic of animals trapped in the midst of battle, the screams of women and children, the moans of the dying. Year after year, century after century, the legacy of man's rage, jealousy, and greed has spilled blood across the pages of history.

Time and progress march hand in hand through the centuries, and as mankind has learned to harness the power of steam, coal, electricity, oil, and nuclear fuels, his capacity for carnage has continually multiplied. Is it any wonder that as war grows ever more terrible, more and more men of goodwill should seek the ways of peace?

As we scan the pages of history, can we be surprised to discover that people would gladly accept the rule of tyrants when their only recourse was anarchy? As Rome conquered the Mediterranean world, the people gladly accepted the laws of the Roman dictators, for the legions also brought the Pax Romana—a measured peace under the hegemony of Rome.

In the ninth century, European nations submitted themselves to the Holy Roman Empire, which historians assert was neither holy, nor Roman, nor even an empire. But peace remained elusive for the next thousand years as an unending succession of warrior-kings and would-be emperors continued to rise to challenge the world order.

Out of the anarchy of revolution in France arose a twenty-six-year-old general named Bonaparte who brought an illusion of stability for a season. But this vainglorious conqueror wasted the flower of French youth on his own personal dreams of empire and ultimately turned Europe into a charnel house.

The Balance of Power

After Napoleon's final defeat in 1815, the Congress of Vienna met to lay out the new map of Europe. Prince Klemens von Metternich of Austria dominated the conference, and he was certainly no idealist.

Recognizing the cupidity of the various European powers and the ever-present threat of war, he proposed a balance of power—not that dissimilar from the concept of *détente*—by which no group of nations would have the strength to force its will upon another.

Further, preserving the balance in Europe required that no European nation would be permitted to gain added strength in the New World of North and South America. To ensure the European balance of power, England's Lord George Canning persuaded President James Monroe to issue what became known as the Monroe Doctrine, which declared North and South America off-limits to the Europeans. The Monroe Doctrine was honored because it was backed first by British power, then, until the Cuban Missile Crisis of 1962, by the power of the United States.

With balance-of-power politics in place in Europe, and with the incredible ascendancy of British economic power—along with Britain's worldwide naval presence—the nineteenth century became a time of relative peace under what we now recognize as the Pax Britannia.

The most devastating conflict of the period was not between nations but within our own nation. This was, of course, what historians now call the Civil War and what we in Virginia call the War of Northern Aggression!

Indeed, the nineteenth century was a time of great optimism and pride. Mankind was soaring. It was inventing, producing, discovering, transforming, and proving everywhere the eminence of its science and its mind. And in an orgy of self-congratulation, the intellectual, spiritual, and social leaders began moving away from their roots and their heritage of ethical values.

But hadn't twentieth-century man proved himself superior to his ancestors? Shouldn't he naturally discard those ancient traditions and beliefs—and especially those based on the idea that man was an instrument of divine authority—and embrace a newer, grander vision of humanity in charge of its own destiny?

At the very moment we began to see ourselves as too wise for war, our intellectual dreams were shattered by an assassin's bullet at

Sarajevo, Yugoslavia. The assassination of Archduke Ferdinand of Austria immediately ignited World War I and led to four years of terror and carnage beyond anything the human mind could have imagined. Never in history had war been so terrible. Never had weapons of destruction levied such a ghastly toll.

And never has a war spawned such a bloody aftermath. An ailing president of the United States virtually ignored the Treaty of Versailles, which ended the war, while he gave what little strength he had left to the formation of a League of Nations to help ensure a world safe from war. By 1920, after years of angry debate, the plan collapsed. Wilson's health failed, and the peace in Europe began to fray.

Wilson's Tragic Flaw

It is one of the tragic ironies of history that the punitive terms of the Versailles treaty—which emasculated Germany's military power and forced it to pay $5 billion in war reparations—actually paved the way for the rise of Adolf Hitler and foreshadowed a second world war. Meanwhile, Wilson's cherished League of Nations was dying of impotence. His Fourteen Points, which offered a framework for a world without war, failed to keep the peace.

Could people living in 1900 have dreamed of the horrors of Joseph Stalin's starvation of the Soviet Kulaks, of Hitler's concentration camps and the gas ovens of the Final Solution, or of the war in the Pacific? Could anyone have imagined that even worse disasters would grip the entire world only fourteen years after the ratification of the Treaty of Versailles?

Would they have believed the panic and hysteria that ensued only a decade after the end of the first-ever world war, the collapse of the stock market, the Great Depression, and the outbreak of another world war more horrifying and more dehumanizing than the first?

In less than fifty years the world was transformed from the exuberance and whimsy of the Gay Nineties to one seized by the trauma of two terrible wars and a half century of mind-boggling change.

Following the carnage of World War II, nations suddenly numbed by their own capacity for violence yearned for a genuine and lasting peace.

Only such an attitude can explain Franklin Roosevelt's idealistic but incredibly naive explanation of his concessions to Stalin. In his account of Roosevelt's words, Winston Churchill wrote:

> "I think," he said of Stalin, "that if I give him everything I possibly can and ask nothing from him in return, *noblesse oblige*, he won't try to annex anything and will work with me for a world of Democracy and peace."

Although Roosevelt's "Four Freedoms Speech" and the subsequent "Declaration of the Twenty-Six United Nations" on January 1, 1942, gave the impetus for the establishment of the United Nations, Roosevelt did not live to see the founding of the organization itself. Yet he would no doubt have shared the idealistic fervor of those who hailed its creation.

When the United Nations Charter was signed on June 16, 1945, in San Francisco, fifty nations were signatories to the agreement. The official documents were then transported to the White House by none other than Alger Hiss, the presidential adviser who was later charged with giving state secrets to the Soviets and was convicted of perjury in 1949. Five years after the United Nations was founded, the organization participated in its first major action, agreeing to intervene in the civil dispute in Korea.

The United Nations was presented to the American people in glowing terms. In Dean Acheson's words, "As almost holy writ, with the evangelical enthusiasm of a major advertising campaign. It seemed to me," Acheson said, "to raise popular hopes that could only lead to bitter disappointment. . . . The General Assembly appeared to be the town meeting of the world."

The Uncertain Peace

Brief highlights stand out along the road to the "bitter disappointment" of which Acheson spoke. In June 1950, Harry S Truman persuaded the General Assembly to mobilize its police action against North Korea. In 1958, President Dwight Eisenhower broke up the Anglo-French effort to maintain access through the Suez Canal. When he turned the matter over to the United Nations, Dag Hammarskjold used the occasion to blast European imperialism and to extol the virtues of the so-called Afro-Asian nonaligned nations.

It is instructive to note that neither the rhetoric nor the actions of the general secretary were ever directed against the Soviet Union, which had brutally repressed the freedom fighters in Hungary under cover of the Suez Canal Crisis. Hammarskjold's anger was carefully reserved for Western democratic nations.

In 1960, when Belgium began to withdraw from the Congo, civil war broke out. The Belgian government waited for United Nations action. When none was forthcoming, the Belgian army moved in to restore order. Immediately Hammarskjold condemned the Belgians and raised a United Nations force from the nonaligned nations.

Mineral-rich Katanga Province had seceded from the chaos to form a separate state under its nationalist leader, Moise Tshombe. In the melee that followed, the United Nations forces turned on the European settlers and attacked Katanga. Can any of us forget the *Life* magazine photo of a bullet-riddled Volkswagen with a dead woman and child inside and a dazed and blood-spattered Belgian settler raising his head to implore his attackers, or heaven above, to understand why the United Nations "peacekeeping" forces had just done this terrible thing to him and his family?

Since that time, a new philosophy emerged at the United Nations. Right was on the side of the emerging nonaligned nations. Tribal warfare, revolution, dictatorship, terrorism, torture, murder, graft, and corruption within these nations were glossed over. The former Western allies and the United States became, in the words of a later nonaligned leader, "the Great Satan."

The most grotesque example of the United Nations' morality took place on October 1, 1975, when the dictator of Uganda, Idi Amin, who was then chairman of the Organization for African Unity, addressed the General Assembly. This bloodthirsty tyrant denounced an imaginary Zionist-U.S. conspiracy and called not merely for the expulsion of Israel from the United Nations but for its "extinction."

The combined assembly gave him a standing ovation when he arrived, applauded him throughout his address, and rose again to their feet when he left. The following day the secretary-general and the president of the General Assembly hosted a public dinner in Amin's honor.

Dubious Honor

This was the honor given a man who had murdered no fewer than two hundred thousand of his fellow citizens, including Anglican Archbishop Luwum. Julius Nyerere of Tanzania said, "Since Amin usurped power he has murdered more people than Smith in Rhodesia, more than Vorster in South Africa." Yet not once would the United Nations move either to censure the bloody dictator or to prevent his further rape of what was once the loveliest land in all of Africa.

Since the early 1970s, perhaps in a desire to give legitimacy to its bizarre perspectives, the United Nations has brought forth resolutions on the New International Economic Order and the Charter on the Economic Rights and Duties of States.

The thrust of these and related studies was for a world devoid of ideological differences, a built-in poor-versus-rich bias, a new information order severely restricting press freedom, and a new international legal order mandating by fiat world peace as an "inalienable right of humanity." It was a mandate, in effect, for peace at any price, a proposal that could ultimately result in the loss of all other human rights under a one-world dictatorship.

The United Nations' real concern for human rights snaps into clear focus when we realize that from 1980 to 1984 the United Nations' Third Committee concentrated its entire attention on the question of human rights violations in El Salvador, Guatemala, and Chile. Until public outcry finally demanded consideration of human rights violations by the Soviets in Afghanistan in 1986, no communist country had ever been placed on the agenda of the General Assembly or any of its committees.

But why should this be surprising? The nonaligned nations, which make up the majority of United Nations delegations, vote with the communist line fully 85 percent of the time in the General Assembly. In 1987, member nations voted with the United States only 18.7 percent of the time.

From a business standpoint, the fiscal mismanagement and inequity within the United Nations is colossal. The poorest countries contribute less than one-hundredth of 1 percent of the United Nations budget. Together, eighty of these countries, with a numerical voting majority in the General Assembly, contribute less than 1 percent of the United Nations budget.

On the other hand, the United States pays 25 percent of the total United Nations annual budget—in excess of $1 billion each year—and an even larger percentage of the actual costs of some agencies. The United States has contributed $17 billion of the estimated $87 billion spent by the United Nations since its founding in 1945 through 1987. Yet our share amounts to only one-sixth of United Nations Secretariat personnel, and to only 12.6 percent of the agency professional posts.

Where does our money go? In the 1984–85 fiscal year the United Nations funded 2.2 billion pages of documents. The secretariat employs fifty-two thousand civil servants, who are paid 32 percent higher than their American counterparts. After fifteen years of service, employees on the lower levels are guaranteed pensions 80 percent higher than their American counterparts, and those with the rank of under secretary or higher will depart after thirty years service with a $310,000 tax-free farewell bonus—in addition to their generous pensions.

Dean Acheson's warnings were proved correct. The United Nations has led to "bitter disappointment." It has not preserved peace, and it assuredly has not served as a dispassionate forum for the benefit of all mankind.

A Community of Nations

In my 1987 address to the Council on Foreign Relations in New York, I proposed a new organization of nations to supersede and replace the United Nations. Such an organization would be, I suggested, an organization based not on failed utopian idealism but on realism, not on the shifting sands of ideological expediency but on a foundation of time-honored principles.

What I proposed then, and what I still believe would be a much more reasonable forum for international understanding and cooperation, is a community of sovereign nations based on democratic institutions, representative government, and respect for the rule of law. Such an organization would offer respect for the individual freedoms, private property, and the basic rights of free speech, assembly, religion, and the press. And nations that neither use terrorism against other nations nor employ torture and terror against their own citizens would be eligible to join such a body.

The organization, which I called the Community of Democratic Nations, would be open to all nations whose governments have achieved legitimacy by embracing democratic processes. When any nation can show that it has moved from totalitarianism to true democracy for a specified period of time, it would then be eligible for membership in the Community of Democratic Nations.

In such a body, the artificial distinctions of First, Second, and Third World status would disappear. There would be no Eastern or Western power cliques, no nonaligned nations. The international institutional dynamics flowing from the anticolonial period would be superseded by the new realities of the twenty-first century.

Since member nations would represent the lion's share of the world's economic powers, the Community of Democratic Nations would be able to use its power constructively and efficiently. There would be construction without Soviet obstruction. Furthermore, in matters of trade, loans, credit, economic development, and military assistance, the Community of Democratic Nations could use its power to give international support to those governments that do respect democratic principles and promote constructive change.

An organization that would include such diverse nations as Sweden, Costa Rica, and Japan could scarcely be called an American propaganda machine. In my proposal to the CFR, I suggested that the United States reduce its funding to the United Nations by at least $250 million and use that sum for a number of years as seed money for this new organization.

Over the years, the present United Nations could concentrate more on the things it does best in the technological arena, while it continues to serve as a place of discussions between delegates of various opposing camps. Such a move would mean the end of the era of failed idealism and political disappointment and the beginning of a new era of realism and the struggle of freedom against totalitarian tyranny.

A Source of Division

George Bush served as the United States ambassador to the United Nations. He knows what an impractical, unwieldy vehicle it is. The present United Nations was created as a post-World War II mechanism and excluded both Japan and Germany from the Security Council. It also is a vehicle that gave the Soviet Union three seats in the General Assembly (representing the USSR, the Ukraine, and Byelorussia), a veto in the Security Council, and key positions in both the personnel and security offices.

More disturbing, in 1991 the bureaucracy of the United Nations still opposes free enterprise capitalism in favor of government planning and socialism, supporting statist regimes everywhere and withholding assistance from nations that seek to move away from central planning. Christopher Whalen, a Washington, D.C., consultant writing in the July 22, 1991 issue of *Barron's,* reports that the United Nations Development Programme (UNDP), headed by a close friend of President Bush, William Draper III, spends $1.5 billion a year "helping authoritarian governments preserve the status quo."

A few of the shocking misuses of UNDP money include $10.9 million to prop up Fidel Castro in Cuba, $42 million to the Marxist government of Yemen, $99 million to the socialist government of Tanzania, $93 million to communist Vietnam, and $108 million to communist China. Yet those countries that are bravely attempting to move into free market capitalism are being strangled. Poland's UNDP aid was cut from $7.5 million when it was communist to $3.5 million now that it is free. Hungary received $7.5 million when it was under communist control. Now Hungary, which is rapidly moving toward freedom, will receive a tiny $1.7 million.

One veteran United Nations official, according to the *Barron's* report, said, "The underlying theme [at the United Nations] is that the present economic crisis throughout the Soviet Bloc countries is due to the pursuit of ill-conceived free market solutions."

A new world order under the United Nations as it is presently constituted is guaranteed to be a socialist, not a free-market capitalist, world system. The former United Nations ambassador, former CIA director, former ambassador to China, former Republican party chairman must have a pretty good idea of the socialistic and antidemocratic bias of all but a very few members of that assembly. But is he ignoring such facts, as did Franklin Roosevelt in 1944, in order to follow a utopian dream?

Is George Bush merely an idealist or are there plans now under way to merge the interests of the United Sates and the Soviet Union in the United Nations—to substitute "world order" power for "balance of power," and install a socialist "world order" in place of a free market system?

In the Face of Reality

Rest assured, utopian fantasy does not work in the real world. The old balance-of-power strategy is still better. At least the balance-of-power concept is based on opposing cycles of greed! If you recognize that people in power tend to be venal, then a balance of power that counterpoises strong forces with differing views for mutual security is a real-live world system.

When Prince Metternich proposed the idea of a balance of power, he was acknowledging a basic fact of life, namely, the sinful nature of man. He balanced Europe the way we have balanced our government, with checks and balances and the separation of powers.

As scholar and author Michael Novak has observed, the United States Constitution was made for sinners. It was presumed that man was sinful, and sinful man could not be trusted. So the framers of the Constitution locked them up and made things deliberately cumbersome. That was their method of arranging the government so that government could not hurt the people, and so no one group could gain control to the detriment of others. It was an ingenious plan.

Thomas Jefferson warned of an unrestrained Supreme Court. In a letter to an opponent he said, "In matters of Constitutional interpretation you seem to feel that the Supreme Court is the ultimate arbiter." He called such sentiments "a very dangerous doctrine, indeed, and one that could lead us to the despotism of an oligarchy."

Unfortunately, this is precisely what has happened during the past three decades. We have turned the power of the people over to a nonelected body of eight men and one woman, five of whom can effectively control the moral and social destiny of the nation. And along with the Supreme Court, we have empowered another nonelected oligarchy in the form of the Federal Reserve Board. This was not the system the framers of our Constitution intended for this country.

The system of checks and balances they devised included a powerful judiciary, a powerful legislative branch, and a strong executive branch, all balanced in turn by the powerful rights of free citizens. For better or worse, Prince Metternich expressed essentially the same principles in his proposal that strength be limited by strength. His aim was not to take power away from nations, but to balance opposing powers in order to strengthen the resolve growing out of their national self-interest.

That was the old order, and for a time it worked very well. But the world order was bound to change; the seeds of change had been planted around the world during the age of empire. By the mid-nineteenth century those seeds were already bearing fruit.

Spheres of Influence

In an earlier age, when the Spanish and the Portuguese were vying for territory around the globe, powerful nations controlled their "spheres of influence" in the world. These spheres determined the characteristic cultures in parts of Africa, South America, the Southwestern United States, and many island groups from the Azores to the Philippines.

During the nineteenth century colonialism was still a major factor. The spheres of influence carved out by colonial powers in the Third World (to use the modern term) gave today's characteristic shape to the world, but they also laid the foundations for much of the racial strife that continues to this day.

The old world order gave us the adventurism of the eighteenth and nineteenth centuries and the awakening of the Industrial Age. It gave us the Pax Britannia, along with the colonial empires of the Spanish, Portuguese, Dutch, French, Germans, and British. It was essentially a time of peace based on a Christian code of ethics. However, the instinctive bias of the colonists—that the Third World was inherently inferior to the civilized society of Western Europe—would inevitably lead to the collapse of colonialism and the end of the Age of Empire.

Nevertheless, a fair analysis of the colonial policy of England, for example, must show that it was a relatively enlightened time. In terms of bringing to the colonies education, sanitation, the rule of constitutional law, and some kind of economic order, the colonists were genuinely humanitarian.

Before the beginning of the Pax Britannia, America was already a force in the world. The desire of various European nations to manipulate the destiny of the New World had to be dealt with again and again after the British defeat at Yorktown, Virginia, in 1781. Although the French Revolution was still eight years away, the old order of the world was altered there for all time. The old methods of war, the old ambitions of empire, and the old moral code were irrevocably changed.

When America began to flex its muscles, it quickly became the desire of the Europeans to preserve their own balance of power in Europe by keeping America out of "foreign entanglements." When President James Monroe issued his proclamation, he depended on the promise of British support to help keep the others at bay. In fact, if it hadn't been for the support of the European powers, the Monroe Doctrine would never have worked.

Later, the European economic powers began to see the wealth of North America as a great treasure, and some of them still wanted to get their tentacles into America's economy. They eventually did so not by force but by investing their money here, by sending people, and by buying land. Europe could not defeat the United States by military force, but the European financiers knew that they could control the United States economy if they could saddle us with an American equivalent of the German Bundesbank or the Bank of England. Their efforts failed until 1913, when a German banker, Paul Warburg, succeeded in establishing the Federal Reserve Board, America's privately owned central bank.

The old world order was crumbling bit by bit. Monarchies were going out of style. A wave of democratic reform was sweeping across the map. In America, Canada, Great Britain, Switzerland, and France, democracy was working and the atmosphere of change was pervasive. But there were ominous clouds on the horizon.

The twentieth century had hardly begun when the tensions of this changing world brought about a spontaneous eruption, and the assassination of Archduke Franz Ferdinand of Austria at Sarajevo became the pretext for the First World War. With the war, more terrible than any in the history of mankind, the post-Napoleonic world order of kings, nobles, serfs, and small aristocratically led armies came to an end, and a radically different world order began.

4

The Old Order Crumbles

Two attempts to create a new world order arose out of the turmoil surrounding World War I. One was the League of Nations put forward by President Woodrow Wilson; the other was the Communist International put forward by Nikolai Lenin. On the face of it, these two concepts were light-years apart. In this chapter, however, we will see that both plans actually flowed from the same wellspring.

At the beginning of the second decade of the twentieth century Europe was balanced precariously between the French, the British, the Prussian monarchy in Germany, the Hapsburg Austro-Hungarian Empire, and the Tsarist Empire of Russia. Touching Europe at what later became the nation of Yugoslavia was the Ottoman Empire of the Turks, which remained the dominant power in the Middle East until the end of the First World War.

The point of tension that existed in 1917 was back in the news in 1991, when rival factions in Croatia and Slovenia began warring again. These former provinces of the Hapsburg Empire that bordered on the Serbian portion of the Ottoman Empire were joined together to create the nation of Yugoslavia, but it has never been a happy marriage. In fact it was there that the incident which instigated World War I took place in Sarejevo, Yugoslavia, on June 28, 1914.

After the war, the Prussian Kaiser was gone, the Ottoman Empire was gone, the Hapsburg Empire was gone, and the Tsarist Empire was gone. The result was so profound and the excuse for war so flimsy, that casual observers would have reason to suspect that someone had planned the whole thing.

Before the war, monarchies held sway. After the war, socialism and high finance held sway. Was it planned that way or was it merely an "accident" of history?

What was clearly not an accident of history was the entry of the United States into the war. Woodrow Wilson, a Democrat, was elected president of the United States in 1912, primarily because a split developed between the Republican president, William Howard Taft, and the former Republican president, Theodore Roosevelt, who had since formed the Bull Moose party.

Wilson was a devout Presbyterian born in Staunton, Virginia, just thirty-three miles from my hometown of Lexington. Wilson became the president of Princeton University, a Presbyterian school that claims as one of its past presidents the Reverend John Witherspoon. Witherspoon was a member of the Continental Congress and the man who trained James Madison, the author of the U.S. Constitution, in law and theology.

High-Level Maneuvers

According to Georgetown University Professor Carroll Quigley in his provocative tome, *Tragedy and Hope: A History of the World in Our Time,* Wilson was chosen by what was then known as the Money Trust to become governor of New Jersey. From that position, his backers successfully ran him for president. This auspicious group of supporters included the Rockefellers, Jacob Schiff, Bernard Baruch, Thomas Fortune Ryan, and Adolf Ochs.

Since some members of the Money Trust supported Teddy Roosevelt, it is apparent that they deliberately split the Republican party in order to guarantee Wilson's victory. Two agents of J. P. Morgan, Frank Munsey and George Perkins, were pouring in money to support Roosevelt, while at the same time giving large sums to Wilson.

Wilson was dignified, beyond reproach, and a dedicated Christian. However, he was completely naive about the intricacies of international finance and the complex workings of the federal government. He would have been the perfect front man for the financiers of his day, especially when paired with a man of their choosing, Colonel Edward Mandell House, the British-educated son of a Texas financier who represented British financial interests. Scribner's *Concise Dictionary of Biography* says of Colonel House: "No other American of his time was on such close terms with so many men of international fame."

Colonel House handpicked the majority of Wilson's cabinet. But together, Wilson and House quickly paid off their backers when, in 1913, President Wilson helped facilitate the two pillars of the international financial assault on the freedom and integrity of America. The first was the act that created America's privately owned central bank, the Federal Reserve Board; the second was the passage of the federal income tax under the authority of the Internal Revenue Service.

Created by the German banker Paul Warburg, the Morgans, and the Rockefellers, the Federal Reserve Board was custom designed as an instrument of immense power. Colonel House was the key figure in the passage of this legislation, and he was in constant contact with Warburg about it. The companion piece to that play was to change the United States Constitution to force the American citizens to pay for the loans these bankers would make through the Federal Reserve Board to the treasury. The federal income tax would become the most powerful fund-raising mechanism ever devised.

Entangling Alliances

But Colonel House, the "intimate friend of international men of fame," dreamed of much more. He wanted a new world order dominated by American finance—with himself as its head. It was House who talked the president into breaking his campaign pledge to keep the nation out of war and to support a war resolution, which, for the first time in history, broke George Washington's solemn pledge to stay clear of "entangling alliances" in the internecine intrigues of Europe.

Colonel House and his American and European friends undoubtedly hoped for two outcomes from the war. One was the dissolution of the monarchies of the old order—to clear the decks for a new world government. Second, they wanted to be sure that they had a powerful enough seat at the postwar bargaining table to influence the destiny of postwar Europe.

Just prior to the war, House penned a novel entitled *Phillip Dru, Administrator: A Story of Tomorrow.* In this remarkable book, published in 1912, the colonel bared his real soul. Imagine, if you can, the foreign affairs adviser to President Wilson planning a Marxist or socialist economic system as a replacement for monarchy.

Beyond state socialism, House wanted a one-world government, a one-world army, a one-world economy under an Anglo-Saxon financial oligarchy, and a world dictator served by a council of twelve faithful men. The vision of a new world order depicted in this novel included a radically revised United States Constitution and, of course, the United States leading the way, but ultimately submerged into a world government. Clearly, the League of Nations was just one small part of House's grand design.

In a spring 1991 article entitled, "A Much-Deserved Hearing for Wilson's 'New Order,'" *Washington Post* columnist Edwin M. Yoder, Jr., said that it was about time the world gave appropriate credit to President Wilson and Colonel House as the true authors of the new world order. One wonders if Yoder intended to applaud the new world order of *Phillip Dru, Administrator?*

House was a founding member of the Council on Foreign Relations which was conceived in 1919 and established in 1921. This august body of "wise men" has effectively dominated the making of foreign policy by the United States government since before World

War II. The CFR has included virtually every key national security and foreign policy adviser of this nation for the past seventy years. Its impressive roster also includes the former congressman, former ambassador to China and the United Nations, former head of the CIA, and now president, George Bush, who was a CFR director between 1977 and 1979.

Is it not proper, therefore, to ask whether or not the new world order envisaged in 1991 by the Council on Foreign Relations and its former members, Bush and Scowcroft, is indeed the same new world order set forth in detail by the founder of the Council of Foreign Relations in 1921?

In my own opinion, it is highly doubtful that George Bush shares any of the notions of Colonel Edward House. But what about the behind-the-scenes leaders within the CFR who have been promoting and engineering the new world order these past seventy years? Dare we ask?

The Illuminati

The end of World War I brought another world vision more terrible than a mere League of Nations. It brought the triumph of the Bolsheviks in Russia and the rapid growth of international communism. But where did Russian communism get its vision of a new world order?

On May 1, 1776 (May Day is still considered to be the key annual holiday for communists), a Bavarian professor named Adam Weishaupt launched a small secret society called the Order of the Illuminati. Weishaupt's aims were to establish a new world order based on the overthrow of civil governments, the church, and private property and the elevation to world leadership of a group of hand-picked "adepts" or "illumined" ones.

Weishaupt chose as his vehicle for infiltration and takeover the established Continental Order of Freemasons, of which Frederick the Great of Prussia had become sovereign grand commander and the wealthy Philippe of France, Duc d'Orleans, had been elevated to grand master of the grand orient, as his lieutenant. In 1782, Weishaupt succeeded at the international convention of Freemasons held in Wilhelmsbad, Germany, with his planned infiltration of the Continental Masonic Order and the creation of what he termed "Illuminated Freemasonry."

His conspiracy was sufficiently successful from that point on to use French Freemasonary as a vehicle for placing members of the French Illuminati into key governmental positions. Once installed, these members set about to undermine the Bourbon dynasty of France and to prepare the way for the French Revolution. It is believed that several of the key leaders of the French Revolution were members of the Illuminati.

The slaughter that followed was not merely an assault on the king and the aristocracy—what was called the ancien regime—it was an assault against everyone, even the leaders of the Reign of Terror that followed on the heels of the revolution. The satanic carnage that the Illuminati brought to France was the clear predecessor of the bloodbaths and successive party purges visited on the Soviet Union by the communists under both Lenin and Stalin.

When the French Revolution had run its course, more than a million Frenchmen were dead; the government, commerce, and agriculture were destroyed; the currency was debased; and the savings of the people were worthless. France was ready for dictatorship, not by the Illuminati, but by Napoleon. Thus ended the first modern new world order. Lenin later said that the French Revolution did not go far enough. Russian communism showed how much farther it could go.

The League of Just Men

Although Illuminism had been banned in Germany and was discredited in France, it surfaced again in the 1800s through secret revolutionary societies holding to the basic tenets of Illuminism. Operating in France and Germany, these societies commissioned the writing of a militant manifesto.

In the preface to the 1872 German edition of the *Communist Manifesto,* the authors said,

> The Communist League (formerly called the "League of Just Men") . . . which could only be a secret one . . . commissioned the undersigned [Karl Marx and Fredrich Engels], at the Congress held in London in November 1847, to draw up for publication a detailed theoretical and practical program of the party. Such was the origin of the following Manifesto, the manuscript of which traveled to London to be printed a few weeks before the February revolution.

So wrote Marx and Engels themselves!

In 1885, Cardinal Henry Manning wrote that the Communist International was not the work of Karl Marx but that "of secret political societies, which from 1789 to this day have been perfecting their formation, and . . . have drawn closer together in mutual alliance and cooperation. In 1848 they were sufficiently powerful to threaten almost every capital in Europe by a simultaneous rising."

The precise connecting link between the German Illuminati and the beginning of world communism was furnished by a German radical named Moses Hess. According to Eugene H. Methvin, in his book, *Rise of Radicalism: The Social Psychology of Messianic Extremism,*

> [I]n October of 1842 Frederick Engels stopped in Cologne and spent an afternoon with Moses Hess, then 30, who was known as the "communist rabbi" for his missionary zeal in proselyting for *French utopian ideas.*
>
> Hess later wrote a friend: "Engels, an embryonic revolutionary, *parted from me the most enthusiastic communist."* Engels himself credited his conversion to Dr. Hess, and a year later expressly declared that the latter was "the first to make communism plausible to me and my circle."
>
> He goes on to say, "Marx and Engels planned to publish a German edition of Buonarroti's *Conspiration pour l'egalité* [Conspiracy for Equality], translated by Moses Hess. . . . Marx's extensive collection of books on the French Revolution contained a copy of Buonarroti's *Conspiration."*

Further attestation to the link between the communists, the French Revolution, and the Illuminati comes from Saul Padover, in his work, *Karl Marx: An Intimate Biography,* in which he tells of Marx, then aged twenty-three, meeting with the thirty-year-old Moses Hess in Cologne. Hess later wrote, "Dr. Marx is still a very young man, who will give the coup de grace to the medieval religion and politics."

Work of the Masters

In his authoritative book on revolutionary movements, *Fire in the Minds of Men,* James Billington says that the organizational plan that Filipo Michele Buonarroti distilled from two generations of revolutionary experience in Geneva was simply lifted from the teachings of the Bavarian Order of Illuminists. Buonarroti codified the legend of a French Illuminist, François Babeuf, who spoke of "the knights of the order of the equals" and called himself l'HSD (*l'homme sans Dieu*)—by which he meant to imply that he was a man made perfect as a god, without the help of God.

Buonarroti's first revolutionary organization was called the Sublime Perfect Masters. The revolutionary Buonarroti touched the thinking of a group of young Italians who had been influenced by Illuminism while studying in Bavaria. They drew up plans to establish a journal capable of promoting the total transformation of humanity set forth in the Illuminist ideal. The occultic impulses of Illuminism, despite claims to the contrary, were very much alive in European secret societies in the nineteenth century.

The Illuminist streams clearly flowed in Marxist communism in the 1840s. Whether there was a meaningful confluence of these streams in Europe and elsewhere, then and now, remains to be seen.

The atheism, destruction of property, hatred of civil government, ruthless reign of terror, lies and deception, and gross mismanagement of resources of world communism are all mirror images of the French Revolution. Communism draws its spiritual soul from the same impulses that were present in 1789.

In 1988, in a major address to the national convention of the Republican party in New Orleans, I mentioned the atheistic excesses of the French Revolution—a recognized fact of history. Imagine my surprise when the political reporter for *Time* magazine blasted me and called my well-received remarks "a loser" because I had criticized the French Revolution. Apparently those in the United States who want a socialistic new world order are not enthusiastic about hearing criticism of the origins of their concepts.

In 1848, when the *Communist Manifesto* was published, Marx and Engels and their backers looked forward to a new world order that would emerge when the world's urban working classes would lead a revolution against property owners that would one day create a stateless, classless society.

As I have pointed out, the common strain that permeates much of the thinking about a new world order involves four basic premises: (1) the elimination of private property, (2) the elimination of national governments and national sovereignty, (3) the elimination of traditional Judeo-Christian theism, and (4) a world government controlled by an elite made up of those who are considered to be superior, or in the occultic sense, "adepts" or "illuminated."

The Power Behind the Bolsheviks

Americans are appropriately shocked when they find that the one-worlders of the early twentieth-century American Money Trust have financed the one-worlders of the Kremlin, not realizing that both groups hold larger goals and aims for the world that apparently complement one another. Until we understand this commonality of interest between left-wing Bolsheviks and right-wing monopolistic capitalists, we cannot fully comprehend the last seventy years of world history nor the ongoing movement toward world government.

British author Nesta Webster researched and wrote extensively on subversive movements. She described a group in Switzerland claiming direct descent from the founder of the Illuminati, Adam Weishaupt. She says,

[T]he same secret ring of Illuminati is believed to have been intimately connected with the organization of the Bolshevist revolution. . . . None of the leading Bolsheviks are said to have been members of the innermost circle, which is understood to consist of men belonging to the highest intellectual and financial classes, whose names remain absolutely unknown. Outside this absolutely secret ring there existed, however, a semi-secret circle of high initiates of subversive societies drawn from all over the world and belonging to various nationalities.

Authors who expose subversive secret organizations are usually ridiculed because, when asked for proof of the identity of participants in secret societies, they have to answer, "That is impossible, since the names are secret." But, invariably, there is a tiny secret core ring, a larger and slightly less secret middle ring, then a much broader and more public group.

The Illuminati symbol, the dot within the circle, suggests this often-repeated pattern. Nevertheless there is enough evidence and enough unexplained phenomena in the past two hundred years that clearly points to a hidden plan intended to establish the new world order. Looking back, it is possible to discover certain clear links. I believe we can then trust reason and intuition to bridge the gaps.

The Roman pontiff, with his access to worldwide intelligence, made a statement that buttresses this view. Pope Pius XI declared in 1937 that communism has behind it "occult forces which for a long time have been working to overthrow the Christian Social Order." I believe that a statement from a person of such esteem must be given great credence.

The theories of Marx and his backers expressed in 1848 in the *Communist Manifesto,* and later in 1867 in *Das Kapital,* began to take root in the oppressive society of Tsarist Russia. Between 1898 and 1903 the doctrine of Russian communism emerged under the leadership of a young radical named Vladimir Ilyich Ulyanov—later known as Lenin.

Between 1903 and 1917 the Communist party was shaped as an instrument of revolution, with the clear goal of overthrowing the established order in Russia and creating an atheistic command economy ruled by what the communists called the "dictatorship of the proletariat." True to Marx, the new order swept away property, the government, and the outward worship of God. The communists taught a ruthless suppression of their enemies, a radical elimination of the old ways, and the nationalization of not only the means of production but ultimately all private property as well.

The communists, in theory at least, expected that with the end of the class struggle, government would gradually wither away. Instead, their view of utopia led to a totalitarianism in which no sphere of human life was outside the grip of the state. This view of a new world order led almost 2 billion people to enslavement under the most hellish nightmare that the world has ever known, and at least 100 million of those have been ruthlessly killed. Lenin and his disciples indeed went "farther than the French Revolution" by a margin of a hundred to one.

What the average man and woman find so difficult to understand, however, is how a Wall Street banker such as Jacob Schiff of Kuhn, Loeb and Company could personally transport $20 million in gold to help salvage the near-bankrupt, fledgling communist government of the new Soviet Russia—or how a man like Lord Milner of the British Round Table could provide funds in 1917 to get them started again—or how United States industrialists and bankers could repeatedly assist them in receiving massive private and governmental aid over the decades that followed.

The Wail of Oppression

The postwar 1920s brought America prosperity, despite three colorless presidents, Prohibition, and the carefree gaiety of the "flappers." Postwar Germany was a seething cauldron of hyperinflation, desperate poverty, and rising radicalism. Russia, now the Soviet Union, largely isolated from the rest of the world, groaned under the suffering imposed by communism.

The Great Depression of the early thirties crippled the economies of the world and led to a massive disruption of finance and industry. The tragedy of the unemployed and the long bread lines were heartrending. The plaintive voice of crooner Bing Crosby singing, "Once I built the railroads, made 'em run on time; now the work is ended; Buddy, can you spare a dime?" must have convinced millions that free enterprise capitalism could not work.

In the days of the Depression, disillusioned intellectuals like the brilliant, Harvard-educated Alger Hiss apparently turned to an idealistic version of the Marxist-Leninist Communist International, and in the process, decided to betray the United States. Hiss and men like Harry Dexter White and Owen Lattimore began pushing United States foreign policy toward a pro-Soviet tilt, while a succession of New Deal domestic programs began the process of moving Washington, D.C., from a sleepy Southern town on the Potomac housing an $11 billion government to the home of the enormous $1.3 trillion colossus whose tentacles now clutch for control of the life and destiny of every man, woman, and child in the land.

In 1932, an Austrian-born madman determined that he indeed had been chosen by spiritual powers as the anointed savior, not only of Germany but of the world. Adolf Hitler, a man trained in the occult and surrounded by occultists ("demonized" in the words of William L. Shirer, author of the epic *Rise and Fall of the Third Reich*), felt a powerful calling to bring about "a new order" for the world—a thousand-year empire of supremacy that he termed the "Third Reich"—the third kingdom.

It is simply inconceivable to realize that in only thirteen years this poorly educated nobody took control of one of the great nations of the earth, armed it to the teeth, bluffed England and France into letting him dismantle two neighboring democracies, and began a systematic genocide against God's chosen people, the Jews. He subjugated almost all of Continental Europe, while launching a world war of ferocity and barbarity never known in the history of mankind.

After thirteen years of Hitler's madness, Germany was reduced to a heap of rubble, and the world was reminded once again to beware the siren song of utopian dreamers.

The Great Compromise

What remained of the old world order after World War I was indeed demolished after World War II. At Yalta, an ailing President Franklin Roosevelt, with the spy Alger Hiss at his side, surrendered control of the sovereign nations of Lithuania, Latvia, and Estonia to the Soviets. And with these tiny Baltic states came East Germany, Poland, Czechoslovakia, Hungary, Bulgaria, Rumania, Albania, and Manchuria.

But that was not all. Communists threatened the governments of Italy and France. Greece was barely spared a communist take-over. The Labour party socialized major industry in Great Britain. Sweden elected a socialist government. And burdensome government taxes were levied on the rest of Europe to support massive welfare programs.

After Roosevelt's death, his successor, Harry S Truman, barraged by leftist stories about "the corruption of the nationalist government of China," turned his back on Chiang Kai-shek, our staunch friend and World War II ally. America then allowed the Chinese communists under Mao Tse Tung to subjugate, communize, and brutally purge the Chinese people.

The world order after World War II was different from any other, because for the first time in the history of mankind, two great nations had developed weapons capable of destroying all life on the planet.

Since 1945, the American people were told that this nation and the Soviet Union were engaged in a Cold War. The official policy of the government was the "containment of communism," enunciated by what came to be known as the Truman Doctrine. In Fulton, Missouri, the great world strategist Winston Churchill uttered the famous line, "From Stetin in the Baltic to Trieste in the Adriatic, an iron curtain has fallen across Europe."

We were told that behind the Iron Curtain—and later the Bamboo Curtain—lived the enemy. The Cold War required constant massive expenditures for arms, maintaining large numbers of

United States ground forces in Europe and Asia, and stockpiling an ever-growing arsenal of thermonuclear weapons.

The post-World War II world order was characterized by the global nuclear standoff between the two superpowers, the United States and the Soviet Union. Each side developed increasingly powerful bombs whose destructiveness was measured in million of tons (megatons). Our leaders talked of the "throw weight" of missiles, then missiles that could carry up to ten nuclear warheads to separate targets, the so-called MIRV missiles.

Along the way we developed extraordinary accuracy in submarine-launched nuclear devices. We improved on that with a D-2 missile. We developed and deployed the most accurate intermediate-range (twelve hundred miles) missile in the world, the Pershing II. Missiles were placed in silos, on trucks, and on railroad cars. Our latest generation of "smart" bombs, cruise missiles, stealth aircraft, night vision equipment, and satellite surveillance is nothing short of awesome—and, I must add, awesomely expensive.

After we had spent the money developing these weapons, our leaders then negotiated with the Soviets to limit or destroy them. The buzzword that characterized the Strategic Arms Limitation Treaties (SALT I and SALT II) was "strategic parity." In other words, the United States that came out of World War II as the undisputed military and industrial power of the world had agreed to permit the Soviet Union, which came out of World War II as a ravaged, backward, Third World power, to build a nuclear arsenal that would be essentially equal to our own.

Build and Destroy

After months of debate in the early 1970s, Richard Nixon signed the so-called Anti-Ballistic Missile (ABM) Treaty in 1972, which limited the right of the United States to defend itself against nuclear attack. The operative buzzword here was an acronym, MAD, or Mutual Assured Destruction. In other words, neither the Soviets nor the United States were permitted to defend their civilian populations against the nuclear attack of the other.

The theory was that if the civilian populations of both parties were vulnerable, neither nation would launch an attack on the other. That was a nice theory, except we learned that not only did the Soviets prepare massive installations to protect against nuclear war, they also cheated on the ABM treaty by building the famed Krasnoyarsk phased-radar array.

In 1987, Ronald Reagan signed the Intermediate Nuclear Forces (INF) Treaty, which required that the United States destroy its deadly accurate Pershing II missiles and that the Soviet Union destroy its SS-20, SS-4, and SS-5 missiles. On the face of it, this treaty seemed equitable, but underneath, it was another trap for the United States.

Under the INF Treaty, the United States removed forever the nuclear shield protecting Europe from potential aggression by Soviet conventional forces and, in the process, the only meaningful U.S. linkage to European security. The Soviets, on the other hand, removed the obsolete SS-20 missile launchers but were permitted by the treaty to keep their SS-20 nuclear warheads—the bombs—which they have since been installing in their own territory on ultramodern SS-25 hidden, rail-mounted launchers.

The events surrounding the INF treaty are particularly poignant to me, because during the presidential debates I personally challenged then Vice President Bush on a key provision of the treaty which he was vigorously advocating. I discovered, to my shock, that he was completely ignorant of the fact that this treaty permitted the Soviets to keep their SS-20 nuclear warheads.

I also asserted that the treaty should include on-site verification of the presence of intermediate nuclear missiles in Cuba. At the mere suggestion of missiles in Cuba, I was castigated by Fidel Castro and the liberal press in this country for making what they considered an outrageous suggestion. I was interested to read, three years later, a column by Robert Evans and Michael Novak carried in the *Washington Post* which stated that SS-20 missiles were sighted in Cuba in the spring of 1991—missiles, I might add, that are entirely capable of hitting Washington, D.C.

By the summer of 1991, our president had signed a treaty that promised to destroy even more of our nuclear arsenal. Instead of SALT, or strategic arms *limitation,* the new acronym is START for Strategic Arms *Reduction* Treaty. Time will tell what American strategic advantages will be destroyed by a treaty whose verification procedures are perceived by experts to be seriously flawed. I suspect, as has happened all too often before, the United States will carefully abide by the spirit and letter of the START Treaty, and the Soviets will be free to break both the spirit and letter when it serves their interests to do so.

Unwinnable Wars

During the unfolding of the post-World War II world order, our leaders sent United States ground forces into battle to fight Soviet and Chinese communist surrogates in Korea in 1950 and in Vietnam in 1965. For the first time in the history of the United States, our armed forces were not allowed to win a war.

I served with the First Marine Division in Korea under the overall command of General Douglas MacArthur, and later General Matthew Ridgeway. Korea is a small peninsula, joined to China at its extreme northern border on the Yalu River. There is absolutely no question that if General MacArthur had been permitted to bomb Chinese troops and supplies north of the Yalu River, our armed forces in Korea could easily have sealed off the Korean Peninsula and then systematically, by air and ground action, destroyed the North Korean army.

But MacArthur, who insisted on the only intelligent military option, was instead fired by President Truman. His offense was that of failing to acknowledge civilian authority. In truth he was fired for the unpardonable sin of wanting to win the war.

At the time, I felt that the end of the Korean War, which followed so closely World War II, could be explained in part by war weariness. To me this was a mistake that would not be repeated. After Korea, it was clear that the United States should never allow itself to be drawn into another land war in Asia. Yet when the Vietnam War broke out, I could not believe what was happening! It was Korea all over again, only many times worse.

Civilian authorities were actually prohibiting our troops from winning. They conceived incredible rules of engagement, which meant that we could jeopardize *our* troops, *our* aircraft, and *our* ally, South Vietnam, but we gave privileged sanctuary to the North Vietnamese nation and communist troops in Cambodia. I strongly believe that had the United States mined Haiphong Harbor, bombed Hanoi extensively, cut the North Vietnamese dikes, and then launched an amphibious operation against North Vietnam itself, that country would have collapsed and the Vietcong would have been without support in no time at all.

MacArthur had warned, "In war, there is no substitute for victory." Instead of victory, in Vietnam we played at war, and we bled our young men and women to death. We bled our treasury. And worst of all, we bled our national resolve. In Vietnam, the United States was forced by its leaders to suffer the first military loss in its history.

Above all else, we showed the world daily in the world press that the foreign policy establishment of the United States and its allies would not permit this nation ever to "defeat" communism. We could struggle against communism; we could arm against communism; but we could not win against communism.

Their plan for this country was not victory over communism but ultimate union with the Soviet Union in a one-world government. Roman Gaither, former head of the Ford Foundation, was quoted as saying that the resources of his foundation were to be used to "comfortably merge the United States with the Soviet Union."

Impenetrable Logic

During the postwar years the obvious plan was to drain the resources of the United States in preparation for a war that was never to be. This accomplished, the time would be ripe for—in the words of Bruce Russett (the Dean Acheson Professor of International Relations and Political Science at Yale) and James Sutterlin (former director of the executive office of the United Nations secretary-general), writing in the Spring 1991 issue of Foreign Affairs, the official organ of the Council on Foreign Relations—"a new world order envision by Presidents Bush and Gorbachev."

Military preparation for the Cold War during the last forty-five years kept our economy on such a wartime footing that our government will owe an amount approaching $4 trillion in direct debt at the end of the fiscal year. This same economy is sufficiently weakened to accept joyfully the promised end of the Cold War. Now that our former communist "enemy" has been converted to *perestroika* and *glasnost,* we are being prepared for the beginning of a new world order under the aegis of the United Nations. This is the "Bush-Gorbachev world order" into which America and the Soviet Union are being "comfortably merged."

During the Cold War and *détente,* we were told that the Soviet Union was an economic powerhouse between one-quarter and one-half the size of the United States. The ruble was convertible into dollars at the rate of $1.60 per ruble. We were told that the Soviet Army was formidable, Soviet weapons virtually invincible, and that the threat of this colossus justified a $300 billion defense budget, on the one hand, and military parity and shared global leadership, on the other.

Then in 1989, just as the United States of Europe prepared for its 1992 debut, as if some silent director gave the signal, all of our preconceptions were dashed. Suddenly we learned that the awesome Soviet colossus is, in reality, a broken-down Third World economy.

Six million Soviets are homeless and another 13 million live in communal apartments of two or more families and must share a bathroom and kitchen. Less than a third of Soviet households have telephones; only half have refrigerators. The number of blacks in South Africa who own automobiles is greater than the total of all the automobiles in the Soviet Union. There are chronic food shortages.

Health care and sanitation are appalling. The rate of alcoholism is eleven times that of the West. And the people are totally dispirited.

From $1.60 a few years ago, the ruble is now worth less than five cents. The gross national product of the Soviet Union has been shriveling for decades, and the country is in absolute economic, political, humanitarian, and moral chaos.

So where were the CIA, the State Department, and all those government agencies charged with keeping tabs on the economic and military status of other nations while all this was happening? Why weren't we receiving year-by-year assessments of the Soviet decline? The first such official report I ever saw was in 1989. If there has been such a dramatic Soviet decline, it did not happen overnight.

One of two things is certain: Either the CIA and the foreign policy establishment deliberately misled the American people about the strength of the Soviet Union so that the United States would continue its Cold War levels of wasteful spending, or the communists (like the Gideonites of biblical times) have deliberately sabotaged the consumer economy for the purpose of lulling the West into letting down its military, intellectual, and spiritual guard so that aid would flow, treaties would be signed, and (more particularly) alliances would form. In light of the abortive "coup" of 1991, the latter alternative seems much more likely.

The Lessons of History

Consider these news headlines from the *New York Times:* AMERICANS TRADE WITH RUSSIA DESPITE BANS, SOVIET OIL OFFER TO AMERICAN FIRM, AMERICANS TO WORK RUSSIAN OIL TRACT, SOVIET GRANT TO BRITISH-PRELIMINARY AGREEMENT FOR DEVELOPMENT OF OIL FIELDS IS REACHED. These are legitimate headlines, not from the 1990s but from the 1920s!

One in particular stands out above all the rest. On May 31, 1921, the *New York Times* reported, SOVIETS BANKRUPT, LENIN ADMITS, with the subtitle, MOSCOW DISPATCH QUOTES HIM SAYING THAT CAPITALISM MUST

BE UNFETTERED. The process of candor and capitalism was called, of all things, *glasnost*. Does any of this sound familiar?

In 1937, the butcher Joseph Stalin stopped his bloodthirsty purges long enough to begin a program of liberalization of the communist apparatus in the Soviet Union. To those today who feel the term is unique to Mikhail Gorbachev, Stalin called his new program *perestroika*. Can any thinking person honestly believe that the Soviets under Lenin changed their course because Lenin started *glasnost?* And in the light of history, can anyone believe that the Soviet menace was any less intense under Stalin because of *perestroika?* But we may yet see the unfolding of a more repressive regime within the Soviet Union. When that happens, the dreamer's who believed the communist reformers' cries of "Peace, peace!" will have to find some new explanations for their gullibility.

The apparent dismantling of communism in Poland, East Germany, Hungary, Rumania, Bulgaria, Albania, and Czechoslovakia seems genuine enough. Changes there have been monumental, and the failure of the August 1991 "coup" in the Soviet Union has put their hopes for reform into high gear. But lest we become too giddy, let us remember that Gorbachev, the architect of "reform," is the protégé of Yuri Andropov, former head of the KGB and the man who is believed to be responsible for masterminding the assassination attempt against Pope John Paul II.

Despite the rhetoric of *glasnost* and *perestroika*, we should also remember that Gorbachev handpicked all eight of the August 1991 "coup" plotters. He named the hardened KGB operative, Boris Pugo, as minister of the interior, and Gennady Gromov as his deputy. Their front man, Gennady Yanayev, was Gorbachev's own second in command. He placed Vladimir Kryuchkov in charge of the KGB. Wasn't it a bit much to believe that those hard-liners would suddenly become champions of democracy and capitalism, or that their police organization, the KGB, would support a system to take away their own power?

Forbes magazine published an interview with Gorbachev's principal economic adviser, Leonid Abalkin, in its October 19, 1987 issue. Abalkin candidly admitted, as did Lenin before him, "The Soviet economy is in a grave state." However, after discussing *perestroika* and *glasnost,* he made one very telling admission: "We must always bear in mind that we are dealing with two completely different systems. We are a *socialist* country with a *planned economy.* Our *perestroika* will not change this."

Indeed only idealistic dreamers believe it will!

Despite recent events in the Soviet Union, I fervently hope that the move toward democracy in the Eastern Bloc is real. I recognize that within this arena in the present time there exists the greatest opportunity for Christian evangelism that has ever existed since the birth of Jesus Christ. However, our associates who are responsible for placing our animated Bible cartoon series and other programs on Soviet television have been told to work quickly. They may have only months before this window of opportunity is closed by the possibility of new policy changes and restrictions inside the Soviet Union.

The Master Plan

There are some who say that the events since 1989 in Eastern Europe and the Soviet Union were all carefully orchestrated by the KGB. In his gripping book, *New Lies for Old,* published in 1984, Anatoliy Golitsyn, a high-level KGB defector, laid out in meticulous detail—five years in advance of the liberalization movement in Eastern Europe—the precise blueprint for what has occurred over the past two years. Golitsyn's book is taken from knowledge of Soviet intentions gained much earlier.

The American CIA division chief who believed Golitsyn's story was dismissed. Now his words serve as a warning of impending deception. Because what he says is so significant, I would like to quote generously without comment from his chapter entitled, "The Final Phase." Please note again, Golitsyn reported these things to the CIA in the 1970s and published them in 1984, well before any of us had heard of *glasnost* and *perestroika.* He writes:

[T]he communist strategists are now poised to enter into the final, offensive phase of the long-range policy, entailing a joint struggle for the complete triumph of communism. Given the multiplicity of parties in power, the close links between them, and the opportunities they have had to broaden their bases and build up experienced cadres, the communist strategists are equipped, in pursuing their policy, to engage in maneuvers and stratagems beyond the imagination of Marx or the practical reach of Lenin and unthinkable to Stalin. Among such previously unthinkable stratagems are the introduction of false liberalization in Eastern Europe and, probably, in the Soviet Union and the exhibition of spurious independence on the part of the regimes in Romania, Czechoslovakia, and Poland. . . .

Because the West has failed either to understand communist strategy and disinformation or to appreciate the commitment to it of the resources of the bloc security and intelligence services and their high-level agents of political influence, the appearance of Solidarity in Poland has been accepted as a spontaneous occurrence comparable with the Hungarian revolt of 1956 and as portending the demise of communism in Poland. The fact that the Italian, French, and Spanish Communist parties all took up pro-Solidarity positions gives grounds for suspecting the validity of this interpretation.

Western misreading of events led to predictions of Soviet intervention in Poland in 1981, which turned out to be unjustified. It may lead to more serious errors in the future.

There are strong indications that the Polish version of "democratization," based in part on the Czechoslovak model, was prepared and controlled from the outset within the framework of bloc policy and strategy. . . .

As with the "Prague spring" of 1968, the motives for the Polish "renewal" were a combination of the internal and external. Internally it was designed to broaden the political base of the communist party in the trade unions and to convert the narrow, elitist dictatorship of the party into a Leninist dictatorship of the whole working class that would revitalize the Polish political and economic system. The "renewal" followed the lines of Lenin's speech to the Comintern congress in July 1921. "Our only strategy at present," said Lenin, "is to become stronger and therefore wiser, more reasonable, more opportunistic. The more opportunistic, the sooner will you assemble again the masses around you. When we have won over the masses by our reasonable approach, we shall then apply offensive tactics in the strictest sense of the word."

A coalition government in Poland would in fact be totalitarianism under a new, deceptive, and more dangerous guise. Accepted as the spontaneous emergence of a new form of multiparty, semidemocratic regime, it would serve to undermine resistance to communism inside and outside the communist bloc. The need for massive defense expenditure would increasingly be questioned in the West. New possibilities would arise for splitting Western Europe away from the United States, of neutralizing Germany, and destroying NATO. With North American influence in Latin America also undermined, the stage would be set for achieving actual revolutionary changes in the Western world through spurious changes in the communist system. . . .

Externally, the role of dissidents will be to persuade the West that the "liberalization" is spontaneous and not controlled. "Liberalization" will create conditions for establishing solidarity between trade unions and intellectuals in the communist and noncommunist worlds. In time such alliances will generate new forms of pressure against Western "militarism," "racism," and "military-industrial complexes" and in favor of disarmament and the kind of structural changes in the West predicted in [Andrei] Sakharov's writings.

If "liberalization" is successful and accepted by the West as genuine, it may well be followed by the apparent withdrawal of one or more communist countries from the Warsaw Pact to serve as the model of a "neutral" socialist state for the whole of Europe to follow. Some "dissidents" are already speaking in these terms. . . .

The Iraqi attack on Iran looks like a concerted effort by radical Arab states, each of which is in a united front relationship with the Soviet Union against "imperialism," to use dual tactics (hostilities by Iraq, assistance by Syria and Libya) with the single overall objective of bringing Iran into an anti-Western alliance with them. The object of the alliance would be to gain control over a strategically vital area of the Middle East. Its success could but serve the strategic interests of the communist bloc. Despite Saddam Hussein's alleged purges of communists in Iraq and the moderation in his attitude toward the United States, he is continuing to receive arms supplies from communist sources, as are his Iranian opponents.

The overall aim will be to bring about a major and irreversible shift in the balance of world power in favor of the bloc as a preliminary to the final ideological objective of establishing a worldwide federation of communist states.

The suggested European option would be promoted by a revival of controlled "democratization" on the Czechoslovak pattern in Eastern Europe, including probably Czechoslovakia and the Soviet Union. The intensification of hard-line policies and methods in the Soviet Union, exemplified by Sakharov's arrest and the occupation of Afghanistan, presages a switch to "democratization" following, perhaps, [Leonid] Brezhnev's departure from the political scene.

The following observations were made prior to Brezhnev's death. They are followed by comments on developments subsequent to that event.

Brezhnev's successor may well appear to be a kind of Soviet Dubcek. The succession will be important only in a presentational sense. The reality of collective leadership and the leaders' common commitment to the long-range policy will continue unaffected. Conceivably an announcement will be made to the effect that the economic and political foundations of communism in the Soviet Union have been laid and that democratization is therefore possible. This would provide the framework for the introduction of a new set of "reforms."

In the economic field reforms might be expected to bring Soviet practice more into line with Yugoslav, or even, seemingly, with Western socialist models. Some economic ministries might be dissolved; control would be more decentralized; individual self-managing firms might be created from existing plants and factories; material incentives would be increased; the independent role of technocrats, workers' councils, and trade unions would be enhanced; the party's control over the economy would be apparently diminished. Such reforms would be based on Soviet experience in the 1920s and 1960s, as well as on Yugoslav experience. The party would be less conspicuous, but would continue to control the economy from behind the scenes as before. The picture being deliberately painted now of stagnation and deficiencies in the Soviet economy should be seen as part of the preparation for deceptive innovations; it is intended to give the innovations greater impact on the West when they are introduced.

Political "liberalization" and "democratization" would follow the general lines of the Czechoslovak rehearsal in 1968. This rehearsal might well have been the kind of political experiment Mironov had in mind as early as 1960. The "liberalization" would be spectacular and impressive. Formal pronouncements might be made about a reduction in the communist party's role; its monopoly would be apparently curtailed. An ostensible separation of powers between the legislative, the executive, and the judiciary might be introduced. The Supreme Soviet would be given greater apparent power and the president and deputies greater apparent independence. The posts of president of the Soviet Union and first secretary of the party might well be separated. The KGB would be "reformed." Dissidents at home would be amnestied; those in exile abroad would be allowed to return, and some would take up positions of leadership in government. Sakharov might be included in some capacity in the government or allowed to teach abroad. The creative arts and cultural and scientific organizations, such as the writers' unions and Academy of Sciences, would become apparently more independent, as would the trade unions. Political clubs would be opened to nonmembers of the communist party. Leading dissidents might form one or more alternative political parties. Censorship would be relaxed; controversial books, plays, films, and art would be published, performed, and exhibited. Many prominent Soviet performing artists now abroad would return to the Soviet Union and resume their professional careers. Constitutional amendments would be adopted to guarantee fulfillment of the provisions of the Helsinki agreements and a semblance of compliance would be maintained. There would be greater freedom for Soviet citizens to travel. Western and United Nations observers would be invited to the Soviet Union to witness the reforms in action.

But, as in the Czechoslovak case, the "liberalization" would be calculated and deceptive in that it would be introduced from above.

Dissolution of the Warsaw Pact would have little effect on the coordination of the communist bloc, but the dissolution of NATO could well mean the departure of American forces from the European continent and a closer European alignment with a "liberalized" Soviet bloc. Perhaps in the longer run, a similar process might affect the relationship between the United States and Japan leading to abrogation of the security pact between them.

"Liberalization" in Eastern Europe on the scale suggested could have a social and political impact on the United States itself, especially if it coincided with a severe economic depression. The communist strategists are on the lookout for such an opportunity. Soviet and other communist economists keep a careful watch on the American economic situation. Since the adoption of the long-range policy, an Institute of World Economy and International Relations, originally under Arzumanyan and now under Inozemtsev, has been analyzing and forecasting for the Central Committee the performance of the noncommunist, and especially the American, economic system. Inozemtsev is a frequent visitor to the United States and was a member of a Soviet delegation received by the U.S. Congress in January 1978. The communist bloc will not repeat its error in failing to exploit a slump as it did in 1929–32. At that time the Soviet Union was weak politically and economically; next time the situation would be different. Politically the bloc would be better poised to exploit economic depression as proof of the failure of the capitalist system.

Information from communist sources that the bloc is short of oil and grain should be treated with particular reserve, since it could well be intended to conceal preparation for the final phase of the policy and to induce the West to underestimate the potency of the bloc's economic weapons.

A Soviet-socialist European coalition, acting in concert with the nonaligned movement in the United Nations, would create favorable conditions for communist strategy on disarmament. The American military-industrial complex would come under heavy fire. "Liberalization" in the Soviet Union and Eastern Europe would provide additional stimulus to disarmament. A massive U.S. defense budget might be found no longer justified. The argument for accommodation would be strengthened. Even China might throw in its weight in favor of a Soviet-socialist line on arms control and disarmament.

These predictions and analyses were made during Brezhnev's tenure in office in anticipation of his departure. Brezhnev's succession and other developments confirm, in essence, the validity of the author's views. For example, the expeditiousness of the appointment of Andropov as Brezhnev's successor confirmed one of the main theses of this book; namely, that the succession problem in the Soviet leadership has been revolved. The practical consideration of the long-term strategies has become the major stabilizing factor in this solution. The promotion of the former KGB chief, who was responsible for the preparation of the false liberalization strategy in the USSR, indicates that this factor was decisive in his selection and further points to the imminent advent of such "liberalization" in the near future.

It is more than likely that these cosmetic steps will be taken as genuine by the West and will trigger a reunification and neutralization of West Germany and further the collapse of NATO. The pressure on the United States for concessions on disarmament and accommodation with the Soviets will increase. During this period there might be an extensive display of the fictional struggle for power in the Soviet leadership. One cannot exclude that at the next party congress or earlier, Andropov will be replaced by a younger leader with a more liberal image who will continue the so-called "liberalization" more intensively.

The Shocking Truth

Are these the ravings of a madman? Is his narrative of detailed, dated political events wild-eyed and radical, or is it calm and precise?

Please note that Golitsyn accurately predicted, detail by detail, the very events that made news in the communist world in 1989, 1990, and 1991. Yet the establishment power block in this country chose to suppress his words so that the American people could not be warned by them. The Soviet Union has 4 million men in arms.

It has been feverishly building modern submarines and ultramodern missiles. Despite the squalor and desperation in Russia, the Soviet government is still spending as much as 25 percent of its entire national output on arms. Somewhere a voice must be raised in warning!

There is one last interesting footnote to what the *Foreign Affairs* journal is now calling the "new world order as conceived by Presidents Bush and Gorbachev." Mikhail Gorbachev was Communist party first secretary in a province known as Stavropol. The party first secretary of the adjoining province of Georgia was Eduard Shevardnadze. Andropov brought Gorbachev to Moscow as minister of agriculture. Gorbachev brought Shevardnadze to Moscow in July of 1985 as minister of the interior, a police function, and then made him minister of foreign affairs.

In his native Georgia, Shevardnadze was minister of internal affairs and a major general in the secret police, reportedly involved in suppression and torture. Shevardnadze has now become a close friend of Secretary of State James Baker and, according to a report given to me personally by an eminent evangelical leader, a born-again Christian. So suddenly Shevardnadze becomes a great champion of democracy and blasts his old friend and mentor Gorbachev publicly for the "specter of dictatorship" arising in the Soviet Union. Such a statement has to be trumped-up nonsense! The Soviet people have known nothing but ruthless dictatorship since 1917. How could a major general in the secret police be surprised by dictatorship? He was a key part of it!

But today the move is on in the establishment press in key places to break tradition and place Eduard Shevardnadze in the post of secretary-general of the United Nations. Just imagine the implications of this *new world order* under the aegis of a fully armed United Nations whose leader is none other than a former major general of the Soviet secret police. The scenario is too much like a chess game! Each move seems logical. Each move seems plausible. Each move has immense consequences and wide-ranging public support because those in charge of foreign policy are also in charge of key segments of the world's press.

What's worse, the America people are buying the concept. An August 1991 *Newsweek* poll shows that over half of the American public, largely in response to the role of the United Nations/United States joint effort in the Persian Gulf, supports the renewed empowerment of the United Nations and the submission of U.S. national interests to a world governing body.

The Devil's Advocate

The old adage is that when things seem too good to be true they usually are. Just think of the good news as seen through the eyes of the average citizen. America has had a fabulous, almost unbelievable victory in the Gulf. The defeatism of what is called the Vietnam Syndrome has been purged from our consciousness by a national festival of patriotic parades and welcome-home celebrations for the troops.

America is now the undisputed leader of the Free World. Our economy has faltered a bit, but our military might is unrivaled. Our industry, which has been mauled by the Japanese, has modernized, reorganized, and is ready to compete with the best in the world.

More than anything, the long Cold War seemed over, and the terrible threat of nuclear annihilation has receded from our national imagination. We seem to be entering an era of peace—the Pax Americana—during which our massive spending on the military establishment could be reduced.

We are living in a time of an unbelievable acceptance of spiritual values in the Soviet Union, Eastern Europe, Latin America, Africa, and Asia. In 1990 alone, the organization I head, the Christian Broadcasting Network, sponsored a gospel media blitz in Nicaragua, El Salvador, Guatemala, and Argentina that resulted in 6 million decisions for Christ. In the Soviet Union our offices have received over 2 million handwritten letters from across the nation. We are planning a television blitz this year, similar to that in Central and South America, which we believe will result in 20 million people receiving Jesus Christ as their Savior in the Soviet Union. A similar effort in Zaire in 1991 is expected to bring comparable results.

With good news like this to bolster our nation, it would be most unwise to embark on a program to surrender the sovereignty of the United States to any world body, and particularly one that is as poorly constituted and inept as the present United Nations.

I know George Bush. I have met with him in the White House, and I personally believe that President Bush is an honorable man and a man of integrity. Nevertheless, I believe that he has become convinced, as Woodrow Wilson was before him, of the idealistic possibilities of a world at peace under the benign leadership of a forum for all nations.

But I am equally convinced that for the past two hundred years the term *new world order* has been the code phrase of those who desired to destroy the Christian faith and what Pope Pius XI termed the "Christian social order." They wish to replace it with an occult-inspired world socialist dictatorship.

The task of good men now will be to fight with all their strength to preserve the gains in liberty and freedom that have recently come to the people of the world, while resisting with equal strength all attempts—however idealistic and well-meaning—to subvert the sovereignty of this great nation and place it into a one-world socialistic order.

To begin this struggle, we must learn more about the idealists, the dreamers, the manipulators, and the money men who through the decades have grasped for such control of the world.

And, more than that, we must learn a better way.

PART 2

Threats to Freedom

5

The Establishment

T HE DISTINGUISHED PRIME MINISTER of England, Benjamin Disraeli, once wrote, "The world is governed by very different personages than what is imagined by those who are not behind the scenes."

Woodrow Wilson, whose principal adviser was a behind-the-scenes operator, said, "There is a power somewhere so organized, so subtle, so watchful, so interlocked, so complete, so pervasive that they better not speak above their breath when they speak in condemnation of it."

Historians normally recount the deeds and exploits of kings, presidents, prime ministers, secretaries, and cabinet ministers. In truth, the real power to choose presidents and prime ministers is not in public view—it is behind the scenes. Such men generally prefer to operate in great secrecy, although some have a certain public face. Invariably, however, they control such enormous wealth that their collective voices can cause rulers to tremble and governments—along with their national economies—to fall.

If indeed there is in the United States a powerful group attempting to control our world, who is it and how did it get its start?

Rest assured, there is a behind-the-scenes Establishment in this nation, as in every other. It has enormous power. It has controlled the economic and foreign policy objectives of the United States for the past seventy years, whether the man sitting in the White House is a Democrat or a Republican, a liberal or a conservative, a moderate or an extremist. This power is above elections, but it has been able to control the results of elections. Beyond the control of wealth, its principal goal is the establishment of a one-world government where the control of money is in the hands of one or more privately owned but government-chartered central banks.

The visible home of the Establishment is Pratt House, on the corner of Park Avenue and Sixty-Eighth Street in New York City, right across the street from the Soviet embassy to the United Nations. This is the headquarters of the Council on Foreign Relations, and from here the Establishment reaches out to the many power centers. Here are just a few: the U.S. State Department, the U.S. Treasury Department, the Federal Reserve Board, the Export-Import Bank, the Rockefeller Foundation, the Rockefeller family, the Rockefeller Brothers Fund, the Ford Foundation, the Carnegie Foundation, the Chase Manhattan Bank, First National City Bank, J. P. Morgan and Company, Harvard University, Columbia University, Yale University, the University of Chicago, the *Washington Post,* the *New York Times,* the *Los Angeles Times,* and scores of international corporations, investment banking houses, private foundations, and media outlets in this country, in England, and on the continent of Europe.

Making Foreign Policy

In government policy, the most visible expression of the Establishment is the Council on Foreign Relations and its publication, *Foreign Affairs.* Out of some twenty-nine hundred members, at least five hundred are very powerful, another five hundred are from centers of influence, and the rest are influential in academia, the media, business and finance, the military, or government. A few are token conservatives.

According to a man who had been a member for fifteen years, Rear Admiral Chester Ward, former judge advocate general of the navy from 1956 to 1960,

> [T]his purpose of promoting disarmament and submergence of U.S. sovereignty and national independence into an all-powerful one-world government is the only objective revealed to about 95 percent of 1,551 members [in 1975]. There are two other ulterior purposes that CFR influence is being used to promote; but it is improbable that they are known to more than 75 members, or that these purposes ever have even been identified in writing.

The goals of the Establishment are somewhat strange, and we will discuss them in detail. At the central core is a belief in the superiority of their own skill to form a world system in which enlightened monopolistic capitalism can bring all of the diverse currencies, banking systems, credit, manufacturing, and raw materials into one government-supervised whole, policed of course by their own world army.

To accomplish what they perceive as this enlightened goal, they have set out in dozens of ways to weaken the national sovereignty of the United States so that it will be too weak to withstand the coercive pressure of a world government. At the same time, they have perceived that radical Marxism is an important intermediate step toward their goal of a managed world economy, so they have used their influence to promote the communist takeover of Russia, China, Eastern Europe, and parts of Central America and Africa. Some members are genuinely idealistic and feel this is the only way to world peace. Others are simply greedy and power hungry. And some, I fear, are motivated by other powers.

There have been communists or Soviet centers of influence such as Alger Hiss, Owen Lattimore, and Corliss Lamont among them, but on the whole these people are not communists. They are well-bred, highly refined, quite wealthy world leaders. Somewhere along the way they fell victim to the philosophic fallacy that the end justifies the means. And for many of them, the means (communist revolution and world government) became the end itself.

Some political leaders—including Jimmy Carter, Woodrow Wilson, and hopefully George Bush—have spouted the slogans of the Establishment theoreticians without fully understanding what they were saying and doing. Others have used positions of power in the government of the United States for programs that are nothing short of treason.

Special Privilege

Keep in mind, when speaking of the CFR, the *Washington Post,* the *New York Times,* or Harvard University, that these are not left-wing, pinko organizations. They are instead Establishment organizations that desire a one-world government. Many among them feel that supporting world socialism in one of its forms will facilitate their own long-range goals.

The views of these people toward world government are frankly so impractical and bizarre as to earn them a place of shame. Instead, they run huge banks, multinational corporations, the nation's financial system, the State Department, the Treasury Department, and the better part of the entire world.

The power of the Establishment is beyond question. Since 1940 every United States secretary of state except one (former Governor James Byrnes of South Carolina) has been a CFR member. And since 1940, all secretaries of war/defense, from Henry L. Stimson through Richard Cheney, have been CFR members. Here is the list:

SECRETARY OF STATE	SECRETARY OF WAR/DEFENSE
Robert Lansing†	Newton N. Baker†
Charles Evans Hughes	Dwight F. Davis
Frank B. Kellogg	Henry L. Stimson
Henry L. Stimson	Robert Patterson
Cordell Hull	James Forrestal
Edward R. Stettinius	George Marshall
George Marshall	Robert Lovett
Dean Acheson	Charles Wilson
John Foster Dulles	Neal H. McElroy

Christian Herter	Thomas S. Gates, Jr.
Dean Rusk	Robert McNamara
William F. Rogers	Elliott Richardson
Henry Kissinger	James Schlesinger
Cyrus Vance	Donald Rumsfield
Edmund Muskie	Harold Brown
Alexander Haig	Caspar Weinberger
George Schultz	Frank Carlucci
James Baker	Richard Cheney

†CFR Founders

The CIA during most of the years since its creation has been under CFR control, starting with Allen Dulles, founding member of the CFR and brother of another founding CFR member and later secretary of state under President Eisenhower, John Foster Dulles.

Many of these men have held other influential posts. Dean Rusk and Cyrus Vance had been presidents of the Rockefeller Foundation. Charles Evans Hughes, in addition to serving on the board of the Rockefeller Foundation, was appointed chief justice of the U.S. Supreme Court. Admiral James Forrestal became secretary of defense and died some years later under very unusual circumstances.

During the Kennedy and Johnson administrations, more than sixty CFR members held top policy-making positions. McGeorge Bundy was employed on the staff of the Council on Foreign Relations, went from there to be the dean of the faculty of Arts and Sciences at Harvard, then became a key aide and national security adviser to John F. Kennedy. Bundy left that post to head the Ford Foundation. His brother, William Bundy, served as editor of *Foreign Affairs,* the CFR publication deemed so influential that it was even read by Lenin.

Under Richard Nixon the number of CFR members in major policy positions leapt to a hundred, and the story of their selection is mind-boggling. Former Secretary of the Navy William Mittendorf told me that he served as finance chairman of the 1968 Nixon campaign. On the night of the election he occupied a hotel room across the hall from the candidate. At 5:30 A.M. on the morning after Nixon's election victory, Mittendorf saw Nelson Rockefeller and William

Rogers come down the hotel corridor and enter Nixon's room. Later Rogers told Mittendorf that they were there to help select the cabinet.

Inside Information

What is not known is that Richard Nixon joined the CFR in 1961 and then resigned in 1965. He worked as a partner in the law firm of Nelson Rockefeller's bond counsel, John Mitchell, and occupied an apartment at 810 Fifth Avenue that was owned by Nelson Rockefeller, which adjoined the place where Rockefeller lived. During the mid-1960s, for the first time in his life, Nixon was making substantial sums of money. To quote another commentator on that subject, "Nelson Rockefeller was Nixon's employer, benefactor, landlord, and neighbor" during this period.

Insiders, like Mittendorf, were not surprised when Nixon chose Henry Kissinger, a man whom he had reportedly never met, to become his national security adviser and later secretary of state. Kissinger, as it turned out, was a protégé of Nelson Rockefeller and entered the White House straight from the staff of the Council on Foreign Relations—with, I might add, a $50,000 Rockefeller check to help with the expenses of the transition.

Nixon appointed Charles Yost, another paid CFR staff member, to be United Nations ambassador. He chose CFR members Arthur Burns to head the Federal Reserve Board, Gerald Smith to be director of the Arms Control and Disarmament Agency, Dr. Paul McCracken to head the Council of Economic Advisers, Joseph J. Sisco to be assistant secretary of state for the Middle East and South Asia, and, of course, Bill Rogers became secretary of state. Nixon actually detached, on September 7, 1970, Brigadier General Robert L. Gard, Jr., from the office of the assistant chief of staff for force development for assignment to the headquarters of the Council on Foreign Relations in New York.

We must not forget that it was Nixon who also selected a young former Texas congressman, who had lost a Senate race against

Democrat Lloyd Bentsen, to be chairman of the Republican party, ambassador to the United Nations, ambassador to China, and director of the CIA. That former congressman was a longtime CFR member and a CFR director in the late 1970s. He was none other than George Bush.

Perhaps knowing who his foreign policy advisers were may help explain why Nixon, the strong anticommunist, faithfully carried out major CFR goals—recognition of Communist China, signing the Anti-Ballistic Missile Treaty and the Strategic Arms Limitation treaty with the Soviets, continuing a Keynesian economic policy, and decoupling the U.S. dollar from gold.

Nixon, as you may remember, rose to power as the vice president under the Eastern Establishment candidate Dwight Eisenhower, who ran for the presidency as a Republican against another CFR member, Adlai Stevenson, who later became John Kennedy's ambassador to (you guessed it) the United Nations.

Long-Range Control

Of course, the present United Nations organization is actually the creation of the CFR and is housed on land in Manhattan donated to it by the family of current CFR chairman David Rockefeller. According to State Department Publication 2349, entitled "Report to the President on the Results of the San Francisco Conference" submitted by CFR member and then Secretary of State Edward R. Stettinius, "a committee on post-war problems was set up before the end of 1939 at the suggestion of the CFR."

Imagine! *Two years before the United States entered World War II, the CFR was already planning how to order the world when the war was over.* We may assume from this initiative that the entry of the United States into World War II was certain to these people two years before the "dastardly attack" at Pearl Harbor on December 7, 1941. How reminiscent this was of the entry of the United States into World War I at the urging of a founder of the CFR, President Wilson's key aide, Colonel Edward House.

The American delegation to the San Francisco meeting that drafted the charter of the United Nations included CFR members Nelson Rockefeller, John Foster Dulles, John McCloy, and CFR members who were communist agents—Alger Hiss, Harry Dexter White, and Owen Lattimore. In all, the Council sent forty-seven of its members in the United States delegation, effectively controlling the outcome.

For better or worse, the United Nations as we now have it, the International Monetary Fund, the World Bank, and the Bretton Woods monetary agreement were not the work of the United States government, per se, but that of the members of the Council on Foreign Relations carrying out the stated (and perhaps unstated) goals of that organization.

Perhaps the most blatant exercise of the power of the Establishment occured in the selection of their 1976 presidential candidate.

In 1970 a young Polish intellectual named Zbigniew Brezinski foresaw the rising economic power of Japan and postwar Europe. Brezinski idealized the theories of Karl Marx. In his book, *Between Two Ages,* as in subsequent writings, he argued that balance-of-power politics was out and world-order politics was in. The initial world order was to be a trilateral economic linkage between Japan, Europe, and the United States. David Rockefeller funded Brezinski and called together an organization, named the Trilateral Commission, with Brezinski as its first executive secretary and director.

The stated goals of the Trilateral Commission are: "Close Trilateral cooperation in keeping the peace, *in managing the world economy,* in fostering economic re-development and alleviating world poverty will improve the chances of a *smooth and peaceful evolution of the global system."* (Emphasis added.)

In other words, a three-cornered world system to "manage the world economy" will pave the way to world government. Senator Barry Goldwater's critique was scathing.

What the Trilaterals truly intend is the creation of a *worldwide economic power superior to the political government of the nation states involved. As managers and creators of the system, they will rule the future.* (Emphasis added.)

Brezinski took under his wing a born-again Baptist peanut farmer from South Georgia named Jimmy Carter, who had served one term as governor of that state. Brezinski took Carter as his pupil, filled him full of the philosophy of global government, and then brought him on as a member of the Trilateral Commission. Carter was an eager pupil who later wrote in his book, *Why Not the Best?* "Membership on this Commission has provided me with a splendid learning opportunity, and many of the other members have helped me in my study of foreign affairs."

Changing Horses

It was obvious that after the Watergate scandal the Republican nominee, Gerald Ford, was in trouble going into the 1976 election. The population of the country had been moving south and west. After Vietnam and Watergate, there was a search for honesty and integrity. What better candidate for president than an unknown Southerner, an outsider, and a born-again Christian whose principal campaign pledge was, "You can trust me!"

Sometime in 1973, David Rockefeller picked Carter, and soon after the Establishment machinery went to work on his behalf. I learned in 1989, a long time after the fact, that a private security agency had been hired to meet a private plane at the Des Moines, Iowa, airport one night and to bring the passenger, Jimmy Carter, to a private meeting at the offices of the *Des Moines Register,* presumably for a briefing on the crucial 1976 Iowa presidential caucuses. The *Register* was formerly part of the Cowles Publishing empire, the owner of which was an ardent CFR member. My source in Des Moines said that in those days the *Des Moines Register* considered itself the Midwest outpost of the CFR.

Given a favorable press umbrella by the state's most powerful newspaper and by dint of incredible personal exertion, the man who had been called "Jimmy who?" won the Iowa caucuses and was whisked by jet that night to New York City for appearances on all three of the morning national network television programs. The next crucial test was the New Hampshire primary where Carter won in a crowded field with only about twenty-eight thousand votes for a 33 percent plurality. From then on "front runner" Carter was covered with favorable press by the CFR media.

I personally was thrilled to think that a born-again Christian might gain the White House, and I gave Carter a boost with some friends of mine who were active in organized labor in Pennsylvania. After Carter won the Pennsylvania primary (believed, incorrectly I might add, to be a Northern, liberal, industrial state), the Southern peanut farmer had effectively won the Democratic nomination.

After the general election in November, I spoke to President-Elect Carter during a three-way telephone conversation along with pro-family activist Lou Sheldon of California. I suggested to Governor Carter that he, as a strong evangelical, might want to include some evangelical Christians among his appointments. He greeted the idea with enthusiasm and agreed to receive a list if we could get it to him within two weeks.

Lou Sheldon and I worked night and day to put together a short roster of names and résumés. The finished product was outstanding. All of the candidates were Democrats. All were highly distinguished in government, business, or education. The composition of the group looked like what Jesse Jackson sometime later called the Rainbow Coalition.

We had included male and female blacks, whites, Hispanics, native Hawaiians, and, I believe, a Chinese-American. A friend of a friend even obtained a preliminary thumbs up/thumbs down FBI screening to keep us from wasting the president-elect's time. (We had to omit one born-again Democratic governor from the South because of alleged campaign contributions by reputed Mafia figures.)

When the document was ready, I chartered a small aircraft to take Lou Sheldon to the grassy strip in Georgia we laughingly called

"Plains International." Sheldon arrived at the Carter residence to find the next president barefoot and in blue jeans. They greeted each other warmly, and Sheldon proudly presented the booklet. Carter took it, read it, and began to cry.

When he got back to Virginia Beach, Sheldon said, "Jimmy was so touched by all the work that we did that tears came to his eyes." I said, "Lou, you are wrong. The reason he cried is because the appointment process is out of his hands, and he is not going to appoint any of those people." And indeed my words were true. Not one of our recommendations—men and women who on the surface shared every principle that Jimmy Carter espoused—was appointed to public office, or even seriously considered.

Rash Promises

Hamilton Jordan, Carter's brilliant but socially obnoxious campaign manager, was also surprised. Jordan reportedly said, "If, after the inauguration you find Cy Vance as secretary of state and Zbigniew Brezinski as head of national security, then I would say that we failed, and I'd quit."

But, in fact, that is precisely what happened. Carter's teacher, Brezinski, took the national security council post. Cyrus Vance who, like John Kennedy's secretary of state, Dean Rusk, had previously served as president of the Rockefeller Foundation, was made secretary of state.

Trilateral Commission member Walter Mondale, whose brother had signed the first *Humanist Manifesto*, was selected as vice president. CFR member Stansfield Turner was placed in charge of the CIA. Trilateral member Mike Blumenthal, whose family connections went back to internationalist banker Lazard Freres, was put in charge of the treasury. But more significant to the average American, Paul Volcker, a former employee of Rockefeller's Chase Manhattan Bank, was given the powerful role of chairman of the Federal Reserve Board. Out of only sixty-five American members on the Trilateral Commission, thirteen, including the president and vice president, were given top posts in the Carter administration.

Lest we forget, the Trilateral Commission, tagged by Senator Barry Goldwater as a scheme to place control of the world in the hands of "a worldwide economic power superior to the political government of the nation states involved," included in its membership (until he resigned about the time of the 1980 election) George Bush.

Jimmy Carter, who seems to be a decent enough person, was by aptitude and training totally unsuited for the presidency of the most powerful nation on earth. But in his four short years, he served his backers well.

Carter chose CFR member Sol Linowitz, a board member of a bank that had made loans to Panama, to be his emissary to negotiate away the United States ownership of the vital Panama Canal to Panamanian Dictator Omar Torrijos. Torrijos was succeeded in office by that paragon of virtue, accused drug smuggler Manuel Noriega.

In 1977, Panama owed $1.7 billion, much of it to U.S. banks, which included Chase Manhattan, First National City Bank (now Citicorp), Bank of America, Banker's Trust, First National Bank of Chicago, and Marine Midland Bank (where Sol Linowitz was a director). Revenues from canal fees would be used to pay down the bank loans. Later Panama created a tax-free banking haven to reward its friends for their help.

The Panama Canal is a vital link for shipping from the West Coast of the United States to the East Coast and vice versa. It is one of the strategic choke points of the world. A look at the map quickly reveals that no other waterway exists for that purpose. The other sea route is to go all the way around Tierra del Fuego, at the extreme tip of South America, which is a totally unrealistic option for regular shipping.

The only other likely site for an alternate canal is in Nicaragua, which has two large inland lakes that could easily be connected by an inland waterway from the Pacific to the Caribbean. But under the Carter administration, the second canal option was violently taken away when Carter's people engineered the ouster of the pro-American leader of Nicaragua, West Point-trained Anastasio Somoza, and then brought in the Soviet- and Cuban-backed communist Sandinistas.

The Deadly Truth

Jack Cox's book, *Nicaragua Betrayed*, features a bombshell—an extended interview with Somoza. I interviewed Cox on my television program and learned the shocking truth about the betrayal of a United States ally by the Carter administration's State Department. In Somoza's own words:

> [Carter's] single-minded and overwhelming purpose has been to put Nicaragua in the hands of the communists. . . . Mr. Carter had effectively cut off Nicaragua from any possible source of supply.

At the conclusion of the book General Somoza makes this incredible charge:

> [T]he betrayal of steadfast anti-communist allies places Mr. Carter in the company of worldwide conspiratorial forces. I repeat, the treacherous course charted by Mr. Carter was not through ignorance, but by design.

Then Somoza continued:

> [W]hile I'm privileged to tread this planet called earth, I shall do all within my power to see that other free nations do not suffer the agonizing death which struck Nicaragua. In my own way I am sounding the alarm. It is my wish, it is my impassioned hope that the freedom loving people of the United States will hear the alarm and that they will respond without delay. There is no time for dalliance.

Shortly after *Nicaragua Betrayed* was published, however, General Somoza's time to "tread this earth" was cut short when a rocket fired by an unknown assassin blew up his vehicle on a street in Paraguay, where he had gone seeking asylum. He apparently knew too much to be allowed to live.

I visited Nicaragua just before the recent election. I talked with Violeta Chamorro before she was elected president. I met with various church leaders and a key member of the ruling Sandinista junta. Previously I had visited a Contra camp in Honduras located on the border of Nicaragua. I also have met and interviewed the current president and the past two presidents of El Salvador. I have a first-hand view of the truth in Central America that goes back many years.

Betrayal and Insult

The legacy of the Carter presidency in Central America is horrible. Nicaragua under the Sandinistas is one of the most wretched places I have ever visited. Around the capital of Managua there are miles of wretched hovels that resemble children's tree houses. Annual inflation at the time of my visit was 30,000 percent. The economy has been virtually destroyed. Unemployment is epidemic. The per capita income of the people is, along with Haiti, the lowest in the Western Hemisphere.

But Nicaragua under communism gave Fidel Castro a base for subversion against El Salvador, Guatemala, and Mexico. The flyleaf of *Nicaragua Betrayed* quotes the *Valeurs Actuelles,* a French political and economic weekly that carried on July 23, 1979, a conversation between Henry Kissinger and Lopez Portillo, then president of Mexico. Portillo said that he had told President Carter:

> "I do not particularly like Somoza or his regime, as you know. But if the Sandinistas unseat him and replace him with a Castro-picked government it will touch off a slide to the left in my country."
>
> "What did President Carter reply?"
>
> "It was as though he did not hear a word I said," Portillo confided. "He told me: 'Oh, Mr. President, you must do something to help me get rid of this Somoza.'"

A communist government in Nicaragua gave the Soviets two extraordinarily important military assets. First, air bases to receive long-range bombers and surveillance planes after they had flown from the Soviet Union along the West Coast of the United States. Second, Nicaragua has a superb harbor called El Bluff, which is perfect for submarines that could threaten vital U.S. shipping through the Panama Canal and in and out of the Gulf ports of

Houston, Galveston, and New Orleans. As photographs revealed on national television by President Ronald Reagan showed, Nicaragua also became a key safe haven and staging area for drug trafficking from Colombia into the United States.

Postcommunist Nicaragua is a perfect laboratory for us in 1991 to examine the CFR dreams of a new world order. This single exercise of new order foreign policy brought a ruthless dictatorship, violation of human rights, confiscation of property, state socialism, a wrecked economy, subversion of neighboring democratic nations, and the undermining of the economic health and strategic security of the United States.

When the facts are known it is clear to me that anyone who takes an oath of office to uphold and defend the Constitution of the United States and then deliberately attempts to subvert the sovereignty and the strategic interest of this nation in favor of those of another government—world order or not—is guilty of, in a word, treason. Think again of the words of Richard Gardner, former deputy assistant secretary of state, that appeared in the CFR journal: "We are likely to do better by building our 'house of world order' from bottom up rather than from the top down . . . *an end run around national sovereignty, eroding it piece by piece,* is likely to get us to world order faster than the old fashioned assault." (Emphasis added.)

How dare an official (or even a former official) of the United States government set out to erode the sovereignty of the United States piece by piece! How dare a cabal of elected and unelected officials set out to subvert our constitution, our national sovereignty, and our democratic way of life!

Have any of us been told that the secretaries of state, the secretaries of the treasury, the heads of the CIA, the heads of the National Security Council, the heads of the Federal Reserve Board, and countless others are in agreement that American sovereignty is to be "eroded piece by piece"? When has there ever been a referendum for all of the people to decide whether they want to discard our Constitution in favor of a one-world government? The clear answer is, "Never!" Yet that is what the Establishment was preparing for us well before 1917.

The Work of a Dreamer

Obviously the Establishment was not lowered down from heaven, nor did it rise full blown from hell. The best available records show that it sprang from the minds of an amazing man named John Ruskin and of his most apt pupil, Cecil Rhodes.

It was while he was attending Oxford University that Rhodes came under the influence of Ruskin. Ruskin believed in a platonic ideal society in which the state would control the means of production and distribution and which, in turn, is itself controlled for the benefit of all by those best suited by aptitude for the task. He believed, in other words, in the rule of the elite.

Ruskin taught Rhodes that the British upper classes possessed a "magnificent tradition of education, beauty, rule of law, decency, and self-discipline" that could not be saved unless it were extended to "the lower classes in England and to the non-English masses throughout the world."

The price of failure would be that the minority of upper-class Englishmen would ultimately be submerged by these majorities and their tradition lost. We learn that Ruskin read Plato every day. Plato wanted a ruling class with a powerful army and society subservient to it. Old social classes should be wiped away to give a clean slate for the new world to follow.

What seemingly evolved was an Anglo-Saxon platonic utopianism under which the old order of the world would be stripped away to prepare the world for the benign rule of the Anglo-Saxon aristocratic and monied classes. Most thinking people would say, as I do, that such notions are unadulterated hogwash, but sometimes the aberrant ravings of a so-called scholar, tucked away in a cloistered ivory tower, bear seed in a man of action.

Rhodes was such a man. In his maturity Rhodes exploited the diamond mines and gold fields of South Africa and founded the nation that came to be known as Rhodesia. With financial help from the powerful Rothschild banking interests he founded the DeBeers Consolidated Mines and the Consolidated Gold Fields. He conceived of a telegraph and rail link from the Cape of Good Hope to Cairo. And by the mid-1890s, Rhodes had a personal annual income of 1 million pounds sterling (the probable inflation adjusted equivalent of $100 million today).

Georgetown Professor Carroll Quigley, in his book *Tragedy and Hope,* which has been excerpted so skillfully by my friend Cleon Skousen in his excellent work *The Naked Capitalist,* says that despite this enormous income, Rhodes was spending so much on fulfilling the dreams of Ruskin that he was usually overdrawn on his account. Skousen writes:

> These purposes centered on his desire to federate the English-speaking peoples and to bring *all the habitable portions of the world under their control.* For this purpose Rhodes left part of his great fortune to found the Rhodes Scholarships at Oxford in order to spread the English ruling class tradition. (Emphasis added.)

Again, Quigley tells us that Rhodes and other of Ruskin's pupils formed a secret society. Rhodes was the leader; Lord Esher, Lord Milner, and a man named Stead were the executive committee. Lord Balfour, Sir Henry Johnson, Lord Rothschild, Lord Gray, and others were listed as a circle of initiates. Then an outer circle of initiates was later organized by Lord Milner and called the Round Table.

The British Round Table

The Round Table gained access to Rhodes's money after his death in 1902, and Lord Milner became the trustee of the Rhodes trust. Lord Milner was also governor-general and high commissioner of South Africa from 1897–1905. He gathered young men around him then and placed them in key positions in government and finance.

From 1909–13, Lord Milner organized semi-secret groups, known as Round Table Groups, in the British dependencies and America. In 1919, they founded the Royal Institute of International Affairs (Chatham House), financed by Sir Abe Bailey and the Astor family. The Council on Foreign Relations was conceived of at the same time in Paris by Colonel Edward M. House as the United States affiliate of the Royal Institute of International Affairs and, of course, the various Round Table groups.

According to Quigley:

> From 1884 to about 1915 the members of the group worked valiantly to extend the British empire and to organize it into a federal system. . . . Stead was able to get Rhodes to accept, in principle, a solution which might have made Washington the capital of the whole organization or allow parts of the empire to become states of the American Union.

Quigley continues:

> [T]he American branch of this organization (sometimes called the "Eastern Establishment") has played a very significant role in the United States in the last generation.
>
> The chief backbone of this organization grew up along the already existing financial cooperation running from the Morgan Bank in New York to a group of international financiers in London led by Lazard Brothers. Lord Milner became a director of the precursor to the giant Midland Bank. He became one of the greatest political and financial powers in England with his disciples placed throughout England in significant places, such as the editorship of the *Times,* the editorship of the *Observer,* the managing directorship of Lazard Brothers, various administrative posts, and even Cabinet positions. Ramifications were established in politics, high finance, Oxford and London Universities, periodicals, the civil service, and tax-exempt foundations.

In other words, the pattern of operation was set in England, but the American Establishment has played it out to the letter. Quigley also claimed that, in New York, the Council on Foreign Relations was a front for J. P. Morgan and Company.

> The New York branch was dominated by associates of the Morgan Bank. For example, in 1928 the Council on Foreign Relations had John

W. Davis as president, Paul Cravath as vice president, and a council of thirteen others, which included Owen D. Young, Russell Leffingwell, Norman Davis, Allen Dulles, George Wickersham, Frank L. Polk, Whitney Sheperdson, Isaiah Bowman, Stephen P. Duggan, and Otto Kahn.

The group was "cosmopolitan, Anglophile, internationalist, Ivy League, Eastern seaboard, high Episcopalian, and European-culture conscious."

The Power of Influence

By virtue of large grants and control of endowments, these men came to dominate the Ivy League universities and the selection of their presidents. Closely allied with Morgan, and later the Rockefellers, were the powerful Wall Street lawyers from John W. Davis and Paul Cravath to the Dulles brothers and John J. McCloy. Through direct ownership, use of trust and pension money, or by influence over powerful editors, their thoughts came to dominate the Establishment newspapers, then major broadcast chains, and then major magazines and scholarly periodicals.

First with the Morgan Bank, then with the Rockefellers and their Chase Manhattan and First National City Banks, then with foundations established by Carnegie, Ford, and the Rockefellers, the money power of the CFR has come to be enormous. But why would the big money interests veer away from the goal of Anglo-Saxon world domination to flirt with radical Marxism?

The reason is simple. It is easier to deal with a single autocratic authority than with the divided political forces of a democracy. A few years ago when I began the negotiations for a broadcast outlet in Israel—which ultimately led to CBN's television station on the Lebanese border—a kindly Israeli official suggested, "Why don't you try Jordan? Jordan has a king." In other words, a single powerful ruler can make decrees and enforce them. In the case of Israel, a government can fall because of the disaffection of one or more splinter parties; therefore, some things were not politically feasible even if the government wanted them.

Professor Quigley, who professed admiration for the goals of the Establishment and claimed to have been given access to the papers from their secret inner councils, confessed that the men of power and finance who had set out to remake the world were perfectly confident that they could use their money to acquire the cooperation and eventual control of the communist-socialist groups. Ruskin had taught (and Colonel House had written) that the new world federation was to have all property, industry, agriculture, communications, transportation, education, and political affairs in the hands of a small cadre of financially controlled political leaders.

As Cleon Skousen, commenting on Quigley's exposé, points out:

The master planners have attempted to control the global conspiratorial groups by feeding them vast quantities of money for their revolutionary work and then financing their opposition if they seemed to be getting out of control. This policy has required the leaders of London and Wall Street to deliberately align themselves with dictatorial forces which have committed crimes against humanity in volume and severity unprecedented in history.

Quigley, the historian, makes this final observation:

It was this group of people, whose wealth and influence so exceeded their experience and understanding, who provided much of the framework of influence which the communist sympathizers and fellow travelers took over in the United States in the 1930s. It must be recognized that the power that these energetic left-wingers exercised was never their own power or communist power but was ultimately the power of the international financial coterie.

Thus, we have the unbelievable result of the marriage of money and utopian theory. Earlier I mentioned the hypocrisy of utopian John Lennon calling for the abolition of private property for the human race, then leaving an estate of $250 million to his Japanese-born widow. But consider also David Rockefeller, enjoying a personal fortune in excess of $1 billion, living in a gracious estate and his elegant residences in the capitals of the world, driving in chauffeured limousines, flying private jets, dining on the finest food, yet giving massive financial assistance for decades to demonic tyrants to enable them to crush and grind the poor into the earth.

What possible self-delusion can come upon those with multi-million-dollar incomes, enjoying personally the fruits of a free society, who place their money and influence at the service of utopian fantasies which will doubtlessly create a world of slavery and undermine the nation that brought forth their own wealth? Will it not be one of the supreme ironies of history that the madness they have unleashed on the world will one day consume them, too?

The Driving Force

The stream of world order flowing from the Illuminati is clearly occultic and satanic. The carnage that they have brought about is also understandable, given its ultimate source.

What is not clear is how monied, privileged, ostensibly Christian people could willingly and knowingly support the cruel, the barbaric, and the satanic. Quigley's hypothesis, on the surface, seems to provide the explanation. The power of money, by itself, also explains a great deal.

We have explored the link between Marxist communism and the occult Illuminati. What we have not touched upon is a link between these centers of privilege (which have been paying the bills for the communists in order to bring about a new world order) and the occultic, New Age agenda which, in turn, promises a mystical new world order.

Both groups are moving toward one goal, but at the highest, most secret levels. Is there a tie? But more on that in a later chapter.

6

Follow the Money

T<small>HE ORIGIN OF MONEY IS MYSTERIOUS</small> to most people. It is something they receive as wages and in turn spend for food, clothing, recreation, transportation, and shelter. A sizable portion of their money goes for taxes, but under pay-as-you-go taxation, taxes are not "paid," only deducted.

The international bankers have tried to tell us that money is a commodity, like flour or cement, which rises and falls in price depending on demand. But to most people money consists of pieces of paper printed in numerous denominations with pictures of various presidents and famous men. To some, money is the balance a computer tells them is deposited in their name at a bank or in some money market fund. When asked what the source of money is, they usually reply, "The government."

When the founders of the United States drew up our governing document, the Constitution, they were very specific about the creation of money. The key constitutional provision is Article 1, Section 8, which clearly charges the people's representatives, the Congress, with the "power to coin money and regulate the value thereof." To ensure a national currency, the states of the new union were forbidden to make anything but gold or silver payment for debts.

The power to create money and to regulate its quantity and value is the power to control the life of a nation. If there is too much money, prices rise. Inflation then causes interest rates to rise, and the value of the savings of the people is destroyed. If there is not enough money, the economy will collapse. Debts cannot be paid. Workers will be laid off. Construction and retail activity will slow down or dry up. And poorly funded owners of business or property will lose their businesses and property.

Obviously, if any private group could guarantee easy money to the economy, they would be in a position to loan money, build factories, buy stocks, and participate in growth opportunities. Conversely, if they could guarantee tight money, they could reduce loan exposure, short stocks, sell businesses, and then buy them back later at distressed prices at the bottom of what is called a recession or a depression. All things being equal, the control of money is the ability to bring prosperity or disaster on a nation.

Any nation that gives control of its money creation and regulation to any authority outside itself has effectively turned over control of its own future to that body. Ultimately, this was the battle that cost former British Prime Minister Margaret Thatcher her job.

Thatcher knew that linking the British pound to the European Currency Unit (ECU) and then agreeing to merge the British pound into a European currency would effectively put Great Britain in the hands of the president of the European Community, Jacques DeLors (a socialist), the other European socialist countries, and a European central bank controlled by the German Bundesbank. This would mean the loss of British sovereignty over its economic destiny, and Thatcher wanted no part of it. But powerful forces within her own party, moving toward monetary union, made quick work of her seemingly impregnable political position, and she was forced to resign.

Sources of Wealth

Because most average voters do not understand money, they will blame their economic woes on their political leaders and will, by the same token, credit their leaders for prosperity. Therefore, if any group has control of a nation's money, it has the power to create economic conditions that will bring success or ruin to elected officials.

As a former candidate for the presidential nomination of the Republican party, and later as a surrogate speaker for the successful candidate of the party, George Bush, I made my share of speeches extolling the low inflation rates of the Reagan administration which created 17 million new jobs. I also took my share of digs at the previous Democratic administration that "gave this country inflation at 13.5 percent, a 21.5 percent prime rate, and a major recession." The next line would usually be, "Do you want Michael Dukakis to bring you once again the failed economic policy of Jimmy Carter?" Crowds would cheer Bush and Reagan and boo Carter, then vote for four more years of prosperity.

What a stump speech of this sort would not say, however, is the very simple fact that the United States monetary policy of 1979 and 1980 was out of Jimmy Carter's control. Carter got the blame, but it was Paul Volcker, the man who really controlled America's money, who gave us the 21.5 percent prime interest rate and the recession that beat Carter. It was Paul Volcker who produced the low rate of inflation that allowed Ronald Reagan to begin massive deficit spending, create jobs, spur a powerful stock market rally, and enjoy his own reelection in 1984 and the successful succession of his vice president to the Oval Office in 1988.

If the power to create money is taken away from those whom the nation has elected to guide its destiny—the president and the Congress—then the people will have lost their democratic control. Obviously a nonelected body, serving terms that do not coincide with the terms of the presidents who appoint them and whose actions are not controlled or audited by Congress, does great violence to the carefully crafted system of checks and balances that our founding fathers established in the Constitution.

In fact, Thomas Jefferson said that a private central bank issuing the public currency was "a greater menace to the liberties of the people than a standing army." Except for Alexander Hamilton, all of the founders of this nation and their successors fought any attempt to take the power of money creation away from the people in order to place it in a privately owned or foreign-dominated central bank.

The Central Bank

But what is a central bank? The idea first occurred to a canny Scot named William Paterson, who in 1694 agreed to establish a joint stock company to loan £1.2 million at 8 percent interest to William of Orange to help the king pay the cost of his war with Louis XIV of France. In return, the bank received a royal charter granting a number of privileges, including the right to issue notes payable on demand up to the amount of and against the security of the bank's loan to the crown.

The great secret that Paterson discovered was later blurted out by a London merchant, John Houblon, who became the first governor of the Bank of England. He said, "We will charge interest on money which we create out of nothing." In other words, under the government's authority, the Bank of England would issue paper money created out of thin air, which would in turn be loaned at interest to various borrowers. These notes were not backed by gold or silver, but by a fraction of the note representing its loan to the crown.

American money is also made up of "notes" of the central bank. Take a dollar bill out of your wallet and read what it says. It is not a silver or a gold certificate. It is a "note" issued by America's central bank. If you for any reason don't like it, all you will get in exchange is another Federal Reserve note. It is money created out of nothing, printed paper backed only by a private central bank. Yet it says, contrary to the Constitution, it is "legal tender for all debts, public and private."

All banks today use what is called *fractional reserve banking*. This means that if their starting capital is $1 million, they keep $50,000 in reserve and loan out $950,000. Assuming their borrowers redeposit the amount they borrow, the bank can then reserve 5 percent of the $950,000 in deposits and loan out the rest.

As depositors place money with the bank, the bank in turn reserves 5 percent, and loans out the rest, continuing the process as long as deposits or fresh capital is available. Therefore, by using fractional reserves a bank can ultimately pyramid modest capital into an enormous sum of money. Depending on various banking laws, theoretically at least, with capital of $5 million and reserves of $45 million, a bank can support a loan portfolio of $1 billion that would normally net, after interest payments to depositors and all other expenses, about 1 percent, or $10 million annually. This means that the bank has been receiving about $90 million in gross interest on money which it has created out of nothing.

Wealth by the Numbers

It is easy to see the enormous leverage that is created by the banking system. The multiplication of money through fractional reserve banking is simply incredible, but at the same time the dangers of a debt pyramid are equally incredible. A debt pyramid where $50 million supports $1 billion of loans can be collapsed by five defaulted loans of $10 million each. These two facts explain the opportunity for fraud in the savings-and-loan industry, and the ever-expanding liability of the United States government when it is urged to pay for the improvident mistakes of greedy bankers who try to charge interest on money that they created from nothing.

It also shows what incredible damage can be done to the banking system and the economy in general if a central bank has the power to shrink the money supply, force the default of loans, and collapse weak banks. It also shows clearly the power and leverage that a central bank has when it lowers interest rates and increases the supply of money available for lending by the banks of a nation.

The companion secret to wealth building is compound interest, called by Baron Rothschild "the eighth wonder of the world." If it is possible to create money out of nothing, then loan it at interest. Think how much more wealth can be created if the money is not repaid but allowed to compound year after year.

Money at compound interest doubles according to what is called the Rule of Seventy-Two. The number of years required for doubling is calculated by dividing seventy-two by the rate of interest charged. At 10 percent interest compounded annually, a $1 million loan will become $2 million in 7.2 years, $4 million in 14.4 years, 8 million in 21.6 years, $16 million in 28.8 years, and $32 million in 36 years. Put another way, wealth grows 3,200 percent in 36 years at 10 percent interest. In time, those who can make such loans grow rich beyond imagination, but those who borrow become impoverished.

In fact, no individual has the resources to sustain long-term compounding of interest. Only a sovereign government, armed with the enforcement mechanism of an income tax, can sustain the long-term compounding of debt.

The money barons of Europe, who had established privately owned central banks like the Bank of England, found in war the excuse to make large loans to sovereign nations from money that they created out of nothing to be repaid by taxes from the people of the borrowing nations. The object of the lenders was to stimulate government deficit spending and subsequent borrowing. War served that purpose nicely, but from 1945 to 1990 the full mobilization for the Cold War and the resulting massive national borrowings accomplished the result just as well without a full-scale shooting war.

So the monopoly bankers had two major goals. First, they sought to control the creation of money and the underlying political power of a nation. Second, they needed to encourage actions that would result in large-scale government deficit spending and debt creation at compound interest rates, paid for by taxes and tax increases when they become necessary.

Proportional Blindness

I read many periodicals and frankly I am amazed to read newspaper headlines about the "scandal" of a government official who took a $350 ride from Washington, D.C., to New York City in his government-allocated limousine, or the "scandal" of a patriotic U.S. Marine lieutenant colonel who tried to get some money to help freedom fighters in Central America.

But I never read about the scandal of those who have systematically and legally looted hundreds of billions of dollars from the taxpayers of America over the past seventy-eight years. I am reminded of the writing of Oliver Goldsmith, whose satire impaled those in England who put a man in jail for stealing a goose from off the common, but did nothing to the man who steals the common from under the goose.

History records that shortly after the establishment of the United States, the Rothschild interests attempted to saddle the country with a private central bank. The so-called Bank of the United States (1816–36) was abolished by President Andrew Jackson with these words,

> The bold effort the present bank has made to control the government, the distress it had wantonly produced . . . are but premonitions of the fate that awaits the American people should they be deluded into a perpetuation of this institution or the establishment of another like it.

But the centers of European finance could not rest until they had brought the powerhouse of the New World into their orbit. In 1902, Paul Warburg, an associate of the Rothschilds and an expert on European central banking, came to this country as a partner in the powerful Kuhn, Loeb and Company. He married the daughter of Solomon Loeb, one of the founders of the firm. The head of Kuhn, Loeb was Jacob Schiff, whose gift of $20 million in gold to the struggling Russian communists in 1917 no doubt saved their revolution.

A Capitalist Cartel

Warburg was to become the catalyst, when joined with the Rockefeller and Morgan banking interests, to bring about the creation of a central bank for the United States. Here is how it happened.

In 1907, the Morgan interests were believed to have provoked a national money panic to such a degree that Congress established in 1908 a National Monetary Authority under Senator Nelson Aldrich of Rhode Island (whose daughter married John D. Rockefeller II, and one of whose sons was named Nelson Aldrich Rockefeller). Aldrich was considered a close ally of the Rockefeller interests.

From all indications, the National Monetary Commission wasted two fruitless years, including some aimless travel in Europe. On November 22, 1910, another group was formed, consisting of Senator Nelson Aldrich; A. Piatt Andrews, assistant secretary of the treasury; Frank Vanderlip, president of the Rockefeller National City Bank of New York; Henry P. Davison, senior partner of J. P. Morgan Company; Charles D. Norton, president of the Morgan-dominated First National Bank of New York; Benjamin Strong, another Morgan lieutenant; and Paul Warburg. The group left secretly by rail from Hoboken, New Jersey, and traveled anonymously to a private hunting lodge on Jekyll Island, Georgia.

The meeting was so secret that none referred to the other by his last name. In 1935 Frank Vanderlip wrote in *The Saturday Evening Post,*

> [T]here was an occasion near the close of 1910, when I was secretive, indeed as furtive as any conspirator. . . . since it would have been fatal to Senator Aldrich's plan to have it known that he was calling on anybody from Wall Street to help him in preparing his bill. . . . I do not feel it is any exaggeration to speak of our secret expedition to Jekyll Island as the occasion of the actual conception of what eventually became the Federal Reserve System.

At Jekyll Island, the true draftsman for the Federal Reserve was Warburg. The plan was simple. The new central bank could not be called a central bank because America did not want one, so it had to be given a deceptive name. Ostensibly, the bank was to be controlled by Congress, but a majority of its members were to be selected by the private banks that would own its stock.

To keep the public from thinking that the Federal Reserve would be controlled from New York, there was a system of twelve regional banks. Given the enormous concentration of money and credit in New York, the Federal Reserve Bank of New York controlled the system, making the regional concept initially nothing but a ruse.

The board and chairman were to be selected by the president, but in the words of Colonel Edward House, the board would serve such a term as to "put them out of the power of the president." The power over the creation of money was to be taken from the people and placed in the hands of private bankers who could expand or contract credit as they felt best suited their needs.

Dissenting Voices

Congressman Charles A. Lindbergh, Sr., the father of the famed aviator, was the most vocal critic of the plan. He and others bitterly criticized a private stock company that could use the credit of the government for its own profit, take control of the nation's money and credit resources, and exercise a monopoly on the issue of "bank notes." One witness who testified against the plan said, "Both measures rob the government and the people of all effective control over the public's money, and vest in the banks the power to make money scarce or plenty."

The banking interests felt that President Taft could not manage the passage of the Aldrich Bill, so they engineered the three-party race in 1912 which ensured the election of Woodrow Wilson. Wilson's adviser, Colonel House, wrote in his personal memoranda:

—December 19, 1912.
I talked with Paul Warburg over the phone concerning currency reform. I told of my trip to Washington and what I had done there to get it in working order. I told him that the Senate and the Congressmen seemed anxious to do what he desired, and that President-elect Wilson thought straight concerning the issue.

Intimate Papers of Colonel House

George Sylvester Viereck wrote in *The Strangest Friendship in History: Woodrow Wilson and Colonel House,* "The Schiffs, the Warburgs, the Kahns, the Rockefellers, the Morgans put their faith in House. When the Federal Reserve legislation at last assumed definite shape, House was the intermediary between the White House and the financiers."

The Republican or Aldrich Bill of the Taft Administration was replaced with a virtually identical Democratic bill, signed by Woodrow Wilson, known as the Federal Reserve Act, which had been sponsored by the chairman of the House Banking Committee, Virginia Congressman and later Senator Carter Glass.

As a brief personal note, my father, A. Willis Robertson, succeeded his fellow Virginian, Carter Glass, in the United States Senate in 1946. Glass had chaired the House Banking and Currency Committee, and my father went on to chair its counterpart in the Senate, where he had the hearty support of the banking community. As I write this I am looking at a lovely sterling silver tray given him by the American Bankers Association at their annual meeting in San Francisco, October 25, 1966. My father was also a colleague in the Senate of Prescott Bush, the father of George Bush.

In 1968, I received on my father's behalf the award of the Woodrow Wilson Society in appreciation for his thirty-four years of distinguished service in the United States Congress.

As I am digging through all of the research and analysis in these chapters, some readers might wish to say to me: Pat, you are an Anglo-Saxon and an Ivy League law graduate. Your father was a senior United States Senator, and you have a distinguished heritage that goes from colonial days back to the nobility of England. You qualify to play a leadership role in the Establishment and its plans for a new world order. So why don't you just keep your mouth shut, go along, and take the wealth and privilege that is there to enjoy?

My answer to such a question is very simple. I believe in freedom. I believe in equal opportunity for all people. I believe in free enterprise capitalism. I believe in the wisdom of the market.

Furthermore, I believe in the sovereignty of the United States of America. More than anything I believe in Jesus Christ, and I do not think that a man-made new world order is His will for mankind. I believe that God has never given anyone other than Jesus Christ enough wisdom to run this world, and it is my frank belief that some of these Ivy League characters trying to do so, have up to now made a colossal mess of it.

Looming Disasters

On December 21, 1913, American finance was captured by European finance and their powerful American allies in the Money Trust. How much of a financial benefit this central bank has given us can be judged from the fact that between 1913 (when the debt of the United States government was virtually zero) and October 1991, the nation's debt will have compounded exponentially to a staggering sum approaching $4 trillion, with annual interest charges that will exceed $200 billion per year. The federal debt load upon each family of four now totals roughly $64,000, and the annual tax burden upon every citizen is now calculated to be higher than the percentage exaction demanded of the serfs during the Middle Ages.

As for financial stability, we have only to look at the record of the Federal Reserve Board during the 1920s and early 1930s to realize that its policies were disastrous.

In 1928, Montague Norman, governor of the Bank of England, made the preposterous assertion about his banking power, "I have the hegemony of the world." In 1928 and 1929, the money powers of Britain and the United States coordinated their efforts in behalf of England because Montague Norman's hegemony was fast coming unglued.

The Federal Reserve Board embarked on a rescue effort to save the British gold supplies and the British pound sterling by forcing United States interest rates to an artificially low level. Cheap and plentiful money had the effect it always has: It drove the price of stocks and bonds through the roof. In 1929, because of 10 percent margin requirements for the purchase of stocks, stock buying turned into a speculative orgy.

The prices of securities became overvalued and vulnerable to bad news. Thus, when news of the collapse of the Credit-Anstalt Bank in Austria hit the market, there was a wave of selling, margin calls, more selling, and more margin calls. Instead of stepping in to ease the situation, history records that the Federal Reserve Board, faced with the collapse of many banks in the nation, did little to alleviate the crisis of a 25 percent decline in the money supply.

This shortage of money left the economy prostrate and a full quarter of the labor force out of work. Certainly from 1968 until 1991 the erratic expansion and contraction of the money supply by the Federal Reserve Board has caused serious recessions in 1969, 1973, 1979, 1982, and 1990.

Now in the United States the savings-and-loan industry has collapsed. A thousand banks are in trouble. The insurance industry is falling apart. It seems that by 1993 there may well be a massive stock market sell-off and, very probably, a worldwide credit collapse.

Since 1988 the Federal Reserve Board has restricted the money supply to such an extent that the economy has been placed in a painful recession. The so-called broad (or M-3) money supply—which includes all currency, all demand deposits at banks, plus money market funds, along with overnight repurchase agreements, savings accounts, large time deposits, term repurchase agreements, and bank-held Eurodollars—has actually been shrinking in real inflation-adjusted terms from 1988 until the time of publication of this book.

The Federal Reserve Board's mechanism to deal with a healthy growing economy is to cause its collapse in order to reduce inflation. What I fear is that in order to prepare for the reelection of the president in 1992, the Federal Reserve Board will allow the money supply to grow more vigorously to create the appearance of prosperity and then slam on the money brakes around election time, an action that may well cause a debt collapse, a stock market collapse, and a global depression of unprecedented ferocity.

For that reason I am strongly urging readers of my newsletter, *Pat Robertson's Perspective,* to pay off debts now, take stock market profits by summer 1992, and place the bulk of their holdings in short-term treasury bills until the dust settles.

Calculated Risks

If there is a crash, the Republican party will be blamed for it, and their candidate in 1996 will be defeated. Democrats will then take the White House. The Establishment had originally picked former Virginia Governor and now Senator Chuck Robb as their candidate (Robb was one of two senators invited to Trilateral Commission meetings). Unfortunately for Robb, the revelation of his presence in a sex-and-cocaine scandal in my hometown of Virginia Beach while he was governor, coupled with a criminal investigation into recorded taps of Virginia's current black Democratic governor's cellular telephone conversations, have blown Robb, like Gary Hart before him, completely out of contention for any higher political office.

Now the insiders have determined that a surrogate is not necessary when they can have the real thing. They have begun to move centi-millionaire Senator John D. Rockefeller III of West Virginia into the limelight!

Their first move was to name Rockefeller as chairman of a commission to protect the family, where he put forward proposals that won the support of defenders of the poor on the left and pro-family conservatives on the right. His relatively innocuous criticism of George Bush's European forays and his seeming inattention to domestic policy in mid-1991 was spotlighted on the evening news of all three television networks. Absent a miracle, President Rockefeller has been tapped by the elite to bring us that much closer to world government in 1996.

So much for the benefits of a privately owned, and to my mind unconstitutional, central bank. But since most people are not aware that the Federal Reserve System is owned by member banks, which are in turn owned by private investors, it might be instructive to show who had stock in the Federal Reserve Board at its inception. Since the Federal Reserve Bank of New York was to set interest rates and direct open market operations, this bank was far more powerful than any other. Its first governor was Benjamin Strong, president of the Morgan Bank, and one of the participants at Jekyll Island. He brought the Reserve System into interlocking relations with the Bank of England and the Bank of France.

Of the reportedly 203,053 shares of the Federal Reserve Bank of New York, Rockefeller's National City Bank took 30,000 shares; Morgan's First National Bank took 15,000 shares; Chase National took 6,000 shares; and the National Bank of Commerce, now known as Morgan Guaranty Trust, took 21,000 shares. Any of the banks holding the shares could, in turn, be purchased in whole or in part by foreign interests. As I understand it, such a move would mean that control of the public money supply of the United States was not only in private hands but could be, at least in theory, in foreign hands as well.

The Impact of a United Europe

In 1992, the world will see for the first time since Charlemagne a united Europe. The linchpin of that union will be a European central bank with powers similar to the Federal Reserve Board of the United States and some type of common currency, now called the European Currency Unit or ECU.

Presently the German Bundesbank is calling the shots for the flow of interest rates and currency alignment for all of Europe. But think what would happen if the emerging United States of Europe opts for one central bank with seven members. Then realize that Japan also has a central bank controlling its interest rates, money supply, and banking practices. Perhaps this bank might expand to become an Asian central bank.

Consider what would then happen if, in a Trilateral world, the central bank of Europe, the central bank of Japan, and the central bank of the United States began to coordinate their efforts, or even to merge. If that happened, some twenty-one people, possibly as few as three people, could control the money and credit of essentially the entire world. They would not only be able to affect the fortunes of every human being on earth, but they could create an economic climate to keep in power or take from office any government or public figure.

This is precisely the situation that former Senator Barry Goldwater warned about when he spoke of economic power capable of bypassing or controlling the political power of any nation. If national sovereignty collapses on the money front, then the media and public opinion's power will be available to collapse political and military sovereignty, thus bringing the dreams of the one-worlders to reality.

This day is coming much closer than anyone believes. Only one thing will stop it, and that is the concerted effort of concerned Americans who will vote into office a Congress who will repeal the Federal Reserve Act and restore the constitutional power given to the people's elected officials. The price of apathy on this score means the loss of liberty for every American.

Improvident Loans

The money barons are getting much closer to control of the world's economy than even they may have believed was possible. But like the dog who chased after the bus and didn't know what to do when he had caught it, these men don't really know what to do next.

David Rockefeller's Chase Manhattan Bank is swimming in nonperforming foreign loans and foreclosed domestic real estate. The credit rating of the Chase has been downgraded, and its stock value has collapsed. Although Rockefeller has tremendous political power, his financial acumen has been seriously questioned. A former vice president of the Federal Reserve Board once commented that David Rockefeller spends all morning giving away the assets of the bank, and George Champion (its president at that time) spends all afternoon getting it back again.

Citicorp, which grew out of the Rockefeller-dominated First National City Bank, was so heavily involved with loans to countries like Brazil, Argentina, and Mexico that its continued existence is threatened. Not only was its paper downgraded and its stock value dropped by two-thirds, it was saved, at least temporarily, by a humiliating rescue effort made by a rich Saudi Arabian prince who bought some $750 million in Citicorp convertible preferred stock carrying a usurious guaranteed dividend yield.

The great Bank of America was barely saved from collapse when its longtime chairman, A. W. Clausen, returned from retirement and a stint at the World Bank to assume active management.

Manufacturer's Hanover Bank had shaky Third World loans that exceeded twice its stated capital. If these loans had been marked to market value, the bank would have collapsed. Now Manufacturers Hanover and Chemical Bank are merging in the hope of finding operating savings to continue profitably in the future.

I remember a meeting in the late 1970s at the Morgan Bank on Wall Street where I had gone to acquire some distressed real estate. I found three very troubled middle executives who had shoveled $100 million of the bank's money into three hotel projects that were all in default and were costing the bank millions to carry. There were no guarantees of repayment on any of the projects and the loans were, in a word, improvident. These projects were not unusual but typical of the go-go lending of the early 1970s and certainly of the 1980s.

The giant Continental-Illinois Bank was stuck with a $1 billion bad loan to Penn Square Bank in Oklahoma and would have collapsed but for a government bailout.

Recently the Bank of New England collapsed and was taken over by regulators and sold. The giant Bank of Boston almost went under, but it is trying to struggle back.

The hottest banking news in 1991 concerned the largest bank collapse in history, the Pakistan- and Luxembourg-based Bank of Credit and Commerce International (BCCI), a $20 billion institution. This bank not only made unsecured loans to its friends concerning hundreds of millions of dollars, it had a "black" department that laundered drug money, financed arms shipments, held deposits for the CIA, drug dealers, the PLO, and the terrorist Abu Nidal. It financed secret Israeli arms shipments, engaged in terrorism against its enemies, and reportedly distributed $5 million in bribes to United States congressmen and government officials.

The collapse of BCCI leaves depositors with no way of recovering their deposits. Instead, these deposits in fact may have already been dissipated because of this incredible corrupt Ponzi scheme.

Ironically, the BCCI collapse is accelerating the move toward world banking. An urgent call is being made for global bank regulation to prevent a bank that has been chartered under the lax banking laws of such nations as Luxembourg or the Cayman Islands from committing such massive worldwide fraud again. The vehicle being put forward is the Geneva-based Bank of International Settlements, which is controlled by the major central banks of the world. Again, it is as if an unseen director keeps putting the pieces in place.

In 1991, the world owed an unbelievable $25 trillion dollars in private and public debt. The exponential compounding of debt based on fractional reserve banking has created a monster that no central bank, no combination of banks, no single government, and no world government—especially the inefficient and corrupt United Nations—can solve. When the debt bubble finally bursts, the financial wreckage will be the worst in the history of the world.

Who Can You Trust?

In my view the last people in the world to be entrusted with picking up the pieces will be those who caused the problem in the first place. Think about it. They helped destroy Russia, Poland, Czechoslovakia, Hungary, Rumania, China, Southeast Asia, Ethiopia, Angola, Mozambique, Tanzania, Rhodesia, Cuba, and Nicaragua. They brought us the Great Depression and many subsequent recessions. They have almost destroyed their own banks and financial institutions, and in 1991 they came perilously close to destroying the financial system of the entire world.

For years, to further their utopian one-world plans, they have been trying to undermine American education, moral values, sense of patriotism, and national pride. They will destroy everything else they get their hands on.

In the turbulent pre-Christmas days of 1989, an uprising of Christian people had broken out in the city of Timisoara, Rumania, protesting government abuses. The cry of the tens of thousands of people who filled the city square was, "God is alive!" Their peaceful protest was met with gunfire from members of the state security forces that had stationed themselves on the rooftops of buildings surrounding the public square. Some two thousand of those innocent civilians fell dead and wounded.

The news horrified the nation and the world, and on the next day the dictator, Nicolae Ceausescu, called for a large rally in the main square of the capital city of Bucharest. As the dictator began to speak to what he thought was a friendly crowd, one woman shouted out, "You are a liar!" Those around her began shouting, "You are a liar!" Then the whole crowd began to shout it, and Ceausescu fled the platform. On Christmas Day 1989, he and his wife were executed, and the nation was freed from his abuses.

It is time that a new shout go up against the money barons who use such slick phrases to sell their next plans to ruin the world. Americans need to cry at the top of their lungs, "You are liars! We have had enough! Your time is up!"

The Power of Persuasion

The task of bringing forth a cry of rage that will be clearly heard will not be easy. The power of the Money Trust does not end at the banks. Its goes deep into our largest media corporations, private and federal institutions, and educational establishment. Here is how it works.

All major banks develop relationships with large corporate clients. They make lines of credit available to finance inventories and receivables. They provide construction financing and real estate financing. They make bridge loans and term loans for corporate expansion or acquisitions. They help with cash management, currency transactions, letters of credit, and, of course, depository and

check-writing services. Most banks maintain a private banking service for the executives of their large corporate clients in case these
executives need ready cash for their own personal use.

For the really big loan requirements of their clients, a large
bank may become the lead bank to syndicate a loan among several
other national, regional, or foreign banks.

To cement relationships, the chief executives of the major corporate customers of a bank are invited to sit on the bank's board of
directors, and often key bank officials sit on the boards of the corporations with which they do business. It goes without saying that a
lead bank has firsthand, intimate knowledge of the inner workings
of its corporate clients.

But the interconnection goes even deeper. All banks have trust
departments, but some, like J. P. Morgan, manage trusts and
pension funds in the billions of dollars. Several years ago such funds
were in excess of $25 billion at Morgan alone. If that trust money is in-
vested in the common stock of major corporations, especially those
companies in media, it would in turn buy a great deal of influence.
Because of the dispersal of public ownership of stock, a 5 percent
stake in some corporations is tantamount to outright control.

It is my understanding that the major New York banks, and the
trust funds that they manage, have substantial stock holdings in the
New York Times Corporation, CBS, ABC, General Electric (which owns
NBC), the *Washington Post* Company, the Times Mirror Corporation,
and the Dow Jones Company (which publishes the *Wall Street Journal*).

These corporations, and hundreds more industrial corporations,
cannot afford to have demand loans called, credit lines canceled, essential expansion loans denied, their credit standing impugned, or a
bear raid on their stock. Huge holdings depend on credit. Those who
get it have prospered greatly in the past decades; those without access to credit suffer.

This awesome power—tantamount to the power of financial life
and death—accounts for the fact that there never is a critical article
about David Rockefeller or the CFR in the major national media.
The power is subtle but incredibly intense. In high finance, all it

takes is a quiet word from the right person to destroy the future of
any public company that is carrying substantial debt. Every owner
of every major public media company is fully aware of how the game
is played, and it is hardball.

Taking the Brunt

The coup de grace is always administered in a paneled, deeply
carpeted environment in the most genteel of tones. "I am sorry, but
our loan committee does not believe that this is a bankable proposition." "Our loan committee has voted not to renew your company's
annual line." "Your company's demand note signed last December is
now due and payable. Our loan committee has voted not to renew it."

This is not a court. There is no judge, no jury, and no appeal.
There are, of course, other banks, but a discreet leak for publication,
as follows, will cool their interest.

> This publication has learned from reliable sources that the Chase
> bank has called $50 million in demand loans made by it to the XYZ
> Publishing Corporation. The stock of XYZ plunged five points in active
> trading on the news. Speculation is rife concerning the source of the
> problems at the troubled media concern.

If XYZ Publishing recovers, you can rest assured that the managing editor knows that he will be fired and blackballed throughout
the industry if ever a critical word against the Rockefellers or their
CFR associates appears in the XYZ newspapers or on its television
stations. If anyone else criticizes these people in public, XYZ Publications will polish its Establishment image by branding the critics as
ill-informed, right-wing, fundamentalist reactionaries.

Foundation Resources

By the judicious use of credit, the Establishment has built a
network of interlocking corporate and bank boards in every phase
of American life, including the media, which control close to 60
percent of the total financial assets of the United States. Each of
the leaders of these powerful companies are introduced, in turn,

to the travel settings, the overseas business opportunities, the governmental aid sources, and the academic resources that would lead inescapably toward the philosophy of managed globalism.

When Cecil Rhodes died, he left a huge fortune in a tax-free foundation, the Rhodes Trust, which Lord Milner used to fund multiple causes in furtherance of Rhodes's global schemes. The importance of such tax-free foundations should not be underestimated.

First, they permit enormously wealthy individuals to leave huge fortunes free of inheritance taxes in the hands of family members or trusted allies. The wealth within foundations can compound in perpetuity, free of income or capital gains taxes. Foundations can own stock in banks or business corporations, and through foundation tax-planning techniques, families can retain voting control of large corporations while placing much of the beneficial interest into a tax-free foundation which they also control.

Relatively recent tax laws forced private foundations to pay out in grants up to 5 percent of their assets each year. Serious restrictions and penalties have been imposed on the most blatant forms of self-dealing between foundations and those who control them. But absent these modest restrictions, allowable foundation functions and grant-making power is broad and varied.

Andrew Carnegie, a personal friend of Rhodes, sold his Carnegie Steel Works to J. P. Morgan for $400 million. Most of that money, the equivalent of at least $4 billion today, went into the Carnegie Corporation and the Carnegie Endowment for Peace.

John D. Rockefeller gave away about $530 million in his day, worth billions in today's money, much of it to the Rockefeller Foundation. His son added to the sums, and his grandchildren endowed the Rockefeller Brothers Fund.

The largest foundation on record is the Ford Foundation, funded when Henry Ford, Sr., died in 1947, to allow the Ford family to retain voting control of the Ford Motor Company, and I might add, control of the foundation. The Ford Foundation had starting assets of $3 billion, a huge sum at the time.

Despite the express wishes of Henry Ford, Sr., leadership of the Ford Foundation wound up in the hands of Paul Hoffman, a principal player in the CFR and a trustee of the far-left Institute of Pacific Relations. Although Hoffman was removed from the Ford Foundation, its policies strayed continuously so far to the left that Henry Ford II, grandson of the founder, recently resigned in disgust.

The Enemy Within

It goes without saying that leftists gravitated to the big foundations like flies to a honey pot. But who better to control and manage this money than the finance men and lawyers of the Establishment, like the CFR stalwarts, John McCloy or McGeorge Bundy, who at different times ran the Ford Foundation? Of no small note, for that matter, convicted perjurer Alger Hiss later ran the Carnegie Endowment for International Peace.

In 1989, the Ford Foundation listed assets of $5,832,426,000 and gave grants the previous year of $211,769,514. The foundation listed as one of its major purposes:

[I]nternational affairs—analysis, research, dialogue, and public education on such issues as policies affecting immigrants and refugees, arms control and international security, and the changing world economy and U.S. foreign policy; and governance and public policy—including governmental and public policy issues.

That is their real power. The foundation has the ability to give away up to $164 million however it chooses to study and propagandize the nation on such foreign policy and world economy issues as the CFR and its one-world allies dictate.

For reference, it may be helpful to look at specifics on how some of the Ford Foundation's money is spent:

$1 million to the Council on Foreign Relations. $300,000 to study the influence of communism in contemporary America, with Earl Browder, national secretary of the Communist party as a key staff member

$1,134,000 to the American Friends Service Committee to support a study of the communist takeover of China

$630,000 to the Southwest Council of La Raza, allegedly headed by a known communist

Not only has the Ford Foundation poured out hundreds of millions of tax-free grants to fund leftist and global initiatives, but by 1970 it had given a billion dollars to educational projects in support of the same goals. Of interest is the fact that the Ford Foundation makes no grants at all for any religious purpose.

The Rockefeller Foundation in 1989 listed its assets at $2,140,244,924 with grants of $59,996,580. The goal of this fund is "to promote the well-being of mankind throughout the world."

This fund has been a major contributing source to the Council on Foreign Relations and its affiliate organizations, including the far-left Institute for Pacific Affairs. It also has been a training ground for future public servants. The secretary of state under Jimmy Carter, Cyrus Vance, and the secretary of state under John F. Kennedy, Dean Rusk, who were both, prior to their appointments, presidents of the Rockefeller Foundation.

Funding the One World Agenda

In 1946, immediately after World War II, the report of the Rockefeller Foundation stated clearly, "The challenge of the future is to make this one world." In forty-five years they have not deviated from that course.

It is the Rockefeller Brothers Fund, which was valued in 1989 at $242,120,725 with $7,999,659 in grants where the true purposes of the globalist establishment is seen. The mask is off in this incredible published statement of purpose:

Support of efforts in the U.S. and abroad that contribute ideas, develop leaders, and encourage institutions in the transition to global interdependence.

In other words the resources of the Rockefeller Brothers Fund are to be used to develop propaganda, educate future leaders, and move institutions (including the United Sates government) toward a one-world government.

These three foundations have over $8.2 billion in tax-free wealth placed at the service of propaganda, education, leadership training, and "institutional encouragement" to move toward a one-world government and its companion piece, world socialism.

The Carnegie Corporation of New York in 1989 listed assets of $905,106,313 and annual grants of $47,587,022. Carnegie money was used earlier for extremely beneficial activities like the construction of public libraries and technical colleges. For the past few decades, through a propaganda machine called the Carnegie Endowment for Peace, with 1989 assets of $93,184,721, the Carnegie money has often been used in the service of pro-Soviet initiatives. Three of the stated purposes of the Carnegie Corporation are the diffusion of knowledge and understanding among the peoples of the United States and nations (in the manner of Carnegie's friend, Cecil Rhodes) that have been members of the British Commonwealth, the avoidance of nuclear war, and the improvement of U.S.-Soviet relations.

A listing of such foundation grants is available at any public library. The list is exhaustive and gives many examples of contributions to worthwhile causes. But here are some uses of foundation money that underscore the Establishment goals of influencing the press, Congress, and public policy:

Arms Control Association, $200,000. Toward program on arms control and national security for the Washington, D.C., press corps

Aspen Institute for Humanistic Studies, $550,800. Toward meetings on U.S.-Soviet relations with American lawmakers

Aspen Institute for Humanistic Studies, $300,000. Toward meetings on U.S. relations with South Africa for American lawmakers

Council on Foreign Relations, $208,000. For study of U.S.-Soviet relations

Institute for East-West Security Studies, $50,000. Toward international volume of essays on conventional arms control

United Nations Association of the United States, $300,000. **Toward** project on U.S.-Soviet policy dialogue on the United Nations

American Civil Liberties Union Foundation, $200,000. For national security studies on government secrecy

Council on Foreign Relations, $208,000. To study U.S.-Soviet relations in next decade

Council on Foreign Relations, $445,000. To enable ten U.S. scholars and government officials to serve apprenticeships in U.S. foreign policy agencies

Council on Foreign Relations, $45,000. Organizing symposia in five U.S. cities to bring African issues into mainstream of U.S. foreign policy concerns (multiple foundation grants toward this project)

There are hundreds of grants toward projects like these aimed at disarmament, linkage of the United States and the Soviet Union, and propaganda in support of Establishment global concerns aimed at press, lawmakers, and community groups. All these causes subtly move public opinion toward the preconceived goal of world government.

The Tilt to the Left

The "interlocking nexus of tax-exempt foundations" was so tilted toward left-wing associations that in July 1953 Congress set up a special committee under Representative B. Carroll Reece of Tennessee to investigate them. The pressure and vituperation that came upon this committee from very powerful sources ultimately ended with its unpublicized demise.

In 1958, a book by its counsel, Rene A. Wormser, called *Foundations: Their Power and Influence,* tells the story of what this committee accomplished and releases the evidence it uncovered to the public. The summary finding of the Reece Committee was shockingly simple: tax-exempt foundations were deliberately using their wealth and privilege to attack the basic structure of the U.S. Constitution and the Judeo-Christian American culture.

Wormser said quite eloquently that no society should grant tax exemption to any organizations seeking to destroy it. In his chapter entitled "Foundation Impact on Foreign Policy," Wormser cites the Carnegie Endowment for Peace as one of those attempting to mold public opinion and to decide "what should be read in our schools and colleges." He went on to say:

> Foundation activity has nowhere had a greater impact than in the field of foreign affairs. It has conquered public opinion and has largely established the international political goals of our country. . . . This was comparatively easy to accomplish because there was no organized or foundation supported opposition.

Wormser continued his shocking analysis of the evidence presented to the Reece Committee. He wrote:

> The influence of the foundation complex in internationalism has reached far into government, into the policy-making circles of Congress and into the State Department. This has been effected through the pressure of public opinion, mobilized by the instruments of foundations; through the promotion of foundation favorites as teachers and experts in foreign affairs; through a domination of the learned journals in international affairs; through the frequent appointment of State Department officials to foundation jobs; and through the frequent appointment of foundation officials to State Department jobs.

He then showed how the Carnegie Corporation, the Carnegie Endowment for Peace, the Rockefeller Foundation, and the Ford Foundation jointly sponsored conferences and forums filled with one-sided rhetoric advocating United Nations control of U.S. foreign aid, unilateral disarmament, recognition of Red China, and admission of China to the United Nations.

The Reece Committee came to this conclusion:

> The weight of evidence before this committee . . . indicates that the form of globalism which the foundations have so actively promoted

and from which our foreign policy has suffered seriously, relates definitely to a collectivist point of view.

As to the aid given to communist causes by major foundations, Wormser points out that the predecessor to the Reece Commission, the Cox Commission, discovered one hundred grants that had been made to individuals and organizations with extreme leftist records from the Rockefeller Foundation, the Carnegie Corporation, the Carnegie Endowment for International Peace, the John Simon Guggenheim Foundation, the Russell Sage Foundation, the William C. Whitney Foundation, and the Marshall Field Foundation.

Wormser's conclusion from the lengthy investigations of the Reece Committee probably doesn't ring clearly on American ears of the 1990s, but they are nonetheless true.

> If one accepts the concepts and principles of the Declaration of Independence and the Constitution as *the existing order,* then any attempt to replace them with the concepts and principles of socialism must be considered "subversive" and "un-American."

The blending of the pro-Soviet, monopoly capital, globalism of the Establishment, the Establishment foundations, and the Establishment media—particularly when coupled with secular humanism, radical communism, the human sexuality movement, and New Age religion—makes a strange and potent cocktail in America's universities, high schools, and elementary schools.

Can this nation survive such a concerted and powerful effort to dismantle our sovereignty, our national spirit, and the legacy of self-reliance and independence won for us at such great cost? This is an urgent and troubling question, and the answer is not at all certain.

But before I even attempt to answer or to offer a point of conjecture, we will need to explore a few of these critical issues—the educational, religious, and political objectives of the globalist agenda—and with these insights we will gain a more stable footing for some of the assessments that follow.

I turn now to a discussion of the educational programs designed to prepare our youth for the new world order.

7

School for Scandal

In the book *THE PRICE OF POWER*, written shortly after the Second World War for the Council on Foreign Relations, a group of ranking CFR analysts led by Hanson Baldwin made the contention that "our ultimate objective, even though it may be decades or centuries away, must be one world, and we must constantly try to heal and patch and bind to avoid the final hardening of Europe into two camps."

The fear of atomic war seemed a real enough threat in 1948, and fear of imminent mass destruction was a genuine and powerful enigma, a vision that, unfortunately, elicited sinister responses. Expressing grave misgivings, Baldwin wrote, "The face of tomorrow is a bleak visage; we are embarked on a 'time of troubles.'" The images of mass destruction created by World War II brought a sense of overpowering dread to intellectuals which seemed to overpower their reason with irrational fears of the Apocalypse.

Baldwin went on to say, "We have opened for all time the lid of Pandora's box of evils. We cannot now push the genii back into the box. We may not like it, but we must face it. Atomic bombs, biological agents and other weapons of mass destruction are now a permanent part of man's society; and no perfect physical system of control is possible for all these weapons."

Then he added: "But today war—international war—can mean chaos. And so the face of tomorrow is the face of danger; we must anticipate a 'time of troubles' while man learns to make peace with himself."

In fact, this vision of a troubled world has hardly diminished during the past forty years. Former Attorney General Robert Kennedy, brother of President John Kennedy, wrote a passionate, almost evangelical appeal for world peace and a new world order in his 1967 book *To Seek a Newer World*. The postscript to this book is a virtual paean to the unity of mankind, the homogeneity of all races and cultures, and the necessity of "building a new world society."

It was in this book that the younger Kennedy announced his candidacy for the presidency of the United States, and in it he called on the power and idealism of youth (the most visible power block of the 1960s and early 1970s) to fight against any sense of futility, expediency, timidity, or love of comfort in order to bring about a revolution that would help to reshape the destiny of the world. But that destiny would be a challenge the author would not live to fulfill.

From the White House

A few years later, on February 14, 1977, in his address to representatives from many nations—symbolizing the global community—President-Elect Jimmy Carter said:

> I want to assure you that the relations of the United States with the other countries and peoples of the world will be guided during my own Administration by our desire to shape a world order that is more responsive to human aspirations. The United States will meet its obligation to help create a stable, just, and peaceful world order.

Most Americans hardly noticed the new president's peculiar statement or realized that, as a protégé of David Rockefeller and a member of the Trilateral Commission and the Council on Foreign Relations, this born-again Southern Democrat was communicating a deliberate and articulate statement of a specific vision of world government.

But most Americans are equally surprised to learn that the idea of a new world order and the use of the term is not at all new or novel to hundreds of intellectuals, university professors, and public policy professionals in this country. Entire departments and degree programs in dozens of colleges and universities have been built around the premise of planning "alternative futures" for the world and agitating for elimination of the current system of autonomous statehood in favor of one-world government.

Allied with futurists, ecologists, economists, and specialists in many other academic disciplines, these world-order professionals have created an entire industry and a mythology around themselves. Dozens of textbooks, guides, and reference sources have been published over the past dozen years to support this study and to help facilitate the creation of a system of terminology and rhetoric for peace, justice, and ecology.

From the Ivory Tower

In recent years such idealistic dreams have come in a steady stream from the ivory tower. In their 1983 book, *Perspectives on American Foreign Policy*, Professors Charles W. Kegley, Jr., and Eugene R. Wittkopf assembled a series of essays by a number of intellectuals and commentators on the idea of a world superstate. Prompted by the same apocalyptic visions—world crisis and a troubled future—these scholars argued boldly and without pretense for a one-world government that would supersede national identity.

In one article, Henry Steele Commager wrote:

> The inescapable fact, dramatized by the energy crisis, the population crisis, the armaments race, and so forth, is that nationalism as we have known it in the nineteenth and much of the twentieth century is as much of an anachronism today as was States Rights when Calhoun preached it and Jefferson Davis fought for it. Just as we know, or should

know, that none of our domestic problems can be solved within the artificial boundaries of the states, so none of our global problems can be solved within the largely artificial boundaries of nations—artificial not so much in the eyes of history as in the eyes of Nature.

This writer then goes on to say:

Of all the assumptions I have discussed, that which takes nationalism for granted is perhaps the most deeply rooted and the most tenacious. Yet when we reflect that assumptions, even certainties, no less tenacious in the past—about the very nature of the cosmic system, about the superiority of one race to all others, about the naturalness of women's subordination to men, about the providential order of a class society, about the absolute necessity of a state church or religion—have all given way to the implacable pressure of science and reality, we may conclude that what Tocqueville wrote well over a century ago is still valid:

The world that is rising into existence is still half encumbered by the remains of the world that is waning into decay; and amid the vast perplexity of human affairs none can say how much of ancient institutions and former customs will remain or how much will completely disappear.

If some of our ancient institutions do not disappear [the writer observes darkly], there is little likelihood that we shall remain.

For all the horrifying implications of such statements, by far the most alarming evidence of the widespread influence and the future peril of this kind of idealistic rhetoric in the halls of academia can be found in the guidebooks published by the World Policy Institute (located at the United Nations Plaza in New York) entitled *Peace and World Order Studies: A Curriculum Guide.*

These guidebooks offer a comprehensive view of well over a hundred world-order majors and study programs at American colleges and universities, along with their course synopses, syllabi, and statements of purpose. More than any other single source I have seen, these guides indicate the incredible degree to which new-world-order thinking has infiltrated the academy.

The Revolutionary Gospel

For most of these programs, the language of the new world order is no longer theory or mere rhetoric—it is gospel. The only hesitation in any of the literature presented in these books is in expressing openly their clear consensus that nationalism (or pride in one's nation, state, or region) is an ideological travesty and a political dinosaur.

In the introduction to the fourth edition, Peter Dale Scott, a Berkeley professor and former Canadian delegate to the United Nations, states, "Peace studies, while not necessarily committed to more radical proposals for amendment of global problems, still is committed to an enlarged intellectual viewpoint in which such radical critiques of the status quo can be contemplated and discussed."

The excitement of such programs, the author contends, is that they encourage both "global awareness" and a "self-critical attitude" which foments change. Terms such as *hierarchical order* and *authoritarian rule* are profane concepts in such programs, while ideas such as *global unity* and *anarchy* are ideals to be held in reverence.

The third edition of the series of course guides presented comprehensive course outlines on a wide range of courses in globalist issues currently being taught on campuses, in the editor's words, "from Santa Clara to Harvard." The sixty synopses published in that edition were merely the most comprehensive of more than four hundred course and program outlines submitted by colleges and universities all across America.

At UCLA the aim of the Global Issues Program described in the fourth edition of the guide is to examine issues "which have transformed the globe into an interdependent planet" and to prepare students with "international competence, citizen action and personal values for living in the twenty-first-century 'global village.'"

The aim of the curriculum developers at UCLA and many other campuses is to indoctrinate a new generation of Americans into the globalist and nonstatist mode of thinking. That means creating educational structures for thought modification (read that, "thought control") and accepting idealistic theories that will lead inevitably to revolutionary activism.

One such program directive states that the principal requirement for admission is "an open mind." You will recall that such open-mindedness was precisely the goal of the educators Allan Bloom described in his eye-opening bestseller *The Closing of the American Mind.* Open-minded students are those who believe that everything is relative, that there are no absolutes, and that a socialist vision is the only realistic approach to life and society.

According to Professor Walker Bush, the long-term goal of the World Order Program at UCLA is to provide an introductory course in globalist thinking to every entering student. Their aim is, in short, to refocus the entire ethos of higher education. In addition, the university will offer upper-level degrees in various global issues in order to turn out a cadre of new-world-order scholars and strategists.

Along with required reading from the works of Richard Falk and Buckminster Fuller, students study the writings of Norman Cousins, Margaret Mead, Daniel Ellsberg, and other contributors to the literature and mythology of this revolutionary discipline. These are the voices of those who understand the globalist view. For counterpoint, students read the works of the forerunners from the old world order, such as Henry Kissinger, Zbigniew Brezinski, and Cyrus Vance.

Radical Myths

Christine Sylvester teaches a class entitled Alternative World Futures at Gettysburg College in Pennsylvania. She writes:

> We are endangered by structures which encourage a global war system, gross development disequilia, ecological abuse, the violation of human rights, and a "we-they" view of the species. We are also endangered by our seeming inability or disinclination to think seriously and creatively about our options. We are impaled in a world of structural injustice and intellectual paralysis.

The purpose of her course is (1) to foster a politics of species identity; (2) to highlight our collective sources of endangerment; (3) to gain an appreciation of alternative approaches to global management; and (4) to encourage creative, systematic thought on the future.

Required reading includes *The Third Wave* by Alvin Toffler; the novel *The Dispossessed* by Ursula LeGuin; *Toward a Just World Order* by Richard Falk, Samuel Kim, and Saul Mendlovitz; *Mankind at the Turning Point* by Mihajlo Mesarovic and Edward Pestel; and *The Communist Manifesto* by Karl Marx and Friedrich Engels.

Additional reading includes "Religion, Futurism, and Models of Social Change" by Elise Boulding, and "Constructing Models of Presents, Futures, and Transitions: An Approach to Alternative World Futures" by Harry R. Targ.

Among the solutions explored by students in Sylvester's course are a review of utopian ideologies, such as those in LeGuin's science fiction, a review of behaviorist and social engineering models, and in-depth review and writing on the principles of humanistic transformation.

At Amherst, SUNY, Chapel Hill, and Princeton, world order courses focus specifically on women's issues. At the Universities of Florida, Connecticut, Vermont, Northern Illinois, and Columbia, courses focus directly on the methodology of educating both teachers and students into the vocabulary and doctrines of the new world order. To instill the globalist perspective, the system's promoters believe they must train their future leaders from the ground up.

Florida International University's Global Awareness Program (GAP), housed in the School of Education, attempts to act as "a shaper of global futures" by making students more globally minded. Their explicit goal is to train a generation of teachers to see things globally rather than from the traditional perspective of the community, nation, or region.

Professor Arthur Newman at the University of Florida says,

It is unquestionably wrong to assume naively that the world's schools are able to wave a magic wand and usher in the new millennium.

On the other hand, it is just as inexcusable to suggest the converse, i.e., that the schools are impotent as regards engendering an awareness of, identification with, and commitment to universal humankind.

In application, Newman's thesis is intended to discredit the emotions, habits, and historical beliefs associated with nationalism, national sovereignty, and patriotism in order to form a new generation of globalists.

At Syracuse, Virginia Polytechnic, Duke, Tufts, and Denver, courses focus on human rights issues and on reforming the nation's social policies. At Stanford, Colgate, Boston College, Brown, SUNY, Princeton, and others, the prospective student can focus on militarism and the arms race.

Scholastic Globalists

Other programs focus on ecological concerns, on hunger and the politics of food distribution, or on the theories associated with the new global economics. But consistently, the view is futurist, applying alternative visions, imaging, and other fanciful means of exploring the promised globalist world-view which they believe is just ahead of us.

Supporting the research and development of all these programs are some 150 foundations, funding agencies, and research councils, ranging from Amnesty International to the World Future Society. Dozens of films and media resources are already available, from PBS documentaries to Time-Life films. The services of an immense range of scholars, statisticians, and scientists are also combined with those of medical, legal, economics, publishing, and theology professionals, to help make the entire globalist community one of the most auspicious and formidable emerging industries in the world today.

Professor Richard Falk of Princeton University has been one of the principal contributors to the new lexicon of world order studies. In his writings—such as his book *The End of World Order*—Falk has helped to clarify the aims and goals of world-order politics, calling for a realignment of national and federal policy in favor of a globalist one-world government. The statements of such works are so logical and dispassionate, one hardly notices their flagrant revolutionary implications.

In describing the context of world-order studies, Falk writes:

Founded on dissatisfaction with the professional judgment that a statist framework of world politics is here to stay, the world order approach critically examines the durability and adequacy of statism, proposes alternative political frameworks, and considers strategies and scenarios that might facilitate the transition to a post-statist type of world order. Furthermore, it takes the realization of values (peacefulness, economic well-being, social and political justice, ecological balance, and humane governance), rather than materialistic and technological gains, as the decisive criterion of progress in human affairs.

In other words, this professor is helping to promote and define an academic discipline that proposes a general worldwide revolution against nationhood as we now know it in favor of a one-world socialist government. While discrediting technological progress and private property as tokens of the old, militaristic, nationalistic world order, he is calling for the empowerment of ecology, human rights, and socialist activism.

Throughout this movement, as in some throwback to the hippie culture of the 1960s, three predominant concerns stand out in virtually every discussion:

1. Antiwar and antinuclear activism
2. Ecology and environmental protection
3. Emergence of a global New Age religion

Falk writes:

This movement pits the "oppressed" against the entrenched elites, in and out of government, who continue to affirm, however reluctantly, a nuclear future. It is a matter of prediction, not prophecy, to contend that this struggle will intensify in the future and link antinuclear concerns with these wider antimilitary and ecological quality issues.

The Class Struggle, Again?

What Falk describes is a warfare—not unlike a Marxist class struggle—between the oppressed peoples, prodded by their ideological leaders, and what he perceives as the "imperialists" and "militarists" of the world. It is curious how such spokesmen, (hiding behind a facade of antiwar rhetoric) have absolutely no hesitation to threaten violence to accomplish their purposes. But it is also eye-opening to observe that these idealists foresee the potential of a new religious movement within their cause.

Falk writes:

> Finally, there is the question of whether, beneath the negotiations, a new, globally oriented religiosity will emerge to generate new myths, creeds, and symbols. This remains a major, perhaps decisive, uncertainty.

For his model of leadership, the author has gone back to the seventeenth century, to Hugo Grotius, a Dutch Calvinist reformer who was imprisoned for his ideas. For the scholar, Grotius represents the radical antiwar activist who was willing to speak out and to suffer for his unpopular beliefs. But more significantly, he is also the model for the future spiritual leader whom Falk believes will come forth to lead the nations. He says:

> Perhaps we await a Grotius who can teach us to "see" the shadowland [of political transformation] and, without losing persuasiveness, to accord sufficient status to international developments that depart from the premises of the state system. Grotius came from an independent state in the Protestant north of Europe. . . . One would similarly expect that our Grotius, if he or she emerges, will come from the Third World rather than from the advanced industrial countries. The shadowland is more accessible to those who are victims of the old order

and apostles of the new order. . . . Without indulging illusions, I
believe that the Grotian quest remains our best hope.

Since its founding in 1968, another group, the Institute for World
Order, has been investigating an area called "alternative futures" to
determine how national frontiers and interests can be dissolved. At
the heart of its World Order Models Projects (WOMP and WOMP
II) are a host of related political interests concerning nuclear
nonproliferation, human rights activism, social welfare, and the
implementation of a new international economic order.

Again, the terms and ideologies of the think tanks are synonymous throughout all the various institutional programs. But over and
over, the models and heroes being elevated by these groups are such
forward thinkers as Lenin, Marx, and Trotsky, along with Mao Tse
Tung, Mahatma Gandhi, and even Adolf Hitler.

Inspiration for the models and the turn of mind required by
these disciplines comes most often from Zen and Hinduism, from
New Age clones such as est and Unity, or from science fiction—in
works such as Ursula LeGuin's *The Dispossessed.* Is this really the new
order that awaits us?

The Globalist's Creed

Norman Cousins, the former editor of *Saturday Review* magazine, a bestselling author, and a longtime member of the Council on
Foreign Relations, is another prominent contributor to the vocabulary of the new world order. His last work, revised and rereleased in
early 1991 some months after his death, is entitled *The Celebration
of Life,* and it offers a sort of Socratic dialogue on life and faith and
mystical essences.

In this book, first published in 1974, Cousins holds forth an almost poetic image of the "oneness of all life," which is clearly from
Hindu thought and mysticism. "Human unity," he says, "is the fulfillment of diversity. It is the harmony of opposites. It is a many-
stranded texture, with color and depth."

Together, he reasons, all men and women make up "the one-ness of man," and while our lives and memory are "personal and finite," we are part of a universal substance which is "boundless and infinite."

With such a view, it is not difficult to imagine that Cousins could easily espouse a one-world government that scorns individuality, personality, nationhood, and even private property. He notes that Eastern thought, especially in the teachings of Baha Allah, the founder of the Bahai cult, holds that, "The test of spiritual doctrine was in its application to every aspect of life and government." He says, "Baha Allah anticipated the implications of modern destructive science when he advocated world political unity." A thought apparently attractive to the author.

Cousins concludes this final book of his life, in fact, with his own statement of faith, which is his belief that we are all on a shared journey through some sort of mystical unity of body and spirit. He says:

> Together, we share the quest for a society of the whole equal to our needs, a society in which we neither have to kill nor be killed, a society congenial to the full exercise of the creative intelligence, a society in which we need not live under our moral capacity, and in which justice has a life of its own.
>
> Singly and together, we can live without dread and without helplessness.
>
> We are single cells in a body of five billion cells. The body is humankind.

Is this really immortality? Is this really the life that God has designed for humankind? Absolutely not. But this is the sort of mystical idealism which pervades so much of modern philosophy and science. With such a dehumanized and impersonal belief, it is no wonder supporters of the one-world ideology find it so easy to assault the ideas of national pride and the sovereignty of independent nations.

The Scientist As Mystic

Fritjof Capra, another outspoken proponent of one-worldism, was educated as a physicist in Vienna, Paris, and California before becoming a leader of the New Age movement. His book, *The Tao of Physics,* launched his star among West Coast radicals and New Agers with its attempt to demonstrate the mystical elements of natural science. His most recent book, *Uncommon Wisdom,* includes a rambling account of the author's conversations with various scholars, mystics, and sages.

Through his journeys on several continents, dabbling in everything from quantum physics to economics, this spiritual dilettante superimposes his own wistful imagery upon a desperate search for a mystical reality that he hopes will reveal the cosmic unity of all energy and matter.

Like so many voices from the New Age—seekers lost in time and space—Capra is a victim of his own godlessness, a refugee from the hippie culture of the 1960s straining for some hidden reality beyond the perception of his natural senses. He, too, preaches a "challenge to the existing social order" and a mission to seek out "a new vision of reality."

It is sometimes difficult for Christians to understand the implications of such attitudes, since we believe our faith is strong and vital and very much alive. But it is important to realize that these intellectuals have already acknowledged the death of God and the demise of the church as a force in modern culture. Some claim that the publication of *The Communist Manifesto* in 1848 hailed the symbolic death knell of Christendom. Yet few today fail to recognize the need for moral underpinnings in society and even the need for mystical and spiritual values.

In his classic work, *Introduction to International Relations,* Charles P. Schleicher wrote that traditional religion is a dividing force in modern society that pits one group against another over emotional issues and which encourages bloody rivalries. He suggests that only the "decline in religious faith" in this century has helped to reduce social conflict. But more pointedly, he writes:

There are those who believe that only a universal religion to which men are fervently devoted, one which unites men in devotion to a single god and in a common brotherhood, will serve to overcome divisions among men and the worship of the secular nation-state.

Obviously, Christians agree that faith builds brotherhood and understanding, but the scholar's pragmatic view of religion as a sort of social solvent is not particularly comfortable. Nevertheless, in light of the utopian heritage of today's vision of a new world order, the idea that the state or some other political institutions would aspire to divine authority is not at all surprising.

The Counterculture

In a 1968 work edited by Harvard scholar Stanley Hoffman and entitled *Conditions of World Order,* the European scholar Helio Jaguaribe takes the perspective that the spiritual context of life in the coming world order will be the moral responsibility, not of the church, but of the intellectuals. It is the intellectuals, he says, who have the vision and the objectivity to represent "the spiritual unity of men, beyond any conflict of interests, ideologies, and religions."

More sinister though, Jaguaribe also says that the scholars' task includes "the destruction of all romantic illusions regarding the good old days and the smug security provided by a Christian cosmos." In order to build a religion of the state, the scholar must first work to dismantle the religion of the church.

For an idea of what sort of doctrines a religion of the state would enshrine, it may be helpful to look at the work of one powerful organization, the Club of Rome. Citing the forward-thinking plans of the Club of Rome—the notorious pro-death group that preaches the doctrine of Zero Population Growth—many new order advocates support abortion as a practical means of birth control, and they support euthanasia as a way of ridding the new order of the old, the feeble, the tired, and the unproductive. This is their humanistic spiritual reality.

The Club of Rome in its 1976 report entitled *Reshaping the International Order* said that we live in a divided world: on one side is the rich world of the developed nations, on the other, the poor world of the underdeveloped. In saying that a "poverty curtain" divides these worlds, both materially and philosophically, they write:

> One world is literate, the other largely illiterate; one industrial and urban, the other predominantly agrarian and rural; one consumption oriented, the other striving for survival. In the rich world, there is concern about the quality of life, in the poor world about life itself which is threatened by disease, hunger and malnutrition.

The writers and researchers wrote that today there is a new search for order in the world, a new philosophy in which the rich nations are required to contribute materially to the welfare of the poor. "In a fast shrinking planet," they said, "it was inevitable that this 'new' philosophy would not stop at national borders; and, since there is no world government, the poor nations are bringing this concern to its closest substitute, the United Nations."

They observe, ominously, that "the rich cannot conceal their wealth in a 'global village.' The glaring differences are perceived by the poor thanks, perhaps paradoxically, to the rich world's technological dexterity. And their perception of these differences will, in a shrinking world, exert growing stress on already frail international institutions." Then they add that "the adjustment needed in the long terms is undoubtedly to be found in an increased flow of funds from the rich to the poor nations."

One has to wonder how this differs from outright communism! Their proposal is, in fact, an ideology known as state socialism. They want a world where those who work and produce and enjoy a high standard of living pay, not only taxes to support their own federal bureaucracy and welfare institutions through constantly rising taxes, but additional taxes to support the poor nations of the world who do not work or produce effectively.

But be certain, they do not expect government to take money from existing revenues to support this Third World. They know, without a doubt, that government will simply levy new taxes. What they are saying, then, is that you and I must pay more taxes to the government to support the Third World, and we must trust that our money will be used for good purposes and not simply more guns, more revolution, more graft and corruption, and more of the same folly that has kept the Third World largely unprofitable and unproductive throughout history.

The Club of Rome researchers propose a new international Treaty of Rome that would lay down the "rules of the international game," and which calls for, in its final provisions, a one-world government. This is spelled out in detail, with specific provisions and codes, in the documents of the report.

The Limits of Reason

Predictably, scholars such as Richard Falk have nothing but praise for the Club of Rome's initiative and insight in their search for a world-order hypothesis. He says, "The Club of Rome represents perhaps the most significant effort to date to gain a hearing for an interpretation of the future presented in quantitative forms and offered as new knowledge."

In their Project on the Predicament of Mankind, executed in 1970, the Club hired a group of MIT scholars, headed by Jay Forrester, to conduct a sophisticated research project based on global factors. Falk writes that "their purpose was to design a world model for computer analysis organized around the interactions of dynamic processes such as resource use, food production, population growth, capital investment, and industrial output." Their study was eventually published in the 1972 book *The Limits to Growth*.

Many critical reviewers and analysts said that Forrester's computer was reacting to insufficient data and crying "wolf." Even though Falk commended the research, he admitted that "Futurology is intrinsically flawed by the tension between the methodology and its policy recommendations. The method is not presently capable of producing a convincing argument unless it is supplemented by subjective factors—judgments, values, preferences."

But then the Princeton professor goes on to commend another writer, William Irwin Thompson, who in the process of taking issue with some of the technological failures of the Rome report, calls for a new spiritual dynamic to give vitality to such projections.

Falk writes:

> Thompson believes that a new consciousness, based on a new spiritual awareness and appreciation of the realities of planetary culture, is a necessary precondition for any kind of successful response to the world order crises now being acknowledged even by statesmen. As Thompson put it, "If you are going to humanize technology, you're not going to be able to do it without the limited terms of books and civilization and other older containers. You've got to go very far out."

So what does he mean by "far out"? Specifically he proposes "a reunion of scientific and mystical thinking in small-scale institutions that embody a vision of the future." Suddenly Falk's own imagery is alive with models, and he proposes that Hermann Hesse's mystical novel *Magister Ludi* is the very model of such a spiritual linkage of power which merits closer study.

He goes on to say,

> For America, at least, it is morally and hence intellectually impossible to propose a new Jerusalem and yet at the same time remain agnostic or indifferent about genocide and ecocide in Indochina. . . . These comments about a new consciousness are designed to set the stage for an inquiry into the future of world order. . . . With these considerations in mind, it seems possible and desirable, indeed necessary, to propose new ways of envisioning— really revisioning—the future so as to break the bonds of present constraints on moral and political imagination. My primary purpose is therefore educational, to awaken man's reason to the idea of wholeness as the basis for individual or collective sanity.

Isn't it interesting that Falk, like the European scholars mentioned earlier, links the terms *intellectual* and *moral.* He is in fact contending that the scholar, not the priest, is the arbiter of morality.

The Price of Freedom

In another essay entitled "The Trend Toward World Community," included in the Festschrift *The Search for World Order,* Professor Falk writes, "[T]here are many signs of reaction against traditions of blind patriotism, at least in the liberal democracies of the West—in countries, that is, that are both modern and generally indulgent of political dissent."

The author says further that "traditional political symbols have lost much of their meaning. Partly it arises from the positive appeal of transnational moral and legal norms which embody both a generalized revulsion against unjust war, and a kind of cosmopolitan humanism that extends compassion to any victim [of] society. And partly it reflects the renewed appeal of anarchistic politics, with its opposition to all claims over life asserted on behalf of the sovereign state." Are we to understand such observations as fact, or merely as the scholar's wishful thinking?

But he goes on to say,

> There is also now occasion and need for a reorientation of ideas of national citizenship and national interest. In the socialization process that goes on in principal societies of the world, the essential need is to associate "security" more closely with the attainment of world unity than with national or even regional separatism, and to this, education of the young could make a very large contribution. One may hope that the elites throughout the world will begin to be constituted and served by individuals who have been socialized in such a way that they see global norms as automatically relevant to the choice of means to implement societal goals.

It is interesting to note that this author also glows with the observations that the Teheran Conference of the United Nations on Human Rights passed a resolution declaring that developed countries are under a moral obligation to donate 1 percent of their entire GNP to the poor countries. He also notes that the newly revised charter of the Organization of American States argues for much the same principle. Both of these documents argue for the principles of *community* over those of *sovereignty*.

Falk also says that already, "in all major countries there are developing counter-elite groups with a futuristic and cosmopolitan conception of the proper organization of social and political life." Even if they fail to gain power, such groups will continue to foment revolt, resistance, and dissatisfaction within existing governments, whatever their stripe.

The Wisdom of the Academy

This is the wisdom of the academy. This is the rhetoric professors are drilling into our children at this very moment. Even if only a handful of students buy the rhetoric or respond in some fashion with their lives, what will the long-range implications of such radical ideology be? Remember that Falk is the same man who says that a new religiosity (presumably a New Age-type religion) is needed to shape the "myths, creeds, and symbols" of the new world order.

How will these educators change the world? Can they make a radical change in the way our young men and women behave? Harvard Professor Stanley Hoffman, in his book *Primacy or World Order*, writes, "What will have to take place is a gradual adaptation of the social, economic, and political system of the United States to the imperatives of world order." Clearly, educators are prepared to follow John Dewey's model of a slow, persistent, and relentless re-education of America's values and mores. Having seen the fruit of Dewey's labor, can anyone doubt what havoc the prophets of the new order will wreak?

The American system has lived to see the total collapse of the Soviet economy. Gorbachev, who came to our doorstep begging for aid, survived the apparent threats to his life during the August 1991 "coup," then emerged with the support of the enigmatic Boris Yeltsin. But now, with what appears to be fresh evidence of the Russian democratic spirit, the scholars are racing once again to cede the moral advantage to the Soviets.

Hoffman writes, "[T]he demands of world order entail a painful process of discovery for many Americans. They will have to realize that others do not share all our values and practices and that the world is not a field in which we can go and apply our preferred policies and techniques with impunity."

Education of the young to a new way of thinking must begin in the academy: teaching teachers who teach students who, in turn, grow into predictable products of the system. It is the conviction of these world-order advocates that subtle, patient, and gradual changes in education, shaping the minds of the youth of our democratic nations, will bring the real victory of the new world order.

Hoffman writes, "[A] world order policy is a pattern of education. By trial and error, American leaders must show the people whom they represent why traditional policies must change and obtain enough support to turn these changes into new laws, institutions, and habits. And American intellectuals must keep trying, not to behave as if the world of power were the kingdom of heaven, but to enlighten the public and the leaders about the problems of the present world, about the demands of world order, about the pitfalls of any attempt to meet them, and about the greater peril of politics-as-usual."

False Messiahs

Since Dewey began his notorious career at Columbia, twisting and shaping the values and behaviors of American scholars and teachers, the secular establishment has been patiently and persistently dismantling America's inherited value system and its ethical foundations.

In times past their cause was most clearly identified in the language of communism, socialism, humanism, and anarchy. Today the language of the new world order offers a whole new vocabulary and even more sinister agenda for reshaping our world for its ends. It is universalist, globalist, and spiritual in nature. And since it brings with it, in its very language, the specter of Apocalypse, it may well be the most threatening vision of reality ever conceived.

The false prophets of humanism are committed to their agenda of radical change, and they will not spare any means of bringing about their ends. Whether it is slow, like the work of the wind and rain, or fast, like a military revolution, they are committed to this struggle.

In *The Gold of the Gods,* Erich Von Daniken, a scholar and a dreamer, said,

> I suspect that with the step into the interstellar third millennium the end of terrestrial polytheism will inevitably come.
>
> With the assumption that we are all parts of the mighty IT, God no longer has to be simultaneously good and bad in some inconceivable way; He is no longer responsible for sorrow and happiness, for ordeals and acts of providence. We ourselves have the positive and negative powers within us, because we come from the IT that always was.

Such sentiments are hardly different from those of New Age celebrity Shirley MacLaine who, in *Dancing in the Light,* appropriated the language of God Almighty in her statement at the end of the book, "I AM that I AM." The new mystical order and the new secular order are hardly different in their ultimate ambitions.

In his 1979 book, *Tides Among Nations,* Karl W. Deutsch appropriated the language of the Messiah in his declaration that, through the patient and dedicated effort of reformers, "Humanity will be able to take its own fate into its own hands, and see to it that our children, and our children's children, shall have life and have it more abundantly." Clearly, such visionaries have no need of the kingdom of God or of His Christ, since they are driven by the compelling vision that they "shall be as gods."

What are the implications of such beliefs? In the following chapter I would like to examine these and other promises of the new secular agenda in greater detail and review the long-range implications of the ongoing manipulation of America's hopes, dreams, and its place in the world.

8

New Order for the New Age

A SIGNIFICANT SEGMENT OF THE FORCES birthing the new world order is not motivated merely by economic, sociological, or ecological concerns. To be sure, the most highly placed players are clearly centered around the banking-corporate-foundation nexus of big money, and their principal goal appears to be control of the banking power of a world government, along with the power such authority would give them over elected politicians and their policies.

However, when the spiritual dimensions of the new world order are discussed, they invariably take on the appearance of what we have come to know as the New Age. Author Tal Brooke, whose book *When the World Will Be As One* details the satanic background of the New Age, was at one time a disciple of a Hindu holy man, Sai Baba. Sai Baba was possessed by one of a group of powerful demons known to New Agers as "ascended masters."

Brooke wrote in July 1991, in his *SCP Journal,*

> One of the dangers of the New Age Movement is that it is the perfect creed for globalism. It can syncretize with any faith except Christianity. It does not use the language of judgment or sin, but speaks in sweeping terms—about the sacredness of nature and the spark of divinity in the

human race. It uses positive language and idealized human potential. It is utterly post modern and outwardly far more attractive to post-Christian baby boomers than the "outmoded" church. It is up to date, vogue, and politically correct. It could also undergird a planetary faith or spawn something else that will—such as Gaia. In brief, the New Age movement, and its progeny, Gaia, are spiritually correct for a new world order. Christianity is not.

A generic spirituality is necessary to fuse diverse, even hostile, cultures and faiths into a unity. To fit the world together, religious boundaries must be eliminated.

To those of us who realize the invisible spiritual dimension of the struggle to overthrow the existing world order and its Christian roots, the emergence of a New Age world religion is of paramount importance, because the human potential movement, as if part of a continuum, invariably leads to psychic power; and occult power leads straight to demonic power; and these lead, in turn, to a single source of evil identified by the Bible as Satan (the adversary), the Devil (the accuser), Lucifer (the light one), or Abaddon (the one who rules over hell and destruction).

To understand this concern, I recommend a careful reading of a 1977 book by Dusty Sklar, called *The Nazis and the Occult,* which details what happens to a government and its people when occultic forces begin to influence its leaders. Occultism was pervasive among the leaders of Nazi Germany, and it clearly influenced their ghastly programs for world domination.

The Spiritual Nation

Regardless of what anyone may say, America is still a religious nation. The court system and various liberal action groups in this country have tried for more than forty years to dismantle America's religious heritage, but they have not entirely succeeded, and by the grace of God they may not if the revival of Christian values continues to surge forth in the coming years as it has in the past decade.

Washington scholar James Reichley, a senior fellow at the Brookings Institute, reported in his book *Religion in American Public Life* that more than 90 percent of all Americans identify with some religious faith, and on any given Sunday more than 40 percent attend church. The common theology of America is not strict Christianity but what Reichley calls "theist-humanism," that is, a general religious view of the world with the specific duality of Christ's admonition to love the Lord thy God and to love thy neighbor as thyself.

Despite the statistical evidence, the dominant value system in American society during this century, Reichley says, has become a sort of *secular egoism* combined with a flexible *economic individualism.* This radical consumerist view has taken such a commanding lead in the world's value system that it has led, irrevocably, to a glorification of the self and to conspicuous self-gratification, as easily seen in advertising, popular psychological therapy, and entertainment.

According to the numbers, mainline Protestant denominations make up roughly 30 percent of the U.S. population; Roman Catholics make up 25 percent; white evangelical Protestants make up about 20 percent; Black Protestant churches add about 8 percent; Jews are about 3 percent; and others, ranging from Mormons to Hare Krishnas, contribute an additional 5 percent. The remainder are presumably unaffiliated with any particular faith.

It was Joseph Schumpeter who pointed out that the doctrine of Marxism was essentially theological in nature, identifying the proletariat as the chosen people and the state as the ultimate ecclesiastical authority. But if Reichley's observations are correct, the doctrine of capitalism is no less theological, only in this case the god of this new secular religion is the self.

We see the teachings of this theology of self in books, magazines, and activities of every description: self-awareness materials; tapes, videos, and seminars for self-actualization; the national fascination with muscles, fitness, health, and beauty; a growing demand for luxury and creature comforts, even in the face of a difficult recession; and magazines such as *Us* and *Self* and many others that glorify the individual man or woman.

Despite the various religious affiliations Americans claim in the polls and surveys, secular civil humanism (what is generally known as secular humanism) has become the prevailing ideology of most of America's intellectuals and cultural elite. This is a doctrine of the self that traces its roots to the ancient Greeks and was perhaps best expressed by Protagoras (who gave the humanists their essential credo) in his statement that "Man is the measure of all things."

Dark Secrets

The theosophist author and founder of the Arcane School, Alice Bailey, was reportedly the first to use the term *New Age* and also the first to expropriate the image of "the Christ" for New Age purposes. As a prototype of the priestly ascended masters—whom Bailey and other occultists claimed to be involved in working out mankind's spiritual destiny from some remote Himalayan retreat—the New Age Christ was transformed from the true Son of God to a convenient symbol. Bailey claimed her own works were transmitted to her telepathically by the Tibetan Djuhal Khul, who predicted the appearance of a new world government and a world religion. She followed a New Age Christ.

Members of Adolf Hitler's occultic organization within the National Socialist party, the Thule-Gesellschaft, had referred to themselves as the founders of *die neue Zeit,* the New Age, and they promised a thousand-year reign and a mystical godlike transcendence. Like the Rosicrucians and the higher orders of Masons, the Nazis practiced secret ceremonies that invoked mystical powers and included the worship of Lucifer, their god of light.

During the 1930s and 1940s, it was clear that Hitler saw himself as the father of a new world order. He preached a doctrine of Aryan supremacy, and he apparently believed himself to be the Messiah, the promised one, who would lead the world out of darkness into the light. That was just *one* false Messiah.

Years later the British New Ager Benjamin Creme proclaimed that the true Messiah—a combination of Jesus Christ, the Buddhist

Lord Meitreya, and the Muslim Mahdi, all rolled into one—was already here and living in east London. Then, with the immense resources of the Tara Center, a New Age headquarters, he paid for full-page ads in many of the leading newspapers of the world in which he declared this millenarian vision.

New Agers of all stripes continue to long for "transcendence" and "transformation," which makes them natural prophets of and contributors to society's insatiable longing for a new world order. In light of the growing spiritual awareness on all fronts in the past two decades, mystics and sages are declaring the imminent arrival of a new spiritual order which coincides with the political vision. According to New Age author Peter Lemesurier of Scotland's Findhorn Institute,

> Extraordinary things are happening. Great and far-reaching changes are afoot. A strange, autonomous transformation is spreading like some irresistible virus through society. . . . Whether founded on factual evidence or merely on a desperate rejection of the idea that things can possibly go on as they are, the word is out that a new age is upon us, a new dispensation ready to begin, a revolutionary World Order about to supervene.

In an effort to correct the drift, so to speak, of the New Age movement and refocus some of its dualistic thinking, Lemesurier has prepared an astonishingly comprehensive overview of the various heresies, treacheries, cults, plots, and counterfeits (although he would not describe them in those terms) that have paraded as theological wisdom over the past thirty-five hundred years. In his book *This New Age Business,* the latest of his half-dozen offerings, he says that the New Age and the new world order are essentially synonymous concepts that have co-existed since man's emergence from Eden. Of this unified order he writes:

> At one time or another, indeed, it has been regarded as only common sense by large parts of the Earth's population. "New Ageism"—or millenarianism in its broadest sense—is in fact one of the oldest and most widespread ideas known to humanity. And to this day

it remains (as the writings of Mikhail Gorbachev explicitly make clear) every bit as basic to the official outlook of the Marxist East as it does to that of the capitalist and science-orientated West.

Kingdoms of God and Man

The idea of a marriage of secular and spiritual images in the new world order is disturbingly real and potentially very dangerous. Certainly Alice Bailey believed in it, and in her 1947 book *Problems of Humanity,* she wrote:

> The Kingdom of God will inaugurate a world which will be one in which it will be realized that—politically speaking—humanity, as a whole, is of far greater importance than any one nation; it will be a new world order, built upon different principles to those in the past, and one in which men will carry the spiritual vision into their national governments, into their economic planning and into all measures taken to bring about security and right human relations.

Bailey's spiritual vision was both sacred and profane, secular and occult, and she held out a metaphysical image of world order in which the individual was to be swallowed up in the state and individual nations were to be subsumed within a global community. This view was the political equivalent of the Hindu oversoul, or, as Norman Cousins described it, the image of a single human cell surrounded by 5 billion identical and anonymous cells of equal shape and value. Bailey said that:

> What we need above all to see—as a result of spiritual maturity—is the abolition of those two principles which have wrought so much evil in the world and which are summed up in the two words: Sovereignty and Nationalism.

That is such a shocking statement for our traditional sensibilities, but isn't it really the same ideology being touted by today's new world order advocates: a globalist world without national sovereignty or independence and a zeal for global political unity of spiritual dimensions?

In the late eighteenth century, the English philosopher Edmund Burke said that man is by nature a religious animal. Burke understood that man has a deep, heartfelt need for spiritual significance and purpose and that these emotions could only be satisfied by religious experience. The French thinker Blaise Pascal had expressed much the same thought a hundred years earlier in his maxim that there exists a God-shaped vacuum in the human heart that only God can fill. But for the passionate seekers in the New Age, the political agenda leaves little room for traditional moral values, and the religious agenda leaves little room for the rights of freedom-loving men.

If you consider the aims and the pervasiveness of such rich and powerful movements as Silva Mind Control, Eckankar, est (or the forum), Scientology, Unity, the Course in Miracles, various forms of ancestor and spirit worship, channeling, ufology, and crystalology—not to mention the renewed interest in more classical Eastern religions, from Zen Buddhism to Taoism—it is easy to see how spiritual visionaries such as Alice Bailey and L. Ron Hubbard could so easily exploit and despoil the historic values of this nation.

As early as 1978, a Gallup Poll reported that more than 10 million Americans were involved in some form of Eastern mysticism or activities associated with the New Age movement, and another 9 million are involved in some form of holistic and spiritual healing. With the continued growth of the human potential movement and sensitivity seminars in hundreds of America's largest corporations, this disturbing trend continues to grow and gain new converts year after year.

A Subversive Agenda

Willis Harman, formerly a social scientist at SRI International and now a consultant to U.S. corporations, government agencies, and various other institutions, is a highly sought-after New Age author and lecturer. His book, *Global Mind Change,* describes the ways that globalist, occultic, and one-world thinking are infiltrating the elite establishments of both Europe and the United States.

Harman is just one of the thousands of "counselors" being invited by training directors into U.S. companies to teach employee seminars on principles of creativity, imagination, and intuition—concepts derived exclusively from occultic practices that promise to enhance both the practical and the spiritual powers of its practitioners.

As with Fritjof Capra, whom I mentioned in the last chapter, such self-styled corporate gurus are trying to bring about a mystical fusion of science and spirituality—to heal the fragmentation of the human soul, in their own terms—which is very much in keeping with the growing belief that the new world order will bring about both a spiritual and a political unity.

In *The Crime of World Power,* Richard A. Aliano writes, "Ideology may be considered merely as the rationalization of self-interest." It has been used as such in times past in order to motivate, inspire, and threaten, but he says that an ideology—whether it is that of a capitalist, socialist, or spiritual regime—is always presented by its proponents as truth and as the ultimate expression of reality.

Seemingly, that is the situation we are confronted with today. Presented as truth and reality, the ideology of a new world order being offered is, in fact, a rationalization for some form of political or spiritual self-interest and a means of achieving a particular end.

As I review the literature of the New Age and examine the self-evident trends within it, I am continually aware of three particular ends that surface again and again:

1. The subversion and denial of divine revelation
2. The deification of the self
3. The submersion of the individual personality within a larger whole

The Daring Hypothesis

If you are a religious skeptic, I invite you to suspend your judgment for a moment and explore a challenging concept with me. If you are a Christian or a Jew, I invite you to think about this scenario.

Suppose that a powerful spiritual being, a supernatural force such as Satan, a being who is contrary to God and opposed to whatever He does, wanted to overthrow the kingdom of God and to install himself in the seat of power. What would be his agenda? How would he go about implementing such a plan?

First, he would have to cast doubts on God's authority and righteousness. He would have to subvert and undermine God's work among men and His guiding principles whenever and wherever possible. In some cases he could do this himself, but to be fully effective in a world such as ours he would need surrogates, agents, and representatives to carry out this mission among his potential subjects—the nearly 5 billion inhabitants of this planet.

Very likely he would use spiritual beings for this duty, and they could be very effective since they would be both unseen and sinister. But to reach effectively into human society he would have to recruit tens of thousands of willing servants among the sons of men to represent him to other men, not as an evil or sinister force, but as an enticing, wise, loving, and powerful force.

Instead of a source of hate and deception, he would want to persuade men and women that his motives were just, that he had been deprived of his rightful place of authority. He would need to show how mankind is, even now, struggling from darkness toward the light that only he can offer. That would, seemingly, be his natural first objective.

Second, he would no doubt feel that he could easily attract followers with the promise that they could share his kingdom. They, too, would be as gods, have power and dominion, rule the air, the sea, the sky, and hold eternity within their grasp. Poetic metaphors could barely grasp the grandness of such a vision, and the human ego could hardly bear the images of joy such a promise would hold out.

But if his first motive were truly subversion—to overthrow the God of the universe and supplant His authority—not all his methods would necessarily be clean and pure. He would have to do some dark and underhanded things from time to time—which is just common sense; after all, all is fair in love and war, isn't it?—so in some cases he would have to make people understand that dark is light and light is dark. In other words, he would need to create an environment in which any subversive and destructive act would be appropriate and irreproachable.

Third, if his ambition were to rise to godship and to wield divine authority in the world, he could not really share his power. To divide his kingdom would be to take away a part of his glory and dominion, so he would quickly need to submerge this divinity he had promised his subjects in some sort of oversoul or some other cosmic disguise which, in reality, is powerless and noncompetitive with him.

As in the objective stated above, he would also have to convince his would-be followers that the loss of their authority and identity would be the beginning of their godlike powers. Jesus Christ once said (under quite different circumstances) that he who would find his life must lose it. Surely the aspiring sovereign could apply Christ's words for his own purposes.

It is not hard to see that this very simple plan, if applied patiently and consistently over time, could be very effective. Were it not for the power of the authentic God and His followers among men, the job would be much easier. The institutions of the church, evangelical Christians (who actually believe what they profess), and any other recognition of God would be obstructions to his plan. But knowing the weak character of man and mankind's tendency to bend to persistent pressure, this supernatural interloper could surely have his way with the world over time.

The Grand Design

It is as if a giant plan is unfolding, everything perfectly on cue. Europe sets the date for its union. Communism collapses. A hugely popular war is fought in the Middle East. The United Nations is rescued from scorn by an easily swayed public. A new world order is announced. Christianity has been battered in the public arena, and New Age religions are in place in the schools and corporations, and among the elite. Then a financial collapse accelerates the move toward a world money system.

The United States cannot afford defense, so it turns its defense requirements over to the United Nations, along with its sovereignty. The United Nations severely limits property rights and clamps down on all Christian evangelism and Christian distinctives under the Declaration of the Elimination of All Forms of Intolerance and Discrimination Based on Religious Belief already adopted by the General Assembly on November 25, 1981.

Then the New Age religion of humanity becomes official, and the new world order leaders embrace it. Then they elect a world president with plenary powers who is totally given to the religion of humanity.

Forty-five years ago such a scenario would have been unthinkable—but the unthinkable is happening. On July 26, 1991, Haynes Johnson wrote a piece in the *Washington Post* reporting a poll which stated "59 percent of the public believes that United Nations resolutions 'should rule over the actions and laws of individual countries, including the United States.'"

He also stated, "They want the United Nations, not the United States, to take the lead in solving international conflicts . . . as head of an international combat force that wages war." This poll may have been rigged to further condition the public toward globalism. But assuming it is accurate, we may presume that the Persian Gulf War has proved to be an enormous success for the globalists in creating a groundswell reversal of public opinion against the interests of this country.

In earlier chapters, we have traced the infiltration of Continental Freemasonry by the new world philosophy of the Order of the Illuminati, and its subsequent role in the French Revolution. We then were able to find clear documentation that the occultic-oriented secret societies claiming descent from Illuminism and the French Revolution played a seminal role in the thinking of Marx and Lenin.

In fact, one historian has asserted that wealthy and influential Europeans with direct roots to Illuminism operated a very secret society out of Geneva, which in fact controlled the Bolshevik movement. We also know that Lord Milner of the British Round Table and Jacob Schiff, of Federal Reserve Board creator Paul Warburg's banking firm, gave the essential seed money to finance the Russian Revolution.

But where is the link between the Continental Illuminati occultic influences on communism and British and American financial support of the same cause? Let's continue.

The Masonic Connection

We do not know whether such a tie does exist; there is not presently any known direct evidence to support it. However, one magazine source, whose data have not been verified, indicated that all of the French membership on the Trilateral Commission were members of French Freemasonry. This may just be a coincidence, or it may mean that prominent Frenchmen are also Masons, or it may actually be the missing link tying these sordid elements together.

In any event, this book would be incomplete without a look at the impact of Freemasonry on the current thought processes moving toward a new world. To quote from the *Encyclopedia Britannica:*

> Having begun in medieval times as an association of craftsmen, hence its name—Freemasonry has been since the eighteenth century a speculative system. It admits adherents of all faiths, claiming to be based upon those fundamentals of religion held in common by all men . . . it is secret in so far as it has rituals and other matters which those admitted take an oath never to divulge.

But then the encyclopedist goes on to say:

> Since 1738 the Roman Catholic Church repeatedly has declared those of its faithful who join the fraternity to be guilty of grave sin and therefore excommunicated; the chief reason for this is that the

church holds that the beliefs of Freemasonry constitute a deistic or pagan religion.

It is obvious from the teachings of Freemasonry that its doctrines are not Christian but indeed track identically with the syncretism of the so-called New Age religions of today. I think it is especially interesting that one of the official publications of American Masons was called until 1990 *The New Age*.

The power of the Masonic Order was extraordinary, and in England it quickly spread among the highest classes. Lord Alexander, General Alexander Hamilton, Quartermaster General Robert Moray, the Earl of Erroll, Lord Pitsligo, and the Duke of Richmond were members in the 1600s. The aristocracy completely took over the leadership. According to the *Britannica*:

> From 1737 to 1907 about sixteen English princes of royal blood joined the order. The list of past grand masters included eight princes who later become monarchs: George IV, Edward VII, Edward VIII and George VI of England; Oscar II and Gustav V of Sweden; and Frederick VIII and Christian X of Denmark.

With this incredible array of royal power associated with Freemasonry, can we believe it possible that the powerful Cecil Rhodes and his secret society did not have some involvement with the Freemasons of England or those on the Continent?

Contrasting Views

In the United States we know the various Masonic lodges as being composed of people who are engaged in a number of projects for community betterment. In my community, the Shriners sponsor the Oyster Bowl, which pits collegiate football teams in a contest to raise money for crippled children. Their slogan, "Strong legs will run, that weak legs may walk," has enormous appeal. Their benevolent traditions are commendable.

Both George Washington and Benjamin Franklin were Masons. If there is a dark side to Freemasonry, and there is, it should be carefully pointed out that the average American Mason—especially those in the lower orders—is not in any way aware of it. If he were a student of the Bible, he would realize that the Masonic rituals are neither biblical nor Christian, but most Americans know very little about the Bible. To them Freemasonry is a family-centered, fraternal, benevolent organization.

Earlier we pointed out that Adam Weishaupt (the founder of the Order of the Illuminati) had determined to infiltrate the Continental branch of Freemasonry. Weishaupt had been indoctrinated into Egyptian occultism in 1771 by a merchant of unknown origin named Kolmer, who had been seeking European converts. It was said that for five years Weishaupt formulated a plan by which all occultic systems could be reduced to a single powerful organization. He launched the Order of the Illuminati just two months prior to the drafting of the American colonies' Declaration of Independence.

Apparently Weishaupt tried assiduously to promote the concept that the Illuminati, whose offices in Bavaria had been raided and closed down, were therefore merely a transitory phenomenon. But Illuminism was not transitory, and Weishaupt's principles, his disciples, and his influence continue to resurface to this day.

Virtually every single proponent of a complete new world order repeats Weishaupt's concepts, virtually word for word. Here are his revolutionary, destructive goals:

1. Abolition of monarchies and all ordered governments
2. Abolition of private property and inheritances
3. Abolition of patriotism and nationalism
4. Abolition of family life and the institution of marriage, and the establishment of communal education for children
5. Abolition of all religion

In 1921, English historian Nesta Webster, author of *World Revolution,* wrote,

This is the precise language of internationalists today, and it is, of course, easy to point out the evils of exaggerated patriotism. But it will not be found that the man who loves his country is less able to respect foreign patriots any more than the man who loves his family is a worse neighbor than one who cares little for wife and children.

Weishaupt's goal was not just the destruction of monarchy, but the destruction of society. In July 1782, Continental Freemasonry was infiltrated and captured by what Weishaupt called Illuminated Freemasonry. I have read a report by a former Mason, Comte de Virieu, who related his shock at the infiltration of Freemasonry in these words:

Tragic secrets. I will not confide them to you. I can only tell you that all this is very much more serious than you think. The conspiracy which is being woven is so well thought out that it will be impossible for the Monarchy and the Church to escape it.

The Missing Link?

That same year, 1782, the headquarters of Illuminated Freemasonry moved to Frankfurt, a center controlled by the Rothschild family. It is reported that in Frankfurt, Jews for the first time were admitted to the order of Freemasons. If indeed members of the Rothschild family or their close associates were polluted by the occultism of Weishaupt's Illuminated Freemasonry, we may have discovered the link between the occult and the world of high finance. Remember, the Rothschilds financed Cecil Rhodes in Africa; Lord Rothschild was a member of the inner circle of Rhodes's English Round Tables; and Paul Warburg, architect of the Federal Reserve System, was a Rothschild agent.

New money suddenly poured into the Frankfurt lodge, and from there a well-funded plan for world revolution was carried forth. During a Masonic congress in 1786, the deaths of both Louis XVI of France and Gustavus III of Sweden were decreed.

William Still, in his book on the new world order, indicates that the Illuminati, with their Masonic front organization, were actually a secret society within a secret society. In 1798, Professor John

Robison, a highly respected British historian and longtime Mason, wrote in his *Proofs of a Conspiracy:*

> I have found that the covert secrecy of a Mason Lodge has been employed in every country for venting and propagating sentiments in religion and politics, that could not have been circulated in public without exposing the author to grave danger. I have observed these doctrines gradually diffusing and mixing with all the different systems of Free Masonry till, at last, AN ASSOCIATION HAS BEEN FORMED FOR THE EXPRESS PURPOSE OF ROOTING OUT ALL OF THE RELIGIOUS ESTABLISHMENTS, AND OVERTURNING ALL THE EXISTING GOVERMENTS OF EUROPE.

The publishers of Robison's book commented, "A conspiracy conceived not by Masons as Masons, but by evil men using Freemasonry as a vehicle for their own purposes."

Weishaupt enticed people into Illuminated Freemasonry with promises of influence, power, and worldly success. But he also ensured that the members were so compromised by personal revelations about themselves or even the commission of crimes, that denying the order could bring disgrace or even prison. He, and the Masons, had lower orders of rank where the initiates were either lied to or kept in the dark about further secrets. But his biggest appeal was to raw, naked power. He wrote,

> The pupils are convinced that the Order will rule the world. Every member therefore becomes a ruler. We all think of ourselves as qualified to rule. It is therefore an alluring thought both to good and bad men. Therefore the Order will spread.

Perhaps more than anything, the following candid admission by Weishaupt can explain the secret of the Illuminati and all those who are seeking world power:

> Do you realize sufficiently what it means to rule—to rule in a secret society? Not only over the lesser or more important of the populace, but over the best men, over men of all ranks, nations, and religions, to rule without external force, to unite them indissolubly, to breathe one spirit and soul into them, men distributed over all parts of the world.

Perhaps this statement answers the question I raised in the first section of this book: how could a concept like world order be kept alive and vital for two hundred years? If successive generations of men indeed bought into Weishaupt's occultic dream of power, they could indeed be willing (or obligated) to perpetuate it.

To Gain the Whole World

Members of the Illuminati at the highest levels of the order were atheists and Satanists. To the public they professed a desire to make mankind "one good and happy family." They made every effort to conceal their true purposes by use of the name of Freemasonry. By every ruse imaginable, the Illuminists were able to attract to their numbers the rich and powerful of Europe, very possibly including Europe's most powerful bankers.

Illuminism reportedly had large wealth at its disposal. Its influence is clearly alive and powerful today in the doctrines of both the one-world communists and the one-world captains of wealth.

Before we leave the influence of Freemasonry on the quest for a New Age and new world order, we should examine the writings of Albert Pike, whose *Morals and Dogma of the Ancient and Accepted Scottish Rite of Freemasonry* was first published in 1871 and subsequently republished in 1966. It was intended for use by the Thirty-Third Degree Masonic Councils. Pike probably was the most prominent expositor of the creed and doctrines of the Masons.

It should be understood that the Scottish Rite is not from Scotland. It was an American adaptation of the Rite of Perfection of the French Freemasons, which were in turn heavily influenced by Illuminated Freemasonry. Keep in mind that Weishaupt learned the Egyptian rites of the occult, so Egyptian symbolism plays a strong role in the Scottish (or French Perfection) Rite of Freemasonry.

Without comment, I will quote directly from the 1966 edition of the principles of the Scottish Rite by its leading expositor in America.

"Every Masonic temple is a temple of religion." (p. 213)

"The first Masonic legislator . . . was Buddha." (p. 277)

"Masonry, around whose altars the Christian, the Hebrew, the Muslim, the Brahmin, the followers of Confucius and Zoroaster, can assemble as brethren and unite in prayer to the one God who is above all the Baalim." (p. 226)

"Everything good in nature comes from Osiris." [the Egyptian sun God; the all-seeing eye is a Masonic representation of Osiris] (p. 476)

"Masonry . . . conceals its mysteries from all except Adepts and Sages, and uses false symbols to mislead those who deserve to be misled." (pp. 104–5)

"Everything scientific and grand in the religious dreams of the Illuminati . . . is borrowed from the Kabalah; all Masonic associations owe to it their secrets and their symbols." (p. 744)

"When the Mason learns that the key to the warrior on the block is the proper application of the dynamo of living power, he has learned the Mystery of his Craft. The seething energies of Lucifer are in his hands."

> Manly Hall, *Lost Keys of Freemasonry,* p. 48

"To you, Sovereign Grand Inspectors General, we say this, that you may repeat it to the Brethren of the 32nd, 31st, and 30th degrees—The Masonic Religion should be, by all of us initiates to the high degrees, maintained in the purity of the Luciferian Doctrine.

"Yes, Lucifer is God, and unfortunately Adonay is also God. . . . Lucifer, God of Light and God of good is struggling for humanity against Adonay, the God of Darkness and Evil."

> Albert Pike, Sovereign Pontiff of Universal Freemasonry, Instructions to the twenty-three Supreme Councils of the World, July 14, 1889

To my mind, there is no more monstrous evil than to bring public-spirited, often churchgoing, men into an organization that looks like a fraternal lodge, then deliberately mislead them until they are solid members. Then move them up thirty degrees to the place where they are ready to learn that Satan is the good god waiting to liberate mankind, and the Creator of the Universe (Yahweh, Elohim, Adonai) is, in their theology, the malicious prince of darkness.

It is my understanding that as part of the initiation for the Thirty-Second Degree, the candidate is told that Hiram, the builder of Solomon's temple, was killed by three assassins. The candidate therefore must strike back at those assassins which are, courtesy of the Illuminati, the government, organized religion, and private property.

This particular ritual is not Egyptian but from the Hung society of China, based on the cult of Amitabha Buddha. The ceremony, which clearly resembles those of the Egyptian *Book of the Dead*, was apparently copied as well by the Freemasons. It involves not a builder named Hiram, but a group of Buddhist monks, all but five of whom were slain by three villains, one of whom was the Manchu Emperor Khang Hsi.

It is self-evident that Masonic beliefs and rituals flow from the occult. Beliefs from Egyptian mysticism, Chinese Buddhism, and the ancient mysteries of the Hebrew Kabalah have been resuscitated to infuse their doctrines. What a splendid training ground for a new world/New Age citizen!

The New Age religions, the beliefs of the Illuminati, and Illuminated Freemasonry all seem to move along parallel tracks with world communism and world finance. Their appeals vary somewhat, but essentially they are striving for the same very frightening vision.

Now that we have taken a closer look at these spiritual and mystical threads which intertwine to form the historic ideology of a new world order, it is time to take a more precise and in-depth look at what this new world will actually be like.

PART 3

---

*A Glimpse of the
Coming World*

9

A Promise of Hope

IT IS TIME NOW FOR US TO CONSIDER the real possibilities that would exist for every human being if we all could indeed craft a world society where there was a wise administration of law, an end to war and oppression, and a guarantee of the basic necessities of life for every human being.

Indeed people have dreamed of such an age for at least three thousand years. Because the philosophers and dreamers leave out the two ingredients that are guaranteed to sabotage their beautiful dreams—the corruptible nature of man and the presence of spiritual evil—these dreams usually are impractical.

Such societies have been given a name—Utopia—from the island with a perfect government and perfect social system envisaged in 1516 by Sir Thomas More of England. The word *utopia* is from one of two almost identical Greek words that mean "good place" or "no place." It has come to mean in our language not only "perfectionism," but "unrealistic" and "impractical."

The earliest concept of a utopian society that we know of was conceived by Hesiod who lived 750 years before Christ. In his *Works and Days,* Hesiod described his dream of a time when "the fruitful earth spontaneously bore abundant fruit without stint. And they lived in ease and peace upon their land with many good things, rich in flocks and beloved of the blessed gods."

Is there any thinking person whose heart doesn't jump in anticipation when he or she reads such words? Is there any sane person who wants war, disease, famine, or injustice? We all want a life of peace and abundant blessing. If utopia were possible, most people would want it.

Plato was more of a realist in his utopian vision, and it is the platonic vision of a new world that our leaders are urging on us. Plato knew that people were too indifferent or lazy or venal to want his version of utopia, so he crafted an ideal society in which the wise men would rule. In turn, they would control every aspect of social existence in the name of justice, order, freedom, peace, strength, stability, and goodness.

The wise philosopher-kings would not work, but would organize the masses in their proper training and for their designated places in society. The contemporary upper-class term of derision for the laboring masses, hoi polloi, comes directly from the Greek words meaning "the people." According to Plato, the elite classes would not only assign the people their places, but would regulate optimal production and would keep the population at an optimal level as well.

As an aside, the late John D. Rockefeller II was obsessed with burgeoning world population growth and the necessity for birth control in the undeveloped nations. His foundation gave at least $50 million to Margaret Sanger. William Draper II, a key internationalist, came from government service in Europe to establish the Draper World Population Fund and to help form the Population Crisis Committee.

It was a Rockefeller Foundation treatise on abortion that served as the only philosophical support for Supreme Court Justice Harry Blackmun's incredible discovery of a "Constitutional right to abortion" in the case of *Roe v. Wade.*

As we watch our world hurtling toward the elite-controlled utopianism of Plato, another Greek utopianism may well come upon us shortly thereafter—that of Sparta. In Sparta, Lycurgus was the charismatic leader who seized dictatorial power and then created social institutions to make the people of Sparta austere, morally upright, simple, self-sacrificing, brave, and hardy. Lycurgus equalized property in Sparta, all but abolished money, and regulated and ordered the lives of the citizens for what he considered their good and the state's good. Plutarch, in his *Life of Lycurgus,* tells us that the Spartans honored Lycurgus as a god and consecrated a temple in his memory.

If the world embraces the platonic utopianism of Cecil Rhodes, the Rockefellers, and their followers, it is absolutely certain (according to the Bible) that the world patterned after the Spartan utopianism of Lycurgus will follow soon after.

The Grand Vision of World Order

The general in the Union Army during the Civil War who was responsible for the scorched-earth policy in Georgia, William Tecumseh Sherman, said it best: "War is hell." When I met with the then prime minister of Israel, Yitzak Rabin, in 1974, he told me that Israel did not want war but a peace treaty. The most prestigious award in our world today is the Nobel Peace Prize—ironically underwritten from the proceeds of the fortune of the inventor of modern explosives. From generals to statesmen, people yearn for peace.

A new world order promises what we all want—world peace. In the Cato Institute volume *Collective Defense or Strategic Independence,* Georgetown Professor Earl C. Ravenal projects that by the year 1998 the U.S. Defense budget will top $451 billion, with cumulative defense spending in excess of $3.6 trillion. At the present time the expenditures on arms for the rest of the world equal or exceed that of the United States. The economies of Europe and Japan may equal or exceed the economy of the United States during this decade, so given a Cold War balance-of-power world, it is not at all unrealistic to project worldwide arms expenditures of $1 trillion per year—$10 trillion over ten years.

If the nations were disarmed, there would be a sum more vast than the mind can readily accommodate available for peacetime development. What would $10 trillion buy? An inexhaustible source of power from the fusion of hydrogen atoms and cheap electricity for every city and village on earth. Forests of billions of trees to reclaim the desert and restore the ecological balance so badly damaged by man. Plenty of clean, pure water for all the people, along with a bountiful food supply and the necessary infrastructure of roads and harbors to transport food from rural areas to the urban dwellers. Medical breakthroughs as well as the distribution of existing medical technology to the poor, who are so ravaged by easily preventable disease. The drastic reduction of infant mortality as levels of prenatal and postnatal care are raised in the so-called Third World.

Yes, the elimination of the spending for war and the preparation for war could free up enough of the world's resources to create what today's poor might consider nothing short of paradise on earth.

Precepts of World Law

The advocates of the new world order hold out a promise of peace, but a true world community promises many other benefits. We all can imagine supposed benefits. Here are my thoughts about some that will undoubtedly be advanced:

The Law of the Sea. A worldwide government could make and enforce a law regulating maritime commerce, shipping, navigation, harbor rights, and fishing rights. By a worldwide regulation of allowable catches and fishing techniques, the world could halt the depletion of various species of fish in the world's waters as well as the needless killing of dolphins in large commercial nets. Not only would shipping be forbidden to dump pollutants in the waters, nations would be forbidden to dump untreated sewage, chemical pollutants, insecticides, and disease-causing bacteria into the oceans. No tanker would be permitted on the world's waterways without a double hull or similar safety mechanism.

The Law of the Skies. Not only would the safety and dimensions of world aviation be protected and regulated, there would be laws preventing air pollution from auto emissions, power plants, chemical factories, steel mills, paper mills, and the like. No nation would be allowed to use ozone-depleting chemicals or any other emissions beyond a specified level. No one would be allowed to pollute the air that the people of the world, its plants, and its animal life must breathe.

The Law of Land and Forest. Trees would be considered the heritage of the human race and no trees could be cut for lumber or fuel unless it was according to the global forestry plan. Rain forests with their valuable exotic and medicinal plants would be preserved inviolate as "the lungs of the world." A global plan would be developed to protect land from erosion, mud slides, and the silting of rivers and harbors.

Of course, there would be a global law to protect fish and marine life, wild animals, and birds. The ecological balance of the earth would be preserved irrespective of national boundaries. There would be an allocation of land for use in agriculture, urban dwelling, and industry. There would be restrictions not only on the use of land, but on the quantity of land that any individuals or company could use. All land would be considered the patrimony of all people and would be allocated for term use according to the global plan.

There would be detailed regulations forbidding the use of dioxin or DDT or other harmful pesticides on the land, plus worldwide laws regulating the transportation and storage of chemical and industrial waste and the safety of industrial factories, nuclear power plants, oil drilling, oil wells, etc.

The Law of Energy Conservation. Fossil fuels would be regarded as a diminishing world resource, so worldwide laws would be enacted to prohibit wasteful energy practices in industry, transportation, and private residences. Stringent mileage requirements would be levied on automobiles along with subsidies to develop electric automobiles, alternate power sources, and safe, cheap nuclear power.

The Law of Industry and Agriculture. Worldwide output would be regulated to prevent overproduction and dumping. Agriculture would be strictly controlled so that only needed supplies of food were available to avoid the buildup of massive agricultural surpluses.

There would be strict standards of industrial safety for workers along with a guaranteed minimum wage for workers everywhere, guaranteed health benefits, and guaranteed retirement.

World standards would be set to warrant product quality and safety. No food, drug, industrial, or consumer product would be sold that did not meet world standards.

Price controls would be in effect for most of the necessities of life. Costs of health care would be limited under a World Medical Board that would certify physicians, who in turn would be employed with regulated wages under a government-operated health care system.

The growing, manufacturing, sale, and use of marijuana, heroin, cocaine, chemical hallucinogens, and tobacco would be prohibited.

Payments for damages arising out of industrial accidents, product defects, traffic accidents, and malpractice would be limited to specific amounts only. Severe penalties would be imposed on lawyers and clients making frivolous claims.

All customs duties would be eliminated, as well as all immigration laws. All people would be registered as citizens of the world and would be free to live and work wherever they wished—until the time comes when the World Peoples Bureau requires permission to work and travel.

The Law of Credit and Finance. There would be one world currency, backed by a central world bank. This bank would have the authority to expand or contract the money supply of the world to permit industrial growth or to prohibit inflation.

There would be no currency imbalances and all prices would be quoted in the world currency. The central bank would, in turn, charter various world banks and would make currency and credit available at a "discount window" to its affiliate branches, which would in turn regulate smaller member banks. This banking arrangement would be intended to eliminate currency imbalances, misallocations of credit, and disparities of wealth. All peoples everywhere would be guaranteed abundant world credit, a guaranteed world currency, and an inflation-free environment.

Most industrial corporations would be organized on a world-wide basis. Therefore there would be a world stock exchange regulated by the world bank with international shares trading in world currency units. The world stock market would be in session twenty-four hours a day as trading would begin in Tokyo, continue in India, the Middle East, Europe, the East Coast of America, the West Coast of America, and finally end the twenty-four-hour Greenwich cycle in Honolulu.

The Law of Arms and Aggression. No nation would be allowed to take aggressive action against another, under penalty of severe sanctions. All chemical, biological, and nuclear weapons would be banned. Only such arms as would be necessary for local police functions would be permitted.

The World Human Rights Organization would prohibit human rights abuses against any citizen of the world. Torture, terrorism, and state oppression would be prohibited. Human rights abuses would be rectified under the aegis of the world court. Obviously, genocide such as happened in recent history against the Jews of Germany, the Ibos of Nigeria, and the Kurds of Iraq would be prohibited and prevented.

Savoring the Dream

Hum quietly to yourself the words of John Lennon's "Imagine," and dozens of laws, rights, and benefits of one world may pop into your head. Rest assured that the finest dream merchants of the world will be employed in the sales job to come. Of course, it would be wonderful if it were all true. So would the vision behind the dream of Marxism, as it has been put out for public consumption:

"A stateless, classless society. From each according to his ability, to each according to his need."

But we see on our television screens almost daily how the reality of Marxist utopianism actually played out in real life. How will the dream merchants get across their vision of new world utopianism? Frankly, the task is easy, because the hope of the new world order answers the most pressing questions on the minds of people everywhere—world peace, relief of suffering, relief of cruelty, the mystery of the future.

The concept *will* move inexorably through world legislatures. Those who oppose it *will* be labeled obstructionist, reactionary, and out of step with the times. Just think about the color brochures, motion pictures, and television documentaries about this new world order and the promise of hope it offers. We will contemplate the wonders to come about when we enter into this beautiful relationship with each other as the United Nations administers all these laws with compassion, justice, and mercy.

As the world begins to deteriorate into warring trade factions and the inequities of the Third World loom larger and more grotesque, you can see that the promise of the new world order is truly within our grasp. And, following the Gulf War, it will be salable as being attainable. Didn't we go in and rescue this poor beleaguered nation? Didn't we use the force of the United Nations to accomplish it? It was little more than a close order drill, carried off with scientific precision.

Unlike the utopian dreams of the seventeenth, eighteenth, and nineteenth centuries, and unlike the utopias at the roots of the two world wars of this century, this will be a bolder, more practical vision. The other utopias did not have the same level of thought and experience behind them, and they did not come at a time when the human race was ready to hear this kind of news. Now it is.

If during this decade there is a worldwide banking collapse and a worldwide crash of the proportions of the Great Depression of the 1930s, people will be ready for a new order. When there are starving people standing in bread lines, when their physical needs are not being met, they will be ready for change.

The world may see a repeat of these words from 1932:

> The streets of our country are in turmoil. The universities are filled with students rebelling and rioting. Communists are seeking to destroy our country. Russia is threatening us with her might. And the Republic is in danger. Yes, danger from within and without. We need law and order. Without law and order our nation cannot survive.

The author of this most reasonable proposal calculated to touch the heart of every German was none other than Adolf Hitler.

Precisely what happened when Franklin Roosevelt offered his New Deal will happen again. Never before in history had both houses of the Congress of the United States agreed to grant a president such wide-ranging and potentially dictatorial powers in the first hundred days of his administration. But our Congress did that in 1932 with Roosevelt. They gave him virtually everything he asked for because he promised a way out of the Great Depression. The sweeping laws rushed through Congress to begin the New Deal radically changed the face of American federal policy. And they passed with virtually no opposition.

A Climate of Fear

Think of the various New Deal agencies Roosevelt created by fiat. His use of executive power was so unprecedented that the Supreme Court initially struck down key parts of the New Deal program. But when Roosevelt threatened to pack the court and change its character, the justices changed their minds. Roosevelt could do whatever he wanted, because the economic crisis created a compliant majority in the Congress who would blindly follow his lead. Any reasonable offer of hope was acceptable.

A worldwide crisis today would create the same environment we saw during the Depression. This would be the first time in history that the entire globe could be made aware of these issues, simultaneously, via satellite communications. The model was set in place with the incredible coverage of the multinational force assembled in the Persian Gulf, ostensibly to curb the expansionist aggression of Iraq—and it demonstrates the ability to mold the world into one.

CNN was seen virtually around the world. Our world speaks English—the leadership of virtually every nation speaks English. United States films, television programs, records, tapes, and books have spread to every nation on the globe. With satellite technology, the ability to mold a world together is here. The international flow of funds is in place—we have never had anything like it before.

The ease of traveling from one nation to another is unprecedented. You can fly from London to New York City in three hours, seventeen minutes and basically outrun the sun. Facsimile machines, high-speed computers, datalinks, twenty-four-hour rolling markets: all these things make immediate communication and response a reality. The entire world can be instantly involved in every decision.

The United States has had a leadership role, not only as a permanent member of the United Nations and its Security Council, but in conceiving and implementing the ideology of the new world order. The fathers of the new world order are virtually all Americans, and they desire to have continuing, profitable international power out of America.

Their power is not limited by American laws or borders. They can exercise it wherever their money is. Frankly, it is easier to exercise arbitrary power overseas than it is in the United States. There are things you cannot possibly do in America that you can do very easily overseas. There are many restrictions on the freedom of commercial activity here that do not exist in other nations. How convenient it would be for them if world laws could override the regulations of the United States.

The rapid and unexpected changes of the past two years have taken the world by surprise. The Soviet Union is a basket case. They have had to send envoys to America, Europe, and Japan to beg for financial assistance. Eastern Europe is in nearly the same predicament. If the debt burden that exists in the world were to suddenly collapse, you can be assured the wheels of change would begin to spin.

In 1990, we saw the virtual collapse of the Japanese Stock Market, the Nikkei Dow. It has leveled out over the past year but is still in a volatile position, not unlike what the United States is going through at this moment. The underlying problems are about as bad as they always were. Loans are made on the strength of stocks; stocks are run up on the basis of appreciation of real estate; and real estate is escalating on the strength of bank loans and stock market prices.

The result is overpriced real estate, overpriced stocks, interconnected stocks, and weak if not insolvent banks, holding loans based on inflated real estate prices and a synthetic stock market, which, combined, have created a pyramiding of wealth that is completely artificial. That is a dangerous and potentially disastrous situation, which has not changed since the 1991 shakeup. The disaster has only been postponed.

Citizens groups were protesting in early 1991, pushing for a gradual readjustment of Japan's inflated markets before conditions worsen, but the balloon only seems to get larger and larger. When the air suddenly goes out of a balloon, it shrinks to nothing with shocking suddenness. That may be what's in store for the Japanese market if their economists don't wise up soon.

Growing Uncertainties

Fear is a compelling force, but the human mind instinctively seeks relief from fear and dread. Christians naturally seek consolation from Scripture and through prayer and faith in God in times of crisis. But sometimes our hopes may be met by a hope, a dream, or an ideology that may be totally unrealistic and irrational. This can produce some curious reactions.

Robert Nisbet, in his provocative little book, *The Present Age: Progress and Anarchy in Modern America,* makes a very interesting observation about the collapse of socialism. He points out, "The death of socialism in the West opened the field of ideology, of 'isms,' to a number of entries which had not been especially noticeable before the Second World War."

These include such things as egalitarianism—meaning equality for women, races, religions, sex, and the like—and a host of other liberal concerns. Nisbet suggests that the void in the minds of intellectuals left by the death of their beloved socialist theories led to the rise of a host of strange cults, radical causes, and utopias. He writes:

> Socialism, held these vagaries—to the extent that they even existed as ideals in the minds of most intellectuals—together or kept them down as mere latencies—for exfoliation perhaps in the very distant future. But when socialism ceased to be the energizing faith of the Left in the West—primarily because of the repulsiveness of the Soviet Union, Fascist Italy, and Nazi Germany, one and all founded by lifelong socialists, but also because of the indisputable fact that the Third World nations that took up capitalism—as in the Pacific Rim countries to the west—were faring immeasurably better than were those that took up socialism—when the socialist dream passed, the result was a mess of new idols in the marketplace.

Is the current fascination with politically correct thinking we read about in the news magazines a passion brought about in the universities by the death of the socialist dream? Possibly. Could it also be true that the defrocking of a political ideology such as socialism could add intensity and urgency to the Establishment hope for a new world order and a one-world government? Probably.

The Coming Revolution

In the conclusion to his book, Nisbet suggests that the climate in America today appears to be as ripe for a revolution in the world of ideas as it was in the eighteenth century, when our Founding Fathers first established a constitutional democracy in the New World. That seems to be precisely where the advocates of a new world order would like us to be. Poised on the threshold of a new era, a new world, and a new political theory.

Another author, Thomas J. McCormick, in his book, *America's Half Century,* argues that the era of American hegemony in the world is long dead and that new international forces will most certainly carry us into, first, a trilateral world and, next, a one-world internationalist system. Writing from a historical, almost prophetic, frame of reference, he says:

> As the 1990s loomed on the horizon, the world that Americans had made after World War II had come to an end. As yet, no new one had taken its place. The outline of world-system decentering had long been clear, but the contours of its recentering were so far murky and problematical. . . .
>
> American hegemony was dead and Russia in crisis and decline. Japan was the new economic giant and Europe was poised on the brink of true community, and China was ready to leapfrog everyone. This composed the new core of a world in which change was dynamic, uneven, multidirectional, and unpredictable.

The image drawn by McCormick, a Wisconsin history professor, is to some degree disconcerting. But not nearly so much as the author's proposals for a replacement for the now-defunct old world system. The two models he finds most interesting are those of Lenin and the German Marxist, Karl Kautsky. Of the two, he prefers Kautsky's, which argued that "world capitalism would transcend its nationalistic competitions and produce a new order of ultra-imperialism. Core countries, tied together by increasing economic interdependence, would integrate and dominate the Third World collectively."

Then the author rhapsodizes, "The gradual replacement of national industry with multinational industry had carried the world a long way toward a degree of oneness and interdependence." The author makes no effort to disguise the identity of this option as the one-world utopian government of the new world order.

10

A Cruel Hoax

T HE ONE THING THE UTOPIAN DREAMERS always omit is actually the centerpiece of the Constitution of the United States—the sinful nature of man. Twenty-six hundred years ago—about the time of the Greek utopians—the Hebrew prophet, Jeremiah, spoke of that missing element when he wrote, "The heart of man is deceitful above all things, and desperately wicked; who can know it?"

Every utopia presumes that it can build a perfect world order with imperfect people. So, like the Marxist dream, it attempts by indoctrination, coercion, torture, and execution to change the hearts of its citizens. Or, in the case of Plato, it puts the citizens in perpetual bondage to a class of rulers whose natural aptitude and understanding of philosophy place them above the people. Or, in the case of the Illuminati and the New Agers, leadership is to be entrusted to those who have had psychic "illumination" and are, in fact, being instructed by demonic beings referred to as "ascended masters."

But despite utopian claims, Lord Acton's dictum still holds true, "Power corrupts; absolute power corrupts absolutely." Unfortunately, the proof of the idiom is not hard to find.

Revelations have recently come out that the "enlightened" Marxist Sandinista leaders of Nicaragua, the Ortega brothers, Thomas Borge, and their allies have stolen $1 billion worth of property, including luxurious homes and estates. Their grab for free wealth is being called "the Piñata," after the name for the children's toy full of goodies.

Erich Honecker of Germany took for himself luxurious accommodations. Some three hundred criminal investigations are under way involving currency manipulation, theft of state property, and embezzlement totaling $2.7 billion by East German communists. While his people were dying of starvation, disease, and squalor, the "enlightened" Rumanian dictator, Nicolae Ceausescu, had thirty-two private residences plus a still unfinished palace carrying at least a $1 billion price tag.

The founders of America created a constitutional republic where power was divided among the people, the state governments, and the federal government. At the federal level, power was again divided across executive, legislative, and judicial lines. Power was then limited again, not only by a written constitution, but by brief terms for officeholders who were forced to face regular elections and potential impeachment for misconduct.

To be sure, in order to form a "more perfect union" the thirteen sovereign states of America merged their sovereignty at that time into that of the United States of America. But we cannot forget this about America: they and their ancestors had lived in this country in harmony for 169 years, all as subjects of another country, Great Britain. They all shared the same language, traditions, and political concepts about the nature of man and the will of God.

All but about five thousand of the total population were recorded as either Protestant or Roman Catholic Christians, and almost all were committed to the biblical world-view. All the early American leaders had been trained in some fashion or other in statecraft. Furthermore, there was a restricted franchise when this country started, so that only property owners could vote in popular elections. People had to have a stake in society before they were allowed to determine its laws.

There was no inherent danger in merging South Carolina with Virginia or Connecticut with Massachusetts, because they were all basically from one common stock and one common philosophy. Benjamin Franklin in Pennsylvania, John Adams in Massachusetts, and Thomas Jefferson in Virginia were all highly educated men who had a tremendous respect, honed over decades of study, for the God-given rights and freedoms of each individual.

They had read broadly and studied the civilizations of the last thirty centuries, all the way back to the Greeks and Romans. The experience of the founding of America is in no way a precedent for forming a world government of totally diverse peoples. To have people of colonial America coming together in federation is one thing, but moving the United Sates of America into a world government on an equal footing with Muslim dictators like Mohamar Qaddafi of Libya and Hashemi Rafsanjani of Iran, or Marxist dictators like Deng Xiaoping of Communist China and Robert Mugabe of Zimbabwe, and then meekly saying, "We are all one, and we, therefore, surrender our sovereignty to you," is sheer, unmitigated nonsense. But that is precisely what a world government will one day insist upon!

Troublesome Facts

Bureaucrats feel that people have a rather annoying tendency of wanting to live their own lives the way they want, where they want, with whom they want. In the United States this drives the social engineers of government into apoplexy, and they cannot rest until they force the citizens to bus their children away from their friends, hire by quota instead of aptitude, make loans to people who won't pay them back, go to doctors who secretly have deadly diseases, and rent their property to undesirables with aberrant sexual habits.

Utopian ideas can only become reality through a change in the human heart or the force of law. Human government can never change people's hearts, so that leaves the fulfillment of the wonderful dreams of the new world order in the hands of a massive military force and an equally massive police power. Of course, world armies, world police, and world bureaucrats don't come cheaply.

Several years ago a close aide of the late Congressman Claude Pepper appeared as a guest on my television program to advocate a federal program to mandate compulsory catastrophic health coverage for the elderly. I felt that the elderly did not favor this program, and I knew that its cost was projected to be $30 billion. I asked Pepper's associate how much his program would cost. His answer was astounding, "I have no idea." The bill passed overwhelmingly, and no one knew for sure what it would cost. But once the tax bill to pay for it hit the elderly, their outrage forced Congress to beat a hasty retreat.

A similar lapse of knowledge was revealed in 1986 when I appeared before the Senate Labor Committee at the request of the chairman, Senator Orin Hatch, to oppose the sweeping government intrusion proposed by Edward Kennedy, under the euphemistic title, The Civil Rights Restoration Act.

Senator Howard Metzenbaum of Ohio was questioning me in a hostile fashion about the bill, when I asked him point-blank, "Senator, has there been any staff study of any nature to determine the cost to the government of this bill?" He stuttered and blustered and said there had not been. The bill passed ultimately by a wide margin, and no one, Democrat or Republican, had the slightest idea of the potential cost to the government or the people affected by it.

Rest assured that the new world order is going to cost plenty. If you like the Internal Revenue Service, you will love the tax police of the new world order.

Imagine that you, a citizen of the United States, are assessed a tax on your income to pay for a project in Africa that you totally disagree with. Since you are "rich," the representatives of the United Nations from the poor countries will now have a claim on your assets. The levy initially would be on the United States government, which would pass it on to you in the form of higher taxes. One day it may be a United Nations levy on you directly.

You want to complain to your representatives at the United Nations, because the entire nation has voted on the selection of our few U.S. representatives to that body. Unfortunately, the United States now has only 5 percent of the world's total population, and therefore would be entitled to 5 percent of the vote. If the United Nations wanted to drain the wealth of America, it would be free to do so by popular vote. By then we would have no choice but to acquiesce, because America would have been disarmed and the United Nations would control all the weapons.

Present Realities

This type of wealth-transfer legislation is not futuristic, however, but already on the books of the present United Nations, which our leaders want to lead the world. In 1974, the Declaration on the Establishment of a New International Economic Order was adopted by the United Nations General Assembly, advocating that "the prevailing disparities in the world be abolished."

According to author Tal Brooke, "This world welfare system would insist on (1) The transfer of wealth from the first to Third World nations; (2) Nationalization by Third World governments, and (3) Economic special protection for poorer countries." In simple language, the Third World in the United Nations has already voted to take away by decree the wealth of Europe and America and give it to themselves. Only the impotence of the current United Nations General Assembly and the veto power of the Security Council has prevented this resolution from being implemented.

The IRS under successive United States laws has been given sweeping powers over the citizens of this nation in order to collect enough money to pay the bill for the federal deficits borrowed from the Establishment bankers. A worldwide IRS under a banking oligarchy would become the American citizen's worst nightmare.

But remember, before the financial bloodsucking begins in earnest on the newly minted American citizens of the world, the monopoly bankers will have placed themselves and their central banks above the law and out of the reach of the taxing power. They did it in 1913 in America, and, rest assured, they plan to do it again in the new world order.

Punitive taxes would just be the beginning. The world government would also need a standing army. The spring 1991 issue of *Foreign Affairs* calls for a United Nations standing army, not under the command of United States officers as was the case of the United Nations-mandated Gulf War, but directly under the control of the United Nations Security Council.

Personnel for such an army would have to come from somewhere. If America wanted a voice in the action, it would either have to provide volunteers or draftees. But what would happen if young Americans did not want to participate in a United Nations war against one of our allies, such as Israel? The answer is simple, they would be forced to serve under penalty of prison.

What would happen if United Nations sanctions were levied against America? Would young Americans serving in a United Nations Army be forced to fire on their own countrymen? If not, who would do the job? As I mentioned earlier, I cannot forget the bloody picture in *Life* magazine of the young Belgian settler in Katanga whose wife and children lay dead behind him in a little Volkswagen, brutally killed by black African soldiers serving in a United Nations contingent. If it happened there, it can happen here.

The True Risks

What are the downside risks of world citizenship? First of all, it would mean that the protection of the U.S. Bill of Rights would no longer apply. The principle of extra-territoriality applies, which means that the American citizen in the new world order could be arrested in this country or out of it and tried for violation of United Nations laws before a world court, which could just as likely operate under the Muslim Sharia as the Judeo-Christian Ten Commandments.

Whatever laws might be passed by Congress or interpreted by the U.S. Supreme Court could be superseded by world government laws and world court decision. This is, of course, what happens now in the United States. I live in Virginia and am governed by Virginia's code of laws, Virginia's police, Virginia's courts, and

Virginia's taxation. But the federal Congress, the federal marshals, the federal courts, and the federal taxing authorities all have jurisdiction over me, which either supplements or supersedes Virginia's claims.

I accept that gladly, for I like being a citizen of the United States. But world citizenship, however wonderful it may sound, clearly means that our unique privileges as American citizens will be ended whenever this nation buys wholly into the concept of a world government with military enforcement power and the disarmament of individual nations.

Just think of this. Suppose you are an American citizen, your name is Salman Rushdie, and you decide to write a book of poems mildly critical of the Shi'ite branch of the Muslim religion. In America, as it is now constituted, you are perfectly free to do so. But suppose the existing world law of genocide is modified slightly to include the politically correct speech in vogue on American college campuses. Under a world government you could be taken from America and tried before a world court for a world crime without necessarily being afforded confrontation by your accusers, a jury of your peers, counsel of your choosing, freedom from cruel punishment, freedom from excessive bail, freedom from unreasonable searches and seizures, or any of the other legal rights you now take for granted.

Just what does it mean not to be tried by a jury of your peers? In America we know that in our local community a jury will have some appreciation of our shared view of right and wrong, freedom, fairness, and longstanding constitutional liberty. People make up our juries whose material possessions and education is not greatly different from those of the one accused of a crime.

How would you feel as one accused of a crime if you appeared before a people's court composed of illiterate peasants, with annual incomes of $300 to $500, to whom your income of $25,000 a year made you out to be a greedy capitalist exploiter? What appeal would you have to justice, reason, or shared values? None!

But there is more. All the wonderful laws that give freedom from air pollution, water pollution, improper land use, respect for the animals, workers' rights, minimum wages, universal health care, and so on must be enforced by administrative oversight and ultimate punitive sanctions. Bureaucracy means forms, paperwork, inspections, appeals, delay, uncertainty, and unbelievable expense. It also means the possibility of shame, disgrace, fines, or prison if a person or company runs afoul of the regulations as interpreted by a low-level bureaucrat and some politically ambitious prosecutor.

Testing the Apparatus

I read to my horror of a landowner who possessed an unsightly piece of land littered with debris. He hauled some dirt onto his land, smoothed it out, and planted grass on it. For this "crime" against the law, he was given three years in a federal prison. Another upstanding businessman, charged and found guilty of a technical violation of recent laws, was given ten years in a federal prison because of the rigid application of federal sentencing guidelines. The judge in that case broke down and cried because he had no discretion over the severity of the sentence.

It is estimated that the *Federal Register* this year will include sixty thousand pages of new federal administrative regulations. The regulations and enforcement proceedings under these regulations have made rich some of America's thousands of lawyers who practice administrative or tax law, but they only do damage to the citizens harassed by them.

The American and European welfare states are bad, but just consider what it will be like when pollution or energy inspectors from Burma and Sri Lanka visit your facility on orders from the World Energy and Pollution Control Authority in New Delhi, whose deputy administrator in charge of Europe and America speaks French and is headquartered in Brussels.

Given the almost universal propensity of Third World officials to look for bribes, will the new set of world laws turn into nothing more or less than a worldwide protection racket? Those who can pay are cleared of "violations." Those who cannot pay are closed down or sent to prison.

Finally, it goes without saying, the world government would of necessity demand a law against sedition and treason. Most of the world knows nothing about the First Amendment freedoms that have been won for those of us who live in America by those who were Christians, who believed the Bible, and who were steeped in the Anglo-Saxon concepts of jurisprudence. In many countries those who criticize the government in the press or in assembly are executed, imprisoned, or muzzled. How can we possibly believe that these people, sharing other concepts of human rights all their lives, will suddenly switch to American concepts of freedom and free enterprise at the stroke of a pen? It is unrealistic to expect it. It just will not happen.

The downside of the promise for a new world order is that for laws to work, they have to be backed up by sanctions, and the sanctions can be disastrous.

Modern technology has performed wonders in this century. In just the last ten years we have seen an exponential increase in the sophistication of global communications. Think of how satellites, microwaves, fiber optics, computers, fax machines, and magnetic recording devices have changed the way we communicate. Think of how this same technology has given a powerful central government the ability to inform, indoctrinate, monitor, and control the will of the people.

The Leveling Process

Some of the popular motion pictures of the last few years have international and intergalactic forces all interacting. Not only do you have different nations and races all flying together, but animals, reptile creatures, and other alien forms, as if they were all equal. The implication of these scenes is that man is no different or better than any other form of life, and certainly Americans are no different or better than any other nation.

Even if it is not popular to say so, the Europeans and the Americans have had a positive influence on world culture because of their religious beliefs, their work habits, their creative ingenuity, and their desire for a peaceful and productive life.

In my book, *The New Millennium,* I suggested that the pendulum of civilization may now be swinging back toward the East, and the Asian cultures may be once again on the rise. The Chinese and Japanese have had high cultures, far beyond those of most Third World nations today. To blur those distinctions and to act as if every culture and every system is of equal quality is absurd.

Of course, we are all sons and daughters of Adam, but nevertheless we have centuries of cultural differences, and those cannot be ignored. But there is every likelihood that the coming world government would make a declaration of equality of all people.

They would also have to have a law of arms control. They could not have a system that allowed people to keep arms, because that would allow dissenters to foment revolution. So our constitutional right to keep and bear arms would be one of the very first casualties of world order legislation.

We have already had a law against so-called hate crimes passed in the United States Congress. The new world government would have to have a law against world hate crimes where the politically correct speech of the college campuses would be magnified a thousand times. No one could speak out against the beliefs of a Muslim, a Hindu, or an animist, or against the beliefs of a communist or a socialist. Christians could not speak out against the sin of homosexuality or pedophilia. What we know as the freedom of religion would be taken away, and Christians would be muzzled.

Equality of all religions, races, sexual practices, and belief systems would be considered paramount, and anyone found guilty of stepping over the line would have to be publicly penalized by the world government. Remember, a court in the District of Columbia has already held that the right to forbid discrimination on the basis of sexual preference overrides existing American First Amendment rights of religious liberty.

Unprecedented Violations

The court clearly violated religious freedom in Washington, D.C., when it forced a Catholic school, Georgetown University, to provide facilities for homosexual groups, even though homosexuality is specifically and historically proscribed both by the university and the tenets of the Christian faith.

The court decided the university would have to give the homosexual groups an office with telephones, access to mailing lists and other services, all free of charge. In essence, the Roman Catholic Church has been forced to subsidize homosexuality, even though this practice is a blatant violation of the essential doctrines of its faith. As educators, Georgetown University cannot choose conduct it considers to be biblical, or reject what is nonbiblical. The school must comply with government-mandated sexual-orientation guidelines or face severe penalties.

I asked Cardinal John O'Connor of New York why the governors of Georgetown University didn't appeal that case to the higher courts. He said that he personally would have shut the university down before compromising the faith in that way. That decision has now set a tragic precedent, undermining freedom of religion and religious conviction, in essence compromising in a measure the rights of Christians everywhere.

If there has been a gross abuse of liberty in Washington, the seat of our government under the Constitution, you can be certain that those without our values will do it worldwide. Whatever violation of freedom has taken place here will take place in a world body, only in a more blatant fashion. They are not going to be less restrictive or more permissive in the world body about Christian values than we are here in the United States.

Even if they don't go beyond what we have done, they will certainly go just as far. Remember that the collapse of morality in Europe in the past thirty years is absolutely staggering. So if Europe plays a major role in world government—which it most certainly will—then we can fully expect moral standards to drop even lower than we know here, and the freedom of religion will be severely limited.

At some point there will be a law of world religion. Instead of the First Amendment concept, which says that the government shall not establish a religion or prohibit the free exercise of religion, the new law would recognize the universal character of religion and probably adopt a syncretistic religion based on the "New Age." The meditation room at the current United Nations headquarters sets the stage for what they have in mind.

Control of Religion

It does not call for much imagination to see that there could be a formal recognition of the universal spirit, a theology that pays lip service to all religions but ends up as a New Age belief. This is the sort of thing that appeals to Buddhists, Hindus, and even some who claim to be Christians. It is like a religion of mankind, based on what they think is humanism and open-mindedness. But at some point, the world body would of necessity make evangelism and active conversion to a set of beliefs so doctrinaire as Christianity undesirable, then severely restricted, then unlawful.

With that kind of system in place, there would also have to be a law of world indoctrination and thought control. The world government wants a law of the press, regulating what criticism of the central government would be allowed in the media, then a muzzle on free speech with restrictions on public and even private expressions of disapproval.

Third World nations have introduced such proposals over and over again in the United Nations, trying to regulate the world's press. Only strong resistance from a powerful, independent United States has kept these measures from passing. But press control has been dear to the hearts of the Soviets and the Third World dictators. They don't want a free, unfettered press.

In 1991, Mikhail Gorbachev, once praised as the champion of democratic reform, convinced the government to tighten the screws on the press and to set up a new government bureau to use its powers of censorship to crack down on criticism of Gorbachev and the Soviet government. Ultimately this law was never implemented, but the intent was clearly there.

When expression is controlled, then there can be public indoctrination. There will be required courses in world citizenship at all levels of society, teaching the rights and obligations of citizens of the world. That is what Plato called for. That is precisely what happened in the Soviet system and in Germany, and isn't that what is happening right now in the public schools of America?

All over this country, children are being indoctrinated as world citizens, with reverence for the earth, the environment, the animals, and for people of all ethnic, religious, and sexual orientations. This would be carried forward with massive indoctrination paid for by the world government.

It would be a type of brainwashing, and that is only a short step from the Orwellian newspeak concept. Only what's good about the leader can be printed. Everybody is indoctrinated with a uniform set of ideas and beliefs. Think of mass meetings of the world on satellite television, where cheering throngs extol the leader and say what a great man he is and how wonderful it is to live in his new world order.

Computer Technology

Those who speak glibly about the benefits of a world government overlook one alarming development of modern-day technology—the new microchips and the supercomputers. In the old days, with population records maintained by hand, there was no practical way to control all of the people. To be sure, totalitarian governments could exercise enormous control over the bulk of their populations, but people could always hide themselves or their money in some way from the authorities. Escape was possible from tyranny to a free country. Revolt was possible with aid from outside.

Under a totalitarian one-world government there will be no island of freedom. No large power like America holding forth democratic ideals.

Every citizen could be given a number, coded with his nation, his region, and his personal identity. Now in the United States parents are forced to obtain social security numbers for their infant children, generally at birth, or lose out on tax deductions.

Super high-speed mainframe computers coupled with modular fileservers hooked together in wide-area networks can hold and process trillions of bits of information with lightning speed and accuracy. There is absolutely no doubt that a world government, for the first time in history, would have the ability to build and recall, in microseconds, the complete vital statistics and life record of every citizen in the world.

If we went to a world currency, then a so-called checkless, cashless society, it would be possible to monitor and control all wealth, other than primitive barter transactions. At some time it would be possible to tax the wealth stored in computers under law, or given a dictatorial environment to freeze the accumulated wealth of any individual or any class of individuals just by simple instructions to a computer.

With existing technology it would be simple to limit the types of purchases that certain people would be permitted to make, or to prohibit all purchases. Never before has our world known a time when the words of the Book of Revelation could be literally fulfilled "that no man could buy or sell without the mark of the beast." The supercomputer in Brussels handling worldwide bank clearings at the Society for Worldwide Interbank Financial Telecommunications (SWIFT) has already been nicknamed the "Beast."

But there is more. Monitoring mechanisms could be put in place and linked by global satellites to monitor the physical movements of every citizen around the world. All that would be necessary would be a cardreader located at permitted points at home and work. If the individual did not check in at the appropriate places at appropriate times, alarm bells would go off and a search would be made, much like that for a convict escaping from prison.

I know that this all sounds too much like a science fiction horror story, but the loss of United States sovereignty opens up the very real possibility that some day in the future a demonized madman like Hitler could seize control of a worldwide, homogenized government and then employ currently existing technology to turn the entire world into a giant prison.

Complex Interdependence

In an agrarian society where each family was essentially self-sufficient, this type of control would have been impossible. Simple organisms are by their nature more resilient than highly interdependent complex ones. If every home has candles for light and wood for heat, it is not nearly as dependent on exterior support as a large city tied into a six-state electric power grid. Remember the panic that hit New York City when its regional power grid failed? Lights went off, subway cars trapped their riders underground, elevators stopped in-between floors in skyscrapers, street lights and burglar alarms went dead, and panic set in as street gangs began widespread looting under cover of darkness.

People in that complex situation were helpless. In a simpler setting, the loss of electric power is easily surmountable. In industry, in distribution, in finance, and in politics, the simpler, more independent systems are always more resilient to disruption and disaster. Obviously the more complex, interdependent systems are more efficient and less costly, but they are much more dangerous.

The globalists see the economies of scale of so-called transnational corporations, universal credit systems, and world banking and currency. They stress global interdependence almost as if it were the holy grail. We must remember what happened during the power failure in New York City when our leaders urge more and more complex global interdependence controlled by a one-world government, instead of our present system of dispersed power and local independence.

It is no secret. Allan Bloom said this years ago. The agenda of the Back-to-Basics movement has been to erase the slate, to erase the minds of the students, to tell them that everything is relative and everything is equal. American values, Judeo-Christian values, the values of Western civilization are no more important than the values of an aborigine in Australia or a communist cell leader in Red China. Consequently, entire generations of American students are perfectly prepared to accept any dominating theory that is presented as truth. They have no relative value system to use as a yardstick for critical analysis of right and wrong, good and evil.

Traditional values are old-fashioned and meaningless; new ideas and new beliefs are okay. The slate is clean, the door of the mind is standing ajar, and any slick, high-gloss, Madison Avenue fad can be pumped in without resistance.

It has been like a machine. For thirty years the minds of our children have been vacuumed and sanitized, leaving them open to anyone capable of exploiting their trained biases, their materialistic desires, and their programmed gullibility. The model is not universally true—particularly for children who have been taught a value system at home—but you don't have to look far to see just how pervasive this model has become.

Our young people are being taught that the American way, the Christian lifestyle, the standard of living of America, along with all the glorious chapters of our history are tainted with oppression and racism and sexism, and we are no better or no more capable than anybody else. Just read the propaganda against Columbus and the white settlers as we prepare for the five hundredth anniversary of his epic voyage of discovery.

This is, of course, conditioning for the new world. You have got a blank slate, young people with no concept of the history of America, no concept of the struggle for freedom or what the relative values are of our ways versus other ways. They are ready pawns for a value-neutral way of thinking.

This kind of brainwashing is incredibly strong in the university setting. You don't dare say America or Christianity is a better way of living. When I said during my presidential bid that I would only bring Christians and Jews into the government, I hit a firestorm. "What do you mean?" the media challenged me. "You're not going to bring atheists into the government? How dare you maintain that those who believe the Judeo-Christian values are better qualified to govern America than Hindus and Muslims?" My simple answer is, "Yes, they are."

Standing on Principles

Both John Locke and Thomas Jefferson refused to allow atheists into their governments because atheists would not keep oaths. Oaths have to be sworn before God, and since atheists acknowledged no God, Locke and Jefferson maintained that they could not be trusted. If anybody understood what Hindus really believe, there would be no doubt that they have no business administering government policies in a country that favors freedom and equality.

Hindu concepts are totally foreign to our system of values. The practice of *suttee,* abolished by the Christian British, required that a Hindu woman whose husband died first had to be cremated alive on her husband's funeral pyre. Hindus have an entire class of people that is considered "untouchable," supposedly cursed by God and given a bad *karma* (a debt of suffering to repay with their lives). Efforts to help the poor out of their misery are nullified by this religious belief. Hindus let people starve rather than kill rats who breed disease and eat the people's food, because they believe rats are reincarnated people.

Can you imagine having the Ayatollah Ruhollah Khomeini as defense minister, or Mahatma Gandhi as minister of health, education, and welfare? The Hindu and Buddhist idea of *karma* and the Muslim idea of *kismet,* or fate, condemn the poor and the disabled to their suffering. If a child is lame and starving to death with flies all over his face, there is no need to help him. It's the will of Allah. These beliefs are nothing but abject fatalism, and they would devastate the social gains this nation has made if they were ever put into practice.

Obviously, we wouldn't want that, but once we believe that the Christian tradition is no better than any other, and once we believe there is no distinction between our systems and those of India, Sri Lanka, China, the Congo, or the Soviet Union, then we will be ready to surrender anything we have.

During the entire history of modern society, since at least the Elizabethan era, the university campus has always been the haven of the intellectual whose primary right is the freedom to think whatever he likes, to learn from any source he chooses, and to come up with his own conclusions and state those in a public forum without restraint. Today that right no longer exists on the college campuses in this country. Students and professors are not free to think what they like or speak openly in a public forum.

You can see how higher education has changed. It began as a system, with a Christian world-view, where a professor or student could openly debate the nature of God and how the principles of science and the mind were supposed to work in relation to Him. Higher education has since become a system where one can deny the existence of God and openly advocate atheism. Now it is heading toward a system where one has no freedom at all, except the freedom to accept the politically correct doctrines of the current fad.

If the new world order must coerce life and thought into its mold, we are suddenly back to communism. The new world order must inevitably become what communism has been, only without any place on earth where freedom can flourish.

From Anarchy to Slavery

For most of the last fifty years the advocates of socialist and liberal institutions have been the most vocal opponents of capital punishment. Ironically, in the world to come they are going to need something like capital punishment to carry out their agenda. Don't be surprised to see some of these people switch sides on this issue in the very near future.

Capital punishment was common in the Soviet Union, and it reached barbaric heights under Adolf Hitler. A dream that is large and unrealistic—which any utopia must be—must be enforced through coercion and intimidation. Carried to its extreme, coercion becomes assassination, and intimidation becomes murder.

Arguments for reinstatement of capital punishment are already coming from the left. For years liberals had no problem with alcoholism; now arguments against alcoholism are coming from the left. These are the old arguments of the Christians—it's like a slow echo—except that we know the only way to change drug abuse and alcoholism is by faith in God to change the hearts of the people.

The way to transform murderers and other criminals into responsible citizens is not by penal reform. Our 85 percent recidivism rate proves that. The only thing that really works is the transforming power of Jesus Christ, working from within the human heart. The coercive utopians are saying, "No, we will force them to follow our way."

Margaret Sanger, in founding Planned Parenthood, advocated unrestrained sexuality, particularly among teenagers. But once they started engaging in widespread promiscuous sex, her solution was sterilization and abortion.

Sanger had an agenda. She wanted unrestrained licentiousness so that she could bring on involuntary sterilization. Perhaps one of the reasons she was so heavily funded by the Rockefeller and Ford Foundations was that Sanger wanted what is called eugenics or "good genes" by which an elite group under her leadership could cull out the undesirables and create a master race. Increased sexuality was a means of getting there, because the only solution to the problem of runaway illegitimacy is through sterilization and abortion. Sanger advocated sterilization of blacks, Jews, Southern Europeans, fundamentalist Christians, mental defectives, and the relatives of mental defectives. Her monograph published in 1920 called *Breeding the Thoroughbred* is a real eyeopener!

Now proponents of the new world order are working under various ruses and pretexts. To achieve ultimate authority over people, they now encourage a full expression of their baser instincts until a time when society rises up against them. Then to counter the anarchy and runaway evil, these manipulators can appear to be public heroes by advocating and implementing oppressive laws that restrain not only perceived anarchy, but the basic freedoms of all the people.

Disturbing Precedents

One of the most disturbing precedents for the new world system of coercion is the recent outcry of liberals and humanists for congressional passage of the United Nations Treaty on the Rights of the Child. Citing the 135 heads of state who had already adopted the treaty, politicians like Connecticut Senator Christopher Dodd said that our government's delay was shameful, reprehensible, and irresponsible.

Even Senators Robert Dole of Kansas, Richard Lugar of Indiana, and Mark Hatfield of Oregon expressed official "concern" that the president could not pull the Senate together to support this bill that had already become law in such enlightened nations as Iran, Iraq, Libya, Ethiopia, and South Africa.

What does this controversial measure promise? It would grant freedom of expression to children, without restriction. It would guarantee children freedom of "thought, conscience, and religion." It would prohibit any restriction of the child's freedom of association. It would grant children the absolute right of privacy, including privacy from their own parents.

This is only a partial list of the "protections" the lawyers and sages of the United Nations have prescribed for children. A key provision is the right of each child to "mass media" intended for his or her social, moral, or intellectual good. This "right" would prevent parents from prohibiting their children from being indoctrinated by government-sponsored mass media—an alarming precedent. This tactic has always been uppermost in totalitarian regimes. Strip children from their parents, then propagandize them by the state, so that children become agents and informers against their parents.

It is not hard to imagine what sort of character such laws would promote. Nor is it hard to imagine what use clever manipulators will make of young people emptied of the values and instruction of their parents. This law strips away morality and posits a godless law of the jungle.

The idea that mass media can educate and inform the moral and mental health needs of children is really the ultimate farce. Just look at what the mass media offer our children today! Popular television is flooded with filth and violence; MTV, VH-1, and pop radio stations are sewers of obscenity, rebellion, and violence; pop magazines promote the vilest forms of pornography and a form of materialism, selfishness, and greed that has fallen to the lowest levels in human history. Are these the custodians of morality and mental hygiene?

But this is the era of the antifamily, anticommunity, antination new world order. The Rights of the Child Treaty is the law before the current United Nations, the body that is planned to guide us into the future. If a man beats up his fiancé before they are married, rest assured that she will become a battered wife. If the one-worlders are trying to ram the antifamily Rights of the Child Treaty down our throats now, just think what is coming after the wedding! The new world order will not be a promise of hope but a bitter, cruel hoax!

11

The Words of the Prophets

INSCRIBED OUTSIDE THE UNITED NATIONS building on the East River in Manhattan are the words of the Prophet Isaiah, who wrote in 720 B.C., some 2,711 years ago, about a time in the future when,

> They shall beat their swords into plowshares,
> And their spears into pruning hooks;
> Nation shall not lift up sword against nation,
> Neither shall they learn war anymore.
>
> Isaiah 2:4

Obviously those who founded the United Nations believed in the lofty words of the prophet. Or at least they believed that the organization that they were establishing would be the human instrument of peace. Implicit in the message of the United Nations was a promise to disarm, to use the resources of war for peace, and to establish a world order in which the nations of the world would not go to war against one another—in fact they would not even study military science and strategy anymore. The great minds that had created atomic weapons, warplanes, tanks, and artillery would now be devoted to the betterment of mankind.

So far I have pointed out some of the dark sides of the new world order, but to be fair there are some in Establishment circles who sincerely and earnestly wanted the blessing to mankind that world peace would bring. As former Secretary of State Dean Acheson said, they embraced the United Nations "with evangelical fervor," only to have their hopes dashed by forty-five years of military confrontation, communist subversion, and countless wars and revolutions.

No, the United Nations founded in 1945 under the words of the prophet did not bring a time when swords became plowshares and spears became pruning hooks. The reason is simple. God and His prophets never promised world peace to mankind through a human world government.

Here are the words of the prophet which precede those carved at the United Nations:

> Now it shall come to pass in the latter days
> That the mountain of the LORD's house
> Shall be established on the top of the mountains,
> And shall be exalted above the hills;
> And all nations shall flow to it.
> Many people shall come and say,
> "Come, and let us go up to the mountain of the LORD.
> To the House of the God of Jacob;
> He will teach us His ways,
> And we shall walk in His paths."
> For out of Zion shall go forth the law,
> And the word of the LORD from Jerusalem.
> He shall judge between the nations,
> And shall rebuke many people;
> They shall beat their swords into plowshares,
> And their spears into pruning hooks.

First, the prophet makes it quite clear that peace will come to the earth "in the latter days." As much as we would like to hurry it up, it will come as was said of the coming of Jesus Christ, "in the fullness of time."

Second, peace will come when "the mountain of the Lord's house shall be established on the top of the mountains." There will never be world peace until God's house and God's people are given their rightful place of leadership at the top of the world. How can there be peace when drunkards, drug dealers, communists, atheists, New Age worshipers of Satan, secular humanists, oppressive dictators, greedy moneychangers, revolutionary assassins, adulterers, and homosexuals are on top? Under their leadership the world will never, I repeat never, experience lasting peace.

True, Lasting Peace

Peace will only come when its source is flowing from the benign influences of Almighty God, through the people given to His service who comprise "His house." As long as the cynical politicians and equally cynical media continue to deny God's people their rightful place in God's order for the world, they are condemning their world to violence, turmoil, oppression, and war.

Adolf Hitler once commented on the efforts of German evangelical clergymen to oppose his programs. "Their task is to prepare men's souls for heaven; they must leave the earth to me," he said. What a job he did on earth without their advice.

In America, a crescendo has been rising for decades, backed up by the power of the liberal members of Congress, the federal courts, and the Internal Revenue Service, to ensure that evangelical Christians stay in their churches, concern themselves with heaven, and leave the earth to them. Although I agree that it is unwise for the organized church as an institution to get itself entwined with government as an institution, there is absolutely no way that government can operate successfully unless led by godly men and women operating under the laws of the God of Jacob.

Yet when God's house is exalted, peace and prosperity will follow. The people of Guatemala recently elected, by an overwhelming majority, my friend Jorge Serrano as their president. Jorge is a dedicated, spirit-filled, evangelical Christian. Hardly was he inaugurated when he successfully concluded negotiations to end the guerrilla insurgency in Guatemala so the land could have peace. Serrano has placed godly people in high positions in his cabinet, and I am convinced that if they are free from outside mischief, they will bring their country to stability and prosperity.

Serrano continues the enlightened leadership of his patron, former President Rios Montt, who insisted on honesty in government and then had every key official sign a pledge that read, "I will not steal; I will not lie; I will not abuse." I was in Guatemala City three days after Rios Montt overthrew the corrupt Lopez Garcia government. The people had been dancing in the street for joy, literally fulfilling the words of Solomon who said, "When the righteous are in authority, the people rejoice."

Third, the Prophet Isaiah tells us that world peace will come when "many people say, 'Come, and let us go up to the mountain of the Lord, to the house of the God of Jacob; He will teach us His ways, and we will walk in His paths.'"

In other words, world peace will come when the people of the world finally reject the hypocritical lies that have been foisted upon them for centuries, whether by utopian dreamers, hot-headed revolutionaries, greedy, power-hungry politicians, or demonic madmen and then turn to the house of the God of Jacob for help.

Notice two elements of the prophetic message. First, the desire of the nations for help is totally voluntary. The philosophy of Thomas Jefferson, who drew up the landmark Virginia Statute of Religious Liberty, made it clear that the duty a man owes his Creator cannot be coerced by the state. The attitude that brings people's hearts into compliance with God's laws and therefore peace with their neighbors is always voluntary. No army and no civil service can compel it, and none should ever try.

Government can only accomplish its task by compulsion and coercion. Every theory of world order being put forth today always includes the force of arms. And every time government tries to bring on utopia by force of arms, it degenerates into the nightmare of Soviet communism or Hitler's Nazism.

Learning God's Ways

We will not have world peace until people begin to come to God or His representatives on earth and say, "Teach us your ways."

This very thing is happening now in many nations. The Soviet government's television network has requested the Christian Broadcasting Network to provide animated Bible stories to teach their children moral values. Our Soviet representative placed a brief spot announcement in the midst of our Russian language version of the popular "Superbook" and "Flying House" programs.

To those who answered three questions—"Where did people come from?" "What is one of the Ten Commandments?" and "Who is Jesus Christ?"—a little, colored, Bible-story book was sent. Imagine our delight when our Moscow office received more than 2 million handwritten letters from Soviet children and their parents, some containing absolutely beautiful hand-colored pictures of Bible stories.

Of special interest to us was the fact that after years of indoctrination in atheism and evolution, over 90 percent of the people responding said that human beings were created by God, not evolved from apes.

I was told by a distinguished pastor from an Eastern European country that the Soviet Academy of Science welcomed a series of lectures on Creationism and then requested further literature and a series of regional lectures to show that Creationism is more valid than the theory of evolution.

In the same vein, a delegation of the leaders of the Rumanian national television network visited our headquarters in Virginia Beach to request religious and family-oriented television programs for their nation. They will begin airing our Bible stories five nights per week at 7:30 P.M. across their entire nation in order to instruct their children in the ways of God.

The Rumanian government has now approached the churches of their land to send teachers of the Christian religion into their schools to instruct their children in the moral and ethical values that had been taken away from them during communism. To help meet the needs of the Christians in Rumania to learn the principles of government in God's kingdom, we had two hundred thousand copies of my book, *The Secret Kingdom,* translated and distributed throughout the country.

More recently, a member of the diplomatic corps from Zaire came to our headquarters at the direction of President Sese Mobutu with an invitation to me to come to his nation to teach the principles of government according to God's laws to his people, including the pastors as well as members of his government. Not only did I enjoy a successful visit, but we are now planning extended television broadcasts this fall on the national television network of Zaire to teach God's laws to all the people.

As more and more governments acknowledge their failures and come to "the house of the God of Jacob" for teaching, there will be increasing peace and prosperity. The natural process foretold by the Prophet Isaiah is beginning to take place, little by little, around the world. I know this because I have been privileged to be a part of it. My fervent prayer is that the big boys, with their weapons, money, and misguided plans for social reform, will not try to wreck what is springing spontaneously from a heartfelt need.

The prophet says that the nations will come not just to "religion," but to the God of Jacob. We read in the Bible that a woman of Samaria, who held a bastardized version of Judaism imposed on her people by the Assyrians, met Jesus Christ at Jacob's Well in Samaria. After some discussion about religious matters, Jesus made an amazing statement to the woman, "You do not know what you believe, for salvation is of the Jews."

Today's open-minded, anything-goes syncretism will not bring world peace. What I am saying may jar some sensibilities, but only the teaching that comes forth from the house of the God of Jacob will bring world peace. The gods of the animist tree worshipers, the gods of the ancestor worshipers, the million gods of the Hindus, and the Allah of the Muslims is not the God of Jacob. The revelation of the one true God came from Abraham to Isaac to Jacob to David and to Jesus. Then Jesus made the bold statement: "I am the way, the truth, and the life. No one comes to the Father but by me."

The Way of the World

The new world order will have as its religion a god of light, whom Bible scholars recognize as Lucifer. Nations who walk in Lucifer's ways will find only suffering and heartache, but never peace!

We should note well that the prophet tells us that world peace will come when the nations not only come to the house of the God of Jacob to learn His ways, but when they agree to walk in His paths. Obviously it would do no good for the people of Zaire who heard me teach the ways of God to them on television if they refused to reorder their lives after the teaching. First there must be revelation, then obedience. Always voluntary, always from the heart, always on the basis of truth, never coerced, and never for purely selfish motives.

How revolutionary it would be if the nations of the world truly walked in the ways of the God of Jacob. The voluntary application of just one of His principles, called the Golden Rule, would cause air and water pollution to cease, crime to cease, divorce and child abuse to cease, economic exploitation to cease, the narcotics traffic to cease, human rights abuse to cease, and war to cease. The potential savings in national budgets from the elimination of police, criminal courts, standing armies, pollution control agencies, drug enforcement, and many poverty programs is almost beyond calculation.

What is this revolutionary law of God? It is one that many children learned in Sunday school: "Do unto others as you would have them do unto you." That is not utopianism, I might add, but reciprocal self-interest. If you don't want pollution dumped on you, don't dump it on someone else. If you don't want your property stolen, don't steal from someone else. If you don't want to be raped, don't rape someone else. If you don't want your country invaded by armies, don't invade someone else's country. If you want someone to help you when you are poor, then help someone else when he is poor.

It is all so simple. So inexpensive. So very practical. The world works because people at every level live out the Golden Rule and make it work. When they do, there is peace, and no huge money machine called the new world order is necessary.

Fourth, the prophet tells us that peace will come when "out of Zion shall go forth the law." In the United States today we have the highest voluntary income tax compliance of any nation on earth. If the American people ever become persuaded that the Internal Revenue Service is incompetent, corrupt, unfair, or ideologically biased, voluntary compliance would plummet and the government would not be able to place enough revenue agents throughout the country to collect the tax revenues due it. Americans voluntarily comply and pay taxes because, despite misgivings, we still trust our government. When the bond of trust is severed, the government will fall apart.

In Zaire, people do not trust their government. Cheating on taxes is pandemic, and the government is in crisis. Trust is an absolutely essential ingredient for successful government.

Think of a world with a tribunal so wise and so fair that all parties in a dispute would obey its decisions without conflict and without coercion. Then there would be no cause for war. Individuals and nations would submit their disputes to a tribunal that they trusted implicitly. Again it should be emphasized that compliance is not coerced. Compliance is voluntary because the law involved is clearly for the good of mankind, and its wisdom commends itself as being in accord with the nature of man and the nature of the universe.

After all, neither the law of gravity nor the law of thermodynamics requires standing armies and security police for enforcement. These laws enforce themselves by the very action of the universe itself. People who "break" the law of gravity injure themselves.

People who "obey" the law of thermodynamics build pumps, and motors, and vehicles. The physical laws are there for our benefit if we are willing to obey them. The moral laws of the God of Jacob are also there for our benefit, if we are willing to submit ourselves to them. As in the case of the physical laws, God's moral laws do not require armies to enforce them. They are self-enforcing. People and societies that break them destroy themselves.

The Universal Moral Law

Through the history of what has been called Christian civilization, the Ten Commandments, given directly by the God of Jacob thirty-four hundred years ago to a great leader of the family of Jacob, named Moses, have been considered the heart of the universal moral law.

In one of the great tragedies of history, the Supreme Court of the supposedly Christian United States guaranteed the moral collapse of this nation when it forbade children in the public schools to pray to the God of Jacob, to learn of His moral law, or even to view in their classrooms the heart of the law, the Ten Commandments, which children must obey for their own good or disobey at their peril.

It is one of the supreme ironies of history that the former communist bloc nations are desperately seeking to repair the moral wreckage brought upon their nations by an official policy of atheism, while irreligious liberal groups like the American Civil Liberties Union, People for the American Way, the American Jewish Congress, Americans United for Separation of Church and State, the National Organization for Women, and the liberal media are doing everything in their power to drive the United States into the same moral abyss that the Eastern Bloc countries are clawing their way out of.

The Ten Commandments are for our own good. As Jesus Christ put it, "The Sabbath was made for man." How do these commandments relate to the world?

The utopians have talked of world order. Without saying so explicitly, the Ten Commandments set the only order that will bring world peace—with devotion to and respect of God at the center, strong family bonds and respect next, and the sanctity of people, property, family, reputation, and peace of mind next.

All of the utopian societies that we have examined operate under a cloak of secrecy and a cloud of lies—every single one! They are furtive and conceal from view their real leaders and their real agenda. Each one has a series of concentric circles of order—from the key few to the enlightened initiates, to a larger front organization, to the agencies that they can manipulate.

Not one places God or the Bible at the center of its world schemes. When someone offers us a new social order, you would think we would have a clear right to ask, "If what you are offering is so good for us, why are you trying to sneak it by us the way you did the Federal Reserve Board?" God did not deliver His plan for world order in secret. He announced it from a smoking mountaintop and has subsequently caused hundreds of millions of copies of the law to be printed in virtually every known language on earth.

The first commandment is key to all the others, **"You shall have no other gods before Me."** Money, power, success, and utopian dreams all can become gods who have baser standards than the God of Jacob. Serving the lesser gods permits ethical lapses under the broad heading, "the end justifies the means." If our god is a Marxist paradise, then killing 60 million human beings is justified, if that is necessary to bring about paradise. If our god is financial success, then wiping out competitors by unethical means is permissible. To have the God of Jacob as the preeminent deity means to gain success that all of his ethical standards must be observed along the way.

Casting Down Idols

The next point in God's world order, **"You shall not make for yourself any carved image, . . . you shall not bow down to them nor serve them,"** prohibits false religious worship. Idolatry sprang from the worship of the sun, moon, snakes, cows, certain mythical creatures, or Satan. The idol was created by man, and therefore the creators of the idol and its priests could change the rules of the idol to suit themselves.

In the Roman Empire, in the Soviet Union, and in Red China enormous statues and portraits of the leaders were displayed everywhere. Wherever the citizenry looked, they saw these bigger-than-life likenesses of Marx, Lenin, and Mao Tse Tung. Once these men were dead, their followers—the priests of their temple—made up any stories they wished about the real meaning of "pure" Marxist-Leninist thought.

In Third World countries that practice idolatry, the idols are representatives of demonic power, and their worship often involves actual demon possession. The barbaric acts that have been committed in the name of idols range from the assassinations committed by worshipers of Kali in India, to the human sacrifices by the Mayans in Mexico, to the sacrifices to the volcano god in Polynesia, to the sacrifice of children to the Canaanite fire god Molech.

The Bible warns us that in the end times a world dictator will arise whose enormous statue will be energized by Satan in league with a false religious system to do signs and wonders. But if people engage in idolatry, there can be only delusion and manipulation in the name of the idol by the "priests of the temple," but never happiness or world peace.

The third commandment establishing God's world order, **"You shall not take the name of the Lord your God in vain,"** means two things. First, those who are serving Him must understand the full extent of His power, and in turn must not appear to be His followers when in truth they are not.

The name of the Lord means "I am." In history He has showed Himself as provider, healer, victor, wisdom, righteousness, shepherd, peace, and savior. When people and nations come to Him to learn His ways, He wants them to look to Him for the supply of all their needs. He wants them to realize it is not necessary to rob, lie, oppress, cheat, and steal in order to receive His bountiful supply.

God's order for the world requires that people look to God directly to meet their needs, not to government, social programs, or conduct that injures others and violates His laws. And when people claim to know Him, He insists that they live according to their profession. For the United States to write "In God We Trust" on its currency while denying public school children the right to pray is not only hypocritical, it breaks the third commandment.

The next obligation that a citizen of God's world order owes is to himself. **"Remember the Sabbath day, to keep it holy,"** is a command for the personal benefit of each citizen. Our minds, spirits, and bodies demand a regular time of rest. Perhaps God's greatest gift to mankind's earthly existence is the ability to be free from work one day a week. Only when people are permitted to rest from their labors, to meditate on God, to consider His way, to dream of a better world can there be progress and genuine human betterment.

Self-Inflicted Wounds

Galley slaves and coolies forced to work seven days a week became no better than beasts of burden. Higher civilizations rise when people can rest, think, and draw inspiration from God. Laws in America that mandated a day of rest from incessant commerce have been nullified as a violation of the separation of church and state. In modern America, shopping centers, malls, and stores of every description carry on their frantic pace seven days a week. As an outright insult to God and His plan, only those policies that can be shown to have a clearly secular purpose are recognized.

What idiocy our society has indulged in by refusing to acknowledge the wisdom of God. Before our eyes we watch the increase of chronic burnout, stress breakdowns, nervous disorders, and mental and spiritual exhaustion cauterizing the souls of our people. We consume billions of tranquilizers. Marriages fall apart, and the business of psychologists is booming. Psychosomatic illnesses make up 70 percent of our medical problems, yet we ignore the clear wisdom and will of God. The answer in God's world order is so easy to find. It is not a mystery. A loving God has made His way so simple, even a child can understand it.

I never gave the issue of a day of rest much thought until I read God's Word spoken through the Prophet Isaiah on the subject:

> If you turn away your foot from the Sabbath,
> From doing your pleasure on My holy day,

And call the Sabbath a delight,
The holy day of the LORD honorable, . . .
[Not] finding your own pleasure,
Nor speaking your own words,
Then you shall delight yourself in the LORD;
And I will cause you to ride on the high hills of the earth,
And feed you with the heritage of Jacob your father.
                                                Isaiah 58:13–14

Since exaltation and promised rewards came from one day of rest and worship, I determined to remake my Sundays according to the biblical model. When I did, concepts began to flow, my strength and vigor during my workdays jumped dramatically, and along with them came the resulting productivity and resulting benefits. Indeed the Sabbath was made for man. If you don't believe me, try working thirty days nonstop with no weekend breaks, then gauge your mental acuity and productivity.

God's Unit of Order

The basic unit of social, local, national, and international organization in God's world order is the family. As William Bennett, former secretary of education, said so eloquently, "The first Department of Health, Education, and Welfare is the family."

The basic responsibility for child rearing, social, and moral education belongs to the family. Every attempt at institutional child care has proved a miserable failure. Experiments with primates and human beings have shown beyond any chance of contradiction that the social and intellectual development of young children depends on extended personal nurturing by their mothers.

Furthermore, landmark studies by the World Health Organization, cited by Professor Armand Nicolai of Harvard University, showed that the prolonged absence of either parent had a dramatically negative impact upon young children, who then grow up lacking in drive, susceptible to peer pressure, and mediocre in studies. Although these clear findings are known and available, they are

suppressed because women either must work or find personal fulfillment in work. Children are often ignored in the rhetoric of the
feminist movement, which for so long denigrated motherhood and
exalted the role of women in professions, in manual labor, and more
recently in armed combat.

Virtually every recent pressure in society has been antifamily.
We have brought in no-fault divorces. We have raised the tax burden on families by an estimated 226 percent. We have subsidized
illegitimate births. We have permitted teenage abortions without
parental consent. We have opened sex clinics in schools to teach il-
licit sex and to pass out contraceptives.

The National Education Association actually prints literature to
show teachers how to subvert parental rights. More than anything,
the number of working mothers has skyrocketed from 32.8 percent
in 1948 to 66.6 percent by 1990, much of that caused by govern-
ment-induced inflation and the resultant drop in the real incomes of
male head-of-family wage earners.

The fifth commandment says, **"Honor your father and
mother, that your days may be long upon the land."** Under
God's order there is to be a family unit of mother, father, and children.
The norm is the nuclear family, where both mother and father supply the material needs and give the appropriate education and
discipline to the children. The family is to transmit the culture
and traditions of the society to the children.

Children in turn are to respect and obey their parents because
parents are God's representatives to them. When parents become
elderly and unable to work, the honor due them includes material
care. As one person said so poignantly to me, "If a mother and father can afford to care for four children, why can't four children afford
to care for their mother and father?"

Instead, in our society we have cut the link given in God's order. We encourage childlessness and abortion that removes younger
wage earners to care for the elderly. Then we, through social security, Medicare, Medicaid, and a host of other impersonal government
assistance programs, have effectively cut the lifeline between

children and their elderly parents. Instead of old age being a time of honor, it is often a time of destitution, as the enlightened humanists of the new world order look for government-funded nursing homes and ways to advertise the Hemlock Society and more efficient euthanasia.

Knowing God

God's world order builds upon a proper relationship with Him, then respect for man made in God's image, and then the nuclear family as the basis of a healthy clan, which naturally makes for a healthy nation and, in turn, a healthy world.

Every healthy society in our world today stresses the importance of healthy cohesive families, loving parents, obedient children, strong traditions, quality education, respect for hard work and thrift, individual self-reliance, and ethnic pride. Every one of these virtues are under attack by the politically correct apostles of the new world order who have been trying to undermine America so it will surrender its sovereignty and willingly enter into a world government.

Once people in the world are in direct contact with God, have rejected satanic counterfeits, have recognized that God can supply all their needs, have established their own dignity and self-worth, and have come to the proper order in their families—then and only then are they in a position to take care of their fellow man.

The Apostle Paul wrote that the next five commandments are summed up in one phrase, **"You shall love your neighbor as yourself,"** because love does no harm to other people.

The sixth commandment in God's order guarantees respect for life: **"You shall not murder."** Human life has been created in God's image, and it is to be inviolate. The founders of the American republic recognized that God had created all men equal in His image and had endowed each of them with the inalienable rights of life, liberty, and the pursuit of happiness.

The basic rights of people in God's order are guaranteed by God Himself and cannot be taken away by any government. In the communist order, people only have the rights that were given them by the state. Under the United States Constitution, the state receives only that portion of the God-given rights which the people, by contract, cede over to it.

If God is removed from the equation, and if human life is not uniquely created in His image, then people can be treated like cattle for the benefit of their masters. Any new world order based on atheism or syncretism will downgrade the right to life of every human being. The unborn may be aborted, the unfit may be eliminated, and the elderly may be given lethal injections. Hitler in his new order called these people "useless eaters" and not fit to live. In the name of humanism, they downgraded the basic rights of human beings.

In God's order, no one has to fear for his life. He is to be safe from murder in his home, his job, and in his travels. Neither private individuals, mobs, nor the state are permitted to murder.

The Marriage Bond

In some utopias, all children are to be raised in common. In some, as in Nazi Germany, certain women are used like broodmares to bear the master race. In some, family life is forbidden except for the procreation of communal children. In today's view of utopia, unbridled sex between men and women, men and men, and women and women in whatever grouping, technique, or circumstance seems desirable. In God's order, sexual relations outside of marriage are forbidden, and marriage is to be for life. The marriage bond is to be so strong that neither partner is to engage in extramarital sex with another, nor is a single man or woman permitted to have sex with a married person.

In God's order, every spouse is to feel secure in the love and fidelity of the other spouse. Every father will know that the children his wife had born within their marriage are his. Every wife is assured that her husband is not sharing what belonged to her and her children with another woman and her children.

Each partner in a marriage is able to rest assured that the life they have built together will not be shattered by some fleeting liaison with someone outside the marriage. A godly marriage is a lifetime investment by both partners, and neither spouse should have to fear that investment will be squandered by the other. At the same time, neither spouse was to worry that a mate is bringing a deadly disease to their marriage bed. Children are to rest assured in the love and fidelity that their parents share and in the stability and honor of their home. The seventh commandment is clear, **"You shall not commit adultery."**

In God's order, the energy of the people is to be directed toward creating a just and happy world. History shows that every civilization in which the creative energies of people were dissipated by sexual promiscuity and drunkenness has quickly gone into decline. Without trust, fidelity, and discipline, families fail and nations fail.

Respect for Property

God's order recognizes the sanctity of private property. The eighth commandment, **"You shall not steal"** means that the God of Jacob forbids a citizen to take what belongs to another citizen. He did not permit a Robin Hood to take from the rich and give to the poor, or the greedy rich to steal the possessions of the poor. What a man had accumulated was his. In God's order there are no schemes of wealth redistribution under which government forces productive citizens to give the fruit of their hard-earned labors to those who are nonproductive.

Opportunity was to be equal for all citizens. Those who were rich were instructed in order to receive God's blessings to give generous voluntary gifts to the poor, and sufficient gleaning was to be set aside so that the poor would have an opportunity to earn a living for themselves.

We hear in today's political jargon that there is a difference between human rights and property rights. This is nonsense. Without property of some sort it is impossible to obtain food, clothing, and shelter. It is certainly impossible to obtain recreation, education, books, music, art, travel, and worry-free retirement—the things that are considered the benefits of civilization.

When the framers of the U.S. Declaration of Independence spoke of the pursuit of happiness, they obviously had in mind the ability to work, to accumulate private material possessions, and to pay for the type of lifestyle such possessions made possible. Remember, though, our founders guaranteed the pursuit of happiness, not happiness itself. No government has the wealth or power to guarantee happiness, but any government can ensure the opportunity of all citizens to pursue their own destiny under God.

Every single utopian vision of world order requires a severe restriction on people's ownership of property and the enjoyment of its fruits. God's world order says that every man should be free to own private property free from the fear of theft by his fellow citizens or confiscation by a greedy government.

False Accusers

In the communist countries, a regular part of life for the citizens was the false trials and perjured accusations before kangaroo courts. Judges were corrupt, prosecutors were corrupt, witnesses were corrupt. In the United States, although there are occasional cases of defendants falsely accused, the only true counterpart of the communist legal system is found in America's liberal press.

Private citizens and public officials are slandered and convicted in the press by so-called investigative reporters who act as prosecutor, judge, and jury. The accused has no ability to question evidence brought against him, no appeal to an impartial tribunal, and no ability to review the accuracy of the indictment against him. Under the U.S. Supreme Court decision of *Sullivan v. The New York Times,* the burden of proof in proving press libel is so onerous that few of those victimized by the press have any option other then to suffer in silence the loss of their reputations.

The price that the vicious, sensational press exacts of public officials is so great that good citizens of ability are increasingly reluctant to enter into any type of public service. After thirty years of being the recipient of libel and scorn at the hands of the print media, I have become a bit more hardened to their tactics. But I often wonder who gave these people the right to destroy, humiliate, and damage the reputation of another human being living at peace with them?

The liberal press has tried repeatedly to take away from Christian people in America the right to run for office, to support candidates, to protest government abuses, or to protect themselves in court. Whatever ultimate victory Christian candidates may win is usually nullified by the torrent of unwarranted vituperation they have to experience in the press. With very few exceptions in America, it is absolutely impossible for an evangelical Christian to receive a fair story in the liberal press when he or she is involved in any unfavorable encounter with a government agency at any level.

Regardless of government abuse, the evangelical knows that the government agency will be portrayed in a favorable light and he will be portrayed unfavorably. In one case in which I was a party, my Jewish attorney could not convince the liberal press that I had been proved completely blameless of the slander that had been brought against me. This was the comment from my lawyer, who has represented worldwide clients and several Israeli government agencies: "I have never encountered such press hostility in my life."

The liberal press represents the Establishment in the United States and Europe. The Nazis used the press to vilify the Jews and make association with them shameful. The communists used the press to undercut their enemies prior to their trial and punishment. In the new world order we can rest assured that those who stand in the way of the Establishment plans will become, like Margaret Thatcher, the victim of unremitting character assassination by the press.

Freedom from Fear

In God's world order, libel and slander are not permitted. The ninth commandment, **"You shall not bear false witness,"** is meant to protect the reputation of every person. People are to be secure against false trials and lies brought against them in court. But they also are to be free from damage to their reputations brought by lying neighbors, lying officials, or lying reporters.

You see, in God's order, people are to live without fear of any kind. Fear for their lives, fear for their property, fear for their marriages, or fear of losing their reputations because of false accusations.

But no man is truly free from fear as long as someone else is looking longingly at his job, his wife, his home, his money, or his reputation. The welfare state and the socialistic systems are based on the politics of envy. The poor are envious of the rich and therefore will use government power to take their riches away from them. Liberal congressmen always define "rich" as anyone who makes more money that they do. Despite objections to congressional pay increases, it is much safer for the middle class when congressional salaries go higher, for we know they will not enact punitive taxes against themselves.

But the new world order promises to elevate the politics of envy and covetousness to a new level, once the Third World nations find the mechanism to loot the accumulated wealth of this nation. Few citizens are without fear in the United States now when faced with the sanctions of the IRS, their state taxing authorities, and local tax assessors. Think of the fear that will come over you when you contemplate two continents of people coveting your possessions and no way to keep them from taking what is yours.

In God's order, the last commandment makes all the others possible. God addresses something that no government can regulate, the power of the human heart. God effectively nips the root of murder, theft, adultery, and slander when He commands, **"You shall not covet."** In God's order, people may have all that they can get morally and ethically from the resources available to all the people, so long as they worship God and not possessions, and give generously to God and those less fortunate. But they cannot even desire what belongs to their neighbor. What is his, is his, sacred, inviolate, protected by the solemn decree of the God of Jacob.

The socialists, communists, and advocates of a managed welfare state all want government to solve the perceived problems of society. Their solutions invariably involve government regulation, government spending, increased government taxes, and stricter sanctions to enforce their decrees. Government for them takes the place of God, and their constituents increasingly look to government to carry them from birth to death. In America today more than 50 percent of the people, from the rich to the poor, receive some financial payment from the government, and therefore, absent a miracle or a political revolution, the process is virtually irreversible.

Government As God

With the government as god, the major crimes in society involve breaking government regulations. Morality becomes whatever a majority in Congress or the Supreme Court says it is at any point of time. The litany of government-sponsored crimes includes failure to pay income taxes, lying to the government, operating your affairs against regulations, failure to make full disclosure to a state or federal agency, violating securities laws, speeding laws, parking laws, zoning laws, pollution laws, fishing laws. In a poll taken by *Seventeen* magazine, parking in a parking space reserved for handicapped people was rated as a worse moral offense than sexual relations out of wedlock.

The moral order at the heart of the universe is broken daily by blasphemy, adulterous sex, lying, disrespect for parents, and coveting. Society in fact encourages, where possible, every imaginable conduct to violate the true moral law, while defending petty regulations against the citizens as if *they* had been handed down on tablets from Mount Sinai, instead of from "Gucci Gulch," as the lobbyist-filled corridors of power in the United States capital are derisively called.

Yet the Apostle Paul tells us that love is the fulfilling of the moral law. Against the one who loves his neighbor, "there is no law." Marx fantasized about a classless, stateless society where government had faded away. His was a pipe dream. But in God's order that is precisely what will happen—government and its wasteful laws and regulations will be unnecessary. All that would be necessary would be an association of the citizens to accomplish tasks in common, such as road building and traffic control, which no individual family could do for itself.

Thomas Jefferson described it well when he said, "That government governs best which governs least." The founders of America—at Plymouth Rock and in the Massachusetts Colony—felt that they were organizing a society based on the Ten Commandments and the Sermon on the Mount. They perceived this new land as a successor to the nation of Israel, and they tried their best to model their institutions of governmental order after the Bible. In fact the man who interpreted the meaning of Scripture to them, the pastor, was given a higher place than the governor of the colony. These people built an incredible society because they exalted "the mountain of the Lord's house" above the other mountains.

The Missing Ingredient

There is no other way to explain the success of this experiment in liberty other than to realize that for almost two hundred years prior to our Constitution, all of the leadership of this nation had been steeped in the biblical principles of the Old and New Testaments. Their new order was a nation founded squarely on concepts of the nature of God, the nature of man, the role of the family, and the moral order as established by the God of Jacob.

They also knew that, although a few Christian settlers had received a change of heart to obey God's laws fully, there was no guarantee that a larger population at a later time would be so inclined. So they anchored their government with strong chains to keep it from acting rashly or in an arbitrary or dictatorial fashion. The wisdom of our biblically based Founding Fathers gave the United States of America the finest concept of ordered liberty the world has ever known.

It is this "Christian order" which the new world order seeks to replace!

The prophets tell us that there will be a time when the missing ingredient to complete God's world order will take place—the hearts of mankind will be changed to want to live a life of love with their fellow man. When that happens, not only will men be at peace with one another, the wild animals will be at peace as well. Instead of the Lex Talionis, the law of the jungle, there will be the law of God's love. Instead of an outward law, there will be an inner law of the heart.

Here is how the prophet Jeremiah related it:

> I will put My law in their minds, and write it on their hearts; and I will be their God, and they shall be My people.
>
> Jeremiah 31:33

When men's hearts have been changed, when from their hearts they want only good for their fellow men, and naturally, as if by instinct, they obey God's laws, then there will be world peace, a universal brotherhood of man, the sharing of wealth, and a paradise on earth.

Until that happens by the sovereign intervention of God's Spirit, any attempt to create a government structure with no godly values and based on corrupt and venal men will either lead to the foolishness and impotence of the current United Nations or, much worse, to a worldwide dictatorship more horrible than anything the world has yet known.

God's New World Order

But God's new world order is coming much nearer than we believe. Jesus Christ said that "the kingdom of God is at hand." At the present time the kingdom of God is not visible, but it is growing every day, day by day, as hundreds, thousands, millions, and tens of millions are coming to Jesus Christ, receiving His forgiveness for their sins, and being born again by the sovereign action of God Almighty into God's kingdom.

These people are called the sons of God. They are everywhere among us. In the lowest tasks, in the highest. People of no learning, some with great learning. Some with no wealth, others with fabled wealth. Some with no political power, others holding high government office. Some with no athletic ability, others world-class champions. Silently, steadily, they are being prepared for their place in God's coming world order.

The world can recognize them by their lives. Other than that, their nature is invisible. They appear on the surface to be just like everyone else. But they are being kept in waiting until the time that God sweeps away the pretense of the satanic and man-made counterfeits and announces His new world order and His anointed leader, Jesus the Messiah.

Then will come the unveiling of the sons and daughters of God to the world. Then these people, who have often been so ridiculed and despised by the world, will be revealed as what they really are and given their place in God's world order. Then, and only then, will the world be at peace.

The Apostle Paul put it this way in his letter to the church at Rome:

> For the earnest expectation of the creation eagerly waits for the revealing of the sons of God. For . . . the creation itself also will be delivered from the bondage of corruption into the glorious liberty of the children of God.
>
> Romans 8:19, 21

Therefore, do not be anxious. God's work is right on schedule. The company of the sons of God is almost complete—perhaps this very decade may finish the task. God sometimes seems to be slow, but He is never late. In the fullness of time, He will announce His kingdom on earth. I do not believe that we have much longer to wait!

12

The Great Divide

MODERN IRAQ NOW OCCUPIES THE LAND at the mouth of the Tigris-Euphrates Rivers, where civilization began. Although modern-day Iraq is a creation of Winston Churchill as colonial secretary of Great Britain on August 23, 1919, its roots trail back into mystery and legend.

The first known urban civilization was located in Sumer near modern Basra, then farther north to Accad. Around the year 2000 B.C., a man called Abram, whose name was changed by God to Abraham ("father of a multitude"), was born in Ur of the Chaldees near the mouth of the Tigris-Euphrates River and near the site of ancient Sumer.

Abraham journeyed with his family from Ur to nearby Syria, and from there he went out under the command of Almighty God to receive the land we now know as Palestine, or Israel, as his permanent possession. From Abraham came two sons. One was born, as if by a miracle, when Abraham was a hundred years old and his beloved wife, Sarah, was ninety years old and past all natural childbearing ability. This child was named Isaac, which means "laughter." The other son, his first, was born to Sarah's servant girl Hagar. The boy was named Ishmael, which means "God hears."

God had promised Abraham that his descendants would be as numerous as the stars of heaven, and indeed they are. Ishmael was the progenitor of the Arab people, who number in the hundreds of millions. But God made an even greater promise to Abraham when He assured him that through his seed all the families of the earth would be blessed. The promise of blessing was transmitted not to Ishmael, but to Isaac, and then to Isaac's son Jacob, and then to Jacob's son Judah, and then to Judah's descendant, King David, and to King David's descendant, Jesus of Nazareth.

The law of the God of Jacob was preserved by the Jewish people, who were the descendants of Jacob's twelve sons, as the true rule of order for all the nations. The salvation offered to all the families on the earth, as foretold by the Jewish prophets, was to be through the person whom the Jews came to call the Messiah, which in Hebrew means "the anointed one of God."

The Anointed One

For Christians and many others, the literal personification of the Messiah is Jesus of Nazareth, a lineal descendant of Abraham, Isaac, Jacob, Judah, and David, who for the past two millennia has been called *Christos,* which is the Greek word translating the Hebrew word, *Meshiach,* or Messiah. Jesus Christ is the final expression to all mankind of the faith of Abraham. He was a truly perfect man, totally yielded to the purposes of God.

His complete obedience even to death and His subsequent resurrection from death made Him the first of the ever-swelling multitude of those who are preparing for God's new world order of peace and justice. The time of this glorious paradise on earth under the divinely conceived Messiah and His chosen people is termed the Millennium, the thousand-year reign.

Those who have submitted themselves to the lordship of the Messiah and invited Him to live within their hearts eagerly look forward to the establishment of God's new world order when evil, hatred, sickness, poverty, and war are taken from the earth. The Apostle

Paul calls the millennial kingdom "the blessed hope and glorious appearing" of our Lord Jesus Christ. The closing words in the Holy Bible, written nineteen hundred years ago, are a fervent prayer for the commencement of God's world order: "Even so, come, Lord Jesus!"

The Seat of Rebellion

Another stream of human life was birthed in Mesopotamia, the cradle of civilization, that was completely opposite to the stream of life flowing from Abraham and his descendants. These people based their lives on human potential, human ability, and human rebellion against God and His order. Abraham was the father of all those on earth who believe that God exists, that His ways are beneficial for mankind, and who are therefore willing to follow Him even to the point of personal sacrifice so that His kingdom can come and His will be done on earth as it is in heaven. The other Mesopotamians rebelled against God and turned their worship to animals, heavenly bodies, demons, and other human beings.

Near the seat of the ancient Babylonian Empire along the Tigris-Euphrates River, people came together from ancient Accad, Babel, Erech, and Calneh to assert their humanity. They believed that a people united could effectively challenge God, and they set out to prove it. United in their labors, they started building a city and a tower "whose top is in the heavens." Their stated purpose was "to make a name for ourselves, lest we be scattered abroad over the face of the whole earth."

To put it another way, these people used their combined energies to exalt themselves for mutual self-defense while they showed themselves the equals of heaven. Nothing in their plans included faith in God or submission to Him. This early experiment in world government was built on pride, self-exaltation, and what the people considered mutual self-interest.

God's reaction is interesting. He acknowledged the power of combined humanity, even in rebellion against Him. His appraisal is fascinating,

The people are one and they all have one language, and this is what they begin to do; now nothing that they propose to do will be withheld from them.

Genesis 11:6

God knew that this first attempt to build a new world order, if allowed to continue unhindered, would succeed beyond the wildest dreams of its founders. The danger of such a plan to future generations and the threat of this man-made order to the people of faith was so great that God determined to stop it at its inception.

Therefore, God confused the speech of the participants and scattered them over the face of all the earth. In the words of the Bible, "they ceased building the city." God took away from them the key ingredient to success—harmony. If they could not communicate successfully with one another, they could not successfully build an embryonic world order. From that day unto this the nations of the world have never been in unity on anything, ever.

Reunited at Babylon

The significance of the Persian Gulf War transcends Kuwait; it even transcends the concept of a new world order enunciated by George Bush. The Gulf War is significant because the action of the United Nations to authorize military action against Iraq was the first time since Babel that all of the nations of the earth acted in concert with one another. I find it fascinating to consider that this union took place against the very place where the nations had been divided, the successor nation to ancient Babel.

It is as if some power reached out from Babel, where the first world rebellion against God was quashed, and once again called the nations of the world to unity. And on the very day the unity of nations was consummated, General Brent Scowcroft, national security adviser to the president of the United States, longtime Council on Foreign Relations member, and former aide and business associate of Henry Kissinger, announced, in an interview with Charles Bierbauer of CNN, the beginning of a new world order.

Once a new world order without God and based on human potential is established, sooner or later the present players will be moved out of the way. Whatever their motives, whether noble or venal, the present one-world crowd of monied aristocrats will find out, as the wealthy Duke of Orleans discovered in the French Revolution, that they were merely expendable pawns being used by a much greater power. Adolf Hitler used the monied industrialists of Germany so long as they served his purposes, then they were cast aside to make way for his demented inner circle.

The silly so-called intellectuals of academia who are spouting their politically correct foolishness will find themselves considered first irrelevant and then expendable when the real power begins to operate.

The danger to the world is not the plan of monied people to establish a world in which it is easier to make more money. The greatest danger is not even that the poor nations of the earth will use their influence to reduce America to poverty.

The real danger is that a revived one-world system, springing forth from the murky past of mankind's evil beginnings, will set spiritual forces into motion which no human being will be strong enough to contain.

In the Book of Revelation there is a cryptic reference to "four angels who are bound at the great river Euphrates." Is it possible that at the Tower of Babel, Almighty God not only confused the language and scattered the people, but He bound the demonic powers that had energized the earliest form of anti-God world order? Our movie screens have been full of stories of explorers who delved beyond the limits permitted to man, and in the process unloosed dreaded forces upon themselves. These plots are obviously fictional, but the Holy Bible is not fiction.

Here is what the Bible says:

Then the sixth angel sounded: And I heard a voice from the four horns of the golden altar which is before God, saying to the sixth angel who had the trumpet, "Release the four angels who are bound at the great river Euphrates." So the four angels, who had been prepared for the hour and day and month and year, were released to kill a third of mankind.

Revelation 9:13–15

This world horror would be motivated by demonic spirits and would be all consuming. The "angels" or demons had been bound by spiritual commandment from sometime in the early days of history until the precise hour, day, month, and year for them to be released. The result of their release would now cost the lives of some 2 billion people.

Fulfilling Prophecy

As ghastly as it may seem, there are New Age advocates of a new world order who have openly advocated recently that up to 2 billion people need to die in the world in order to cleanse it in preparation for the reign of their Messiah—the Lord Meitreya or the Buddha. It is highly unlikely that these demonized people have been reading the Book of Revelation. Yet their ghastly conclusion accords with the activity of the four angels bound in Iraq at the Euphrates River. What power has been putting such macabre thoughts into their souls?

In a slightly different context, the Book of Revelation also speaks of a Dragon, who is the Devil, or Satan, being cast out of heaven and thrown to earth. He is the one we are told "who deceives the whole world." When he is cast down to earth from heaven, he is very angry "because he knows that he has a short time."

According to the biblical account, when the Dragon is near, he begins to persecute a woman who symbolizes the nation of Israel. When he is only partially successful in injuring Israel, the Dragon then begins mass persecution of the spiritual descendants of Israel, the Christians of the world. We are told the method to be used by Satan to fulfill his plans is to energize a world leader, one who arises from among the common people.

To this leader will be given what the Dragon had two thousand years earlier offered to Jesus—"his power, his throne, and great authority." The Bible tells us further that this world leader will be given authority "over every tribe, tongue, and nation. And all who dwell on the earth will worship him, whose names have not been written in the Book of Life of the Lamb."

This powerful world leader will not only be brutal toward people, but he will be totally and absolutely opposed to God. We are told, "he opened his mouth in blasphemy against God, to blaspheme His name, His tabernacle, and those who dwell in heaven."

Just as Jesus Christ, the Son of Man and Son of God, was the consummate example of a man baptized in God's Holy Spirit, yielded to God, and empowered by God; even so this world leader will be the consummate example of a man totally energized by the power of Satan, raging in blasphemy against God and His angels, filled with hatred against the people who are made in God's image. This world leader, who has come to be known as the Antichrist, will be more terrible than any human leader in history. Hitler, Stalin, Genghis Khan, and Caligula are all types of this leader, but no figure from history can match him for utter depravity and evil. Despite his evil, the world will be so caught up in satanic deception and delusion that it will worship the Antichrist as a god.

The good news for us all is that the world dictator is allocated only forty-two months to swagger on the world's stage. Then in the real mother of all battles, Jesus Christ, His holy angels, and all of the sons and daughters of God will fall upon him and will cast him and his followers into the lake of fire reserved for the Devil and his angels. Then the Devil will be bound for a thousand years, and the world will enjoy a time of peace and happiness and health and freedom and prosperity that is more wonderful than any human mind can conceive.

As Handel's exquisite *Messiah* proclaims: "The kingdoms of this world will become the kingdoms of our Lord, and of His Christ, and He shall reign forever and ever." Then and only then, God's new world order will officially begin, as the sons of God take their proper places in the new world.

The Battle Ahead

How does the word of the Bible relate to the events of today? It is clear that the counterfeit world order will be waiting for the satanic dictator. It just doesn't happen spontaneously. Therefore, it must be prepared for him in advance by someone. The next conclusion is inescapable. Satan knows that a world government must soon be prepared for the man whom he is preparing to receive his particular empowerment and authority.

Such a world government can come together only after the Christian United States is out of the way. After all, the rest of the world can federate any time it wants to, but a vital, economically strong, Christian United States would have at its disposal the spiritual and material force to prohibit a worldwide satanic dictator from winning his battle. With America still free and at large, Satan's schemes will at best be only partially successful. From these shores could come the television, radio, and printed matter to counter an otherwise all-out world news blackout. An independent America could point out Satan's lies. If America is free, people everywhere can hope for freedom. And if America goes down, all hope is lost to the rest of the world.

It is also clear that Satan's strategy will include a frontal assault on Israel. Rest assured that the next objective of the presently constituted new world order, under the present United Nations, will be to make Israel its target. The precedent has been set by the action against Iraq.

A recalcitrant nation whose action does not accord with United Nations policy may be disciplined by military force. That is the newest law of world order. The United Nations General Assembly has already voted to brand Zionism as racism. Surely we can expect, sooner or later, an unreasonable demand for Israel to vacate control of the West Bank and the half of her capital city in East Jerusalem.

Although Israel may be reluctantly conciliatory in regard to some territory, it is absolutely adamant about not surrendering the city won by King David almost three thousand years ago, then won again by modern Israel in 1967. And if Israel refuses to vacate the Holy City, there will be war—under the world order as it is even now constituted.

Beyond that, Satan will launch a war against the Christian people. The Book of Revelation speaks of a flood of water coming after Israel and its seed. I see that as false propaganda, ridicule, and demeaning comments—anything to ruin the influence of Christians and their ability to block Satan's plans. The Nazis used this technique against the Jews in Germany. First, they were ridiculed and blamed for the economic collapse of Germany. Then they were denied a few rights of citizenship. Then they were crowded into restricted ghettos. And finally their property and their lives were taken from them.

Above all, the propaganda was intended to make ordinary Germans uncomfortable and afraid to associate with the Jews, then suspicious of them, then hostile toward them, and then glad to be rid of them. This very technique is being used already against Christian people. It will intensify in years to come as the spiritual battle becomes more intense.

The Gathering of Forces

I believe that the Persian Gulf War has now brought into sharp focus the great cleavage that has existed in the human race since the early beginnings of civilization in the Tigris-Euphrates Valley. On the one side are the beliefs of a portion of humanity that flowed from Abraham to the Jewish race and to the Christians of the world. These are the people of faith, the people who are part of God's world order.

On the other side are the people of Babel—those who build monuments to humanity under the inspiration of Satan. Their successors in Babylon included worshipers of the goddess Astarte and the god Baal. These are the people whose religious rites included the worship of sex with cult prostitutes and cult sodomites, whose temples were adorned with eggs and phallic symbols. These are the people who began the Babylonian mystery religions that swept the Roman

Empire. Their pursuit of the occult was so intense that even the name of their region, Chaldean, came to be the identification of a person who was found in the company of conjurers, magicians, sorcerers, and soothsayers.

The people were famous for their astrologers, their signs of the Zodiac, and the monthly prognosticators. They worshiped the planets and consulted demonic spirits. Never in their entire history did they arrive at a higher form of monotheism. In fact, the Bible refers to "Mystery Babylon, the mother of harlots." It is this stream of humanity that asserted itself in the French Revolution, in Marxist communism, and now appears again in world order planning.

So long as the nations were separated by language, customs, and geography, the opportunity did not present itself for all of the people of the Babylonian humanistic and occultic traditions to unify against the people of the Abrahamic, monotheistic tradition. If, however, a one-world order comes forth, it will assuredly come under the control of the humanistic-occultic branch of humanity. When that happens, the humanistic-occultic leaders will then use the power at their disposal to eliminate the influence of the people of faith.

This means very simply that the world government of the new world order will one day become an instrument of oppression against the Christians and Jews around the world.

None of us should suddenly become philosophical determinists or fatalists. The plan to impose world government on us is well funded and far advanced. However, there is power in truth that is greater than money. What the secret planners of the Establishment fear most is the full spotlight of truth. If the full ramifications of what is being planned for every family in America comes out, their house of world order will splinter apart like so many match sticks.

Therefore it is necessary to bring the truth out in every church, in every synagogue, in every piece of literature, in every meeting. All of us must ask the hard question of our leaders: "What are the consequences of the course of action you are asking us to take?"

Whatever happens in world events, the average American, whose instincts are usually very good, should not be intimidated by "experts" on foreign relations. My wife, Dede, was born in the Midwest and raised as a Taft Republican. Her comment on foreign affairs a few years ago was very perceptive: "I don't trust anyone running the foreign affairs of America who speaks with a foreign accent." In fact, how can anyone who spent most of his life in Germany or Poland fully understand the family life, the shared values, the history of free enterprise and free speech, and the intense patriotism of people born in Columbus, Ohio?

For that matter how can a native-born American, educated at Groton, Harvard, and Oxford, who then goes to work on Wall Street, understand what goes on in the hearts of people in Iowa, Nebraska, Texas, or Florida? The Atlanticists on Wall Street may be willing to sell out America, but Main Street wants no part of their plan. It is these people who must hear what is being planned for their America. Then they must act to stop it.

Tactics and Strategies

The American people were overwhelmingly opposed to the giveaway of the Panama Canal by Trilateralist Jimmy Carter. Twenty senators who voted to ratify that ill-advised treaty were voted out of office in subsequent elections.

Since treaties are ratified in the U.S. Senate, they also can be stopped in the Senate. The key is to make every candidate for election to the Senate declare himself in advance on the issues of surrendering the sovereignty of the United States into a world government, on unilateral disarmament of America, on arming the United Nations, on giving the United Nations power over American citizens, and on the role the Federal Reserve Board has in global banking.

Then it is necessary to print hundreds of thousands of leaflets giving the stand of each of the candidates on these and other key issues, and distribute them to every church member and registered voter in every community in America. The average voter may not understand all of my concerns about religious issues, but he or she will certainly understand having his or her money drained away by a world government. And I believe he or she will vote correctly if given the choice.

The effectiveness of leaflets comparing the stands of two candidates for the United States Senate was dramatically underscored in a recent election in North Carolina.

Before the election, the conservative incumbent, Jesse Helms, was trailing his liberal opponent, the black mayor of Charlotte, Harvey Gantt, by as much as eight percentage points in public opinion polls. On the two Sundays prior to the election, a public interest issues group that I had formed, the Christian Coalition, distributed 750,000 church bulletins listing the stands of the candidates on a number of major election issues. When the ballots were counted, Jesse Helms was ahead by almost the same percentage as he had previously been behind. I believe educating the people on the issues affecting them made the difference in that psychologically vital senatorial election.

Recently, evangelical voters have been very limited in their election preferences. They are known as single-issue voters. Their issues, both of which are usually decided by courts and not by elected officials, are school prayer and abortion. Beyond these things, they are not very discriminating about a whole range of issues from tax increases and deficit spending, to national defense and foreign policy.

If you are sensitive about the dangers of one-world globalism, you can make your senator sensitive, too. Most of them are harried, pressured, and completely unable to grasp the details of the hundreds of pieces of legislation that come before them. As a result they hide behind a safe party vote or a vote that the president has done a good job of selling to the public.

However, if they are sure that a vote is so unpopular with their constituents that it will cost them their jobs, then they will listen to the people. A former secretary of the interior told me that the most effective way to lobby a congressman would be to have three or four farmers or factory workers in their work clothes approach him at a political meeting to register their opinion on an upcoming vote. This man has been trained to react to well-dressed paid lobbyists, but he believes that those working people are speaking for thousands of average voters who will react in the same manner. A few such instances will be sufficient to convince him.

The Christian Agenda

The Christian Coalition is launching an effort in selected states to become acquainted with registered voters in every precinct. This is slow, hard work. But it will build a significant database to use to communicate with those people who are regular voters. When they are mobilized in support of vital issues, elected officials listen. Richard Gardner, the former State Department official, spoke of "building the house of world order" from the bottom up. We must rebuild the foundation of a free, sovereign America from the grassroots, precinct by precinct, city by city, and state by state.

This decade will decide the outcome. Events are moving swiftly, but there is still time. My goal is to see a pro-freedom majority in the United States Senate in 1992, and a reversal of leadership in the House of Representatives by 1996. My associates are now publishing a newspaper called the *Christian American*, which is slated for a circulation of 10 million during this decade. Since in most congressional or senatorial elections a 5 percent swing in the vote means victory or defeat, the power of the concept of a free, sovereign America is so strong that, if properly presented, it can sweep the one-worlders out of contention in the public policy arena in a short time.

No group controlled by a narrow spectrum of internationalist money interests, however enlightened they may be, should be allowed to control in perpetuity the foreign policy, the treasury policy, and the defense policy of a great free nation.

The people need to receive a pledge from presidential contenders that they will go outside the Rockefeller-controlled Council on Foreign Relations and Trilateral Commission for their key appointments. Surely out of 250 million people we can find five thousand men and women for high-level presidential appointments who are not part of the ruling Establishment.

Perhaps the people could take control of both of the political parties and insist on party platforms and candidate pledges that will result in a more open appointment process.

People for the American Way and other ultraliberal lobby groups have had extraordinarily success in preventing anyone with conservative Christian values from being confirmed to an appointed position in the government. The *Washington Post* is incredible in the character assassinations it makes against non-Establishment candidates for appointive office.

Establishment Bias

This example of bias occurred after the 1988 election. The former United States ambassador to the Organization of America States, Richard McCormack, was under consideration for the post of under secretary of state for economic affairs. McCormack had worked in the Nixon White House, had been a Republican candidate for Congress from Pennsylvania, and in addition to being an absolutely brilliant student of international finance, possessed a blameless record of distinguished public service. He happens also to be a dedicated Christian. I joined a number of others in strongly recommending his appointment to the president.

After he was nominated for this key foreign policy post, and while he was awaiting confirmation before the Senate, an article appeared in the *Washington Post* about him. I could not believe my eyes as I read how lacking in experience he was, how he failed to meet the minimum expectations required for this position. Line after line poured out denigration against this outstanding man, and praising the qualifications of CFR member Robert Hormats, who is now a vice chairman of the Wall Street investment banking firm of Goldman Sachs.

I was astounded at the blatant misrepresentations in this story, but I did not say anything about it to Richard McCormack. He went on to win confirmation and to serve as the key economic adviser to

President Bush at the various economic summits. When he recently resigned, he received a letter from the president filled with gratitude and praise for his service.

Recently over dinner, I told him of my shock at the *Washington Post* attack on him. He smiled and said that after his appointment, the reporter who wrote the story apologized and confided that he had been ordered by his editors to attack McCormack and to defeat his confirmation.

Have no doubt: Press objectivity about foreign policy does not exist in the two or three key Establishment papers. They are propaganda organs attempting to control and subvert United States policies in order to further their globalist collectivist plans. Therefore it is essential that nominees from the Establishment for key appointive positions receive the same scrutiny that is given on Capital Hill to pro-American conservatives. Action of this type will entail grassroots campaigns to stop the CFR domination of the most powerful branches of our government.

Such a program requires a modest research center to screen key federal appointees to determine, from their speeches, writings, and actions whether or not they support the CFR program of a one-world collectivist government along with a drastically diminished role for United States sovereignty.

There then needs to be a telefax network to activists all over the nation who can relay the truth about the mind-set and plans of those selected for high government office to the senators responsible for their confirmation.

Anyone who gets involved in the struggle for freedom can be assured of being branded by the Establishment as being narrow-minded, provincial, obstructionist, a defender of fortress America, out of touch with the global realities, unskilled in foreign policy and, of course, the usual "bigoted, fundamentalist Christian, right-wing zealot."

The Courage of Conviction

Like it or not, this is an epic struggle for the future. If it were not important, the Establishment would not have committed the better part of a hundred years of labor and billions of dollars of their resources to bring it about. Are the preservation of faith in God throughout the world and the future of our own families not just as important to us as the one-world agenda is to the global planners?

The time has come to mount an all-out assault on the ultimate power of the Establishment—the ability to elect or destroy political leaders through the control of the money supply. In my opinion a privately owned central bank in control of our nation's money is a clear subversion of the United States Constitution. It not only violates the letter of the Constitution, it also violates the clear spirit of the Constitution.

The Federal Reserve System has survived a half-hearted legal attack on its constitutionality. What is needed now is to produce a legal climate of opinion by law journal articles, learned papers, and historical analysis to show that the United States central bank is, like Russian communism, a relatively recent development that rose up at one time and can be put down at another. Its violation of the framework of constitutional government must be made crystal clear. Then a court campaign should be undertaken before judges who would understand the issues involved.

The Federal Reserve System could be abolished by a simple majority vote in the Congress, or a two-thirds vote if the president vetoed the legislation. If a court challenge fails, all that is needed is the political will to sway 51 senators and 218 representatives. The task is not easy, but with education it is not impossible either.

If the Federal Reserve System were abolished, all of the bank-clearing functions could be transferred to the treasury. The power to "coin money and regulate the value thereof" could be placed once again where the Constitution put it, in the hands of Congress.

A Tragic Assassination

President Abraham Lincoln arrived at the very simple concept that it was not necessary under our government to borrow any dollars from any bank. The government, in fact, has the authority to issue money that is in turn backed up by the taxing power of the federal government. Congress could mandate a percentage growth rate of the economy each year, and authorize the treasury to issue enough funds to permit a modest rate of growth in the various indexes of money supply.

Under this system, the government would pay no interest at all, could easily balance its budget, and then create reserves of gold, silver, and other assets to back its paper. In the event of rising inflation, a simple tax increase could sop up excess currency. Given an approaching recession, the people's representatives could increase the supply of money available for the national economy. Banks would operate under treasury regulations with strict limits on excesses in the use of fractional reserve banking. There would be no "discount window" where banks could pick up cheap taxpayer money to loan out at higher rates, and there would be no "open market" operations constantly manipulating the money supply up and down, and in turn bringing periodically painful swings in the economy.

Beyond all else, if Congress and the treasury did not do a good job, every two years we could vote them out of office. No longer would we be voting for or against public officials on the strength of actions taken by a quasi-private agency over which they have no control.

The European bankers and money lords of America do not want interest-free government loans, nor do they want to relinquish the power they now hold over the economic and political destiny of America. Lincoln's plan to print interest-free currency, called "greenbacks," during the Civil War—instead of issuing bonds at interest in exchange for bank loans—was so revolutionary that it would have destroyed the monopoly that European bankers exercised over their nation's money. There is no hard evidence to prove it, but it is my belief that John Wilkes Booth, the man who assassinated Lincoln, was in the employ of the European bankers who wanted to nip this American populist experiment in the bud.

While still in office, Lincoln saw clearly what would happen after his time; here are his words:

The money power preys upon the nation in times of peace and conspires against it in times of adversity. It is more despotic than monarchy, more insolent than autocracy, more selfish than bureaucracy. I see in the near future a crisis approaching that unnerves me and causes me to tremble for the safety of my country. Corporations have been enthroned, an era of corruption in high places will follow, and the money power of the country will endeavor to prolong its reign by working upon the prejudices of the people until the wealth is aggravated in a few hands and the republic is destroyed.

Are these the ravings of a lunatic? No, they are the judicious and heartfelt words of a patriot, a friend of the people, a man of faith who dreamed great things for America and suffered profoundly over its pains.

Except for a brief interlude, the United States operated without a true central bank from the time of its founding under the Constitution in 1789 until 1913, a period of 124 years. We have only operated under a central bank for 78 years, a relatively short time.

Lincoln's plan would be more practical now than it was after the Civil War, because the United States dollar is the reserve currency of the world. A direct issue of our money, given political discipline and restraint, could be as good or better than the present Federal Reserve notes issued to fund government debt evidenced by interest-bearing Treasury bills, notes, and bonds.

For the average person, central banking is very complex. Many feel that it should be left, like foreign policy, "to the experts." I was amazed to learn that Walter Mondale, a lawyer, a former United States senator, a vice president of the United States, when he became the Democratic presidential candidate said, "I think I have finally figured how the Federal Reserve Board works." Obviously when someone is stealing you blind, he is not anxious to let you in on how he's doing it. Few, if any, even those on the inside of government, know how the Federal Reserve Board works. I have in my library a book by Maxwell Newton, the financial editor of the former *New York Post* and a prize winner in economics at Cambridge University. On the jacket of the book published by New York Times Books is the title, *The Fed,* then this line, "Inside the Federal Reserve, the *Secret Power Center* that controls the American Economy." (Emphasis added.)

Toward a Better World

We do not need a secret power center controlling our economy. We need our economy controlled by action of a free market under regulations laid down by those whom we vote into office by free and open elections to serve as our representatives. Nothing else is acceptable in a free society!

Obviously those who believe in freedom and American sovereignty must work toward a better world. We need cooperation with our trading partners and the lowering of barriers to free trade. We need a forum to exchange ideas. We need some world body to handle global weights, measures, and standards; allocation of spectrum space; designation of air corridors; postal regulations, etc.

It is helpful to have a World Health Organization working globally on immunizations, communicable diseases, infant mortality, and similar health concerns. It is helpful to have world libraries for the recording and dissemination of scientific discoveries of benefit to all mankind. Particularly the developed nations need coordinated plans to counter terrorism, the international drug trade, and global conflicts. We clearly need a coordination among the developed nations to alleviate poverty, plant forests, purify water, and stimulate domestic agriculture in Third World nations.

Cooperation to protect the world's air, water, vegetation, and wildlife is vital. In truth, the misuse of these resources damages all and should be protected in some reasonable way by all. Global cooperation of this nature is essential and may be accomplished by mutual limited accords between nations that preserve their own national identity, national beliefs, and national sovereignty. Obviously we must all try to find mechanisms to enable us to live together in peace on Planet Earth.

However, to accomplish all these worthwhile goals does not require the undermining of America economic and political power, nor does it require us to embrace some overarching utopian world vision in which all "become as one." This is where the danger lies, and we must resist every single day the sales pitch trying to lure this nation into a global trap.

Whatever the long-term political and emotional consequences for Mikhail Gorbachev, the failure of the August 1991 "coup" will dramatically reinforce the Establishment's goal of bringing about a new world order. The defeat of the "coup" seemingly eliminated certain threats, but it also signaled the beginning of a new, more volatile stage in Soviet-American relations.

I am reminded of Winston Churchill's words on learning of the British victory over the Nazis in North Africa, at El Alamein. He said, "This is not the end; it is not even the beginning of the end. But undoubtedly it is the end of the beginning." The August "coup" adds an incredible new dimension to the plans for a globalist state. In the months and years ahead we will no doubt see these plans unfold. Only God knows where they will lead.

Finally, let us remember that the triumph of God's world order is certain. Those who believe in Him have truth and power within them which is "greater than that which is in the world." This is the decade of opportunity for the church of Jesus Christ, a decade in which at least 1 billion people will come to faith in Christ. Especially let us not forget the miraculous power of concerted, believing prayer to alter world events.

Indeed, there will be a struggle between people of faith and people of the humanistic-occultic sphere. But as we think of the new world order let us remember the words of Jesus Christ, who said:

> In the world you will have tribulation; but be of good cheer, I have overcome the world.
>
> John 16:33

Bibliography

Aaron, Henry J., ed. *Setting National Priorities: Policy for the Nineties.* Washington, D.C.: Brookings Institute, 1990.

Aliano, Richard A. *The Crime of World Power: Politics Without Government in the International System.* New York: G. P. Putnam's Sons, 1978.

Allen, Frederick Lewis. *Only Yesterday: An Informal History of the 1920s.* New York: Harper & Brothers, 1931. Revised 1962.

Baldwin, Hanson Weightman. *The Price of Power.* New York: Harper & Row for the Council on Foreign Relations, 1948.

Ball, George W. *Diplomacy for a Crowded World: An American Foreign Policy.* Boston: Little, Brown and Co., 1976.

Billington, James. *Fire in the Minds of Men: Origins of the Revolutionary Faith.* New York: Basic Books, 1980.

Boller, Paul F., Jr. *Presidential Anecdotes.* New York: Penguin Books, 1982.

Brooke, Tal. *When the World Will Be As One: The Coming New World Order in the New Age.* Eugene, Oreg.: Harvest House, 1989.

Brown, Seyom. *On the Front Burner: Issues in U.S. Foreign Policy.* Boston: Little, Brown and Co., 1978.

Capra, Fritjof. *Uncommon Wisdom: Conversations with Remarkable People.* New York: Bantam Books, 1988.

Carpenter, Galen Ted, ed. *Collective Defense or Strategic Independence? Alternative Strategies for the Future.* Washington, D.C.: Cato Institute, 1989.

Chandler, Russell. *Understanding the New Age.* Dallas: Word Publishing, 1989.

Commager, Henry Steele. "Misconceptions Governing American Foreign Policy" in *Perspectives on American Foreign Policy.* Edited by Charles W. Kegley and Eugene R. Wittkopf. New York: St. Martin's Press, 1983.

Cord, Robert L. *Separation of Church and State: Historical Fact and Current Fiction*. New York: Lambeth Press, 1982.

Cousins, Normal. *The Celebration of Life: A Dialogue of Hope, Spirit, and the Immortality of the Soul*. Revised edition. New York: Bantam Books, 1991.

Cromartie, Michael, ed. *Evangelicals and Foreign Policy: Four Perspectives*. Washington, D.C.: Ethics and Public Policy Center, 1989.

DeBeus, J. G. *The Future of the West*. New York: Harper & Brothers, 1953.

Deutsch, Karl W. *Tides Among Nations*. New York: Free Press, 1979.

Falk, Richard A. *The End of World Order*. New York: Holmes & Meier, 1982.

———. *A Global Approach to National Policy*. Cambridge, Mass.: Harvard University Press, 1975.

———, Samuel S. Kim, and Saul H. Mendlovitz. *Toward a Just World Order*. Volume 1. Boulder, Colo.: Westview Press, 1982.

———. "The Trend Toward World Community: Issues" in *The Search for World Order*. Edited by Albert Lepawsky, Edward H. Buehrig, and Harold D. Lasswell. New York: Meredith, 1983.

Finder, Joseph. *Red Carpet*. New York: Holt, Rinehart, and Winston, 1983.

Fowle, Eleanor. *Cranston*. Los Angeles: Jeremy Tarcher, 1984.

Friedman, Thomas L. *From Beirut to Jerusalem*. New York: Doubleday, 1990.

Gill, Stephen. *American Hegemony and the Trilateral Commission*. Cambridge: Cambridge University Press, 1990.

Goldwater, Barry. *With No Apologies: The Personal and Political Memoirs of United States Senator Barry M. Goldwater*. With Barry Morris. New York: William Morrow, 1979.

Golitsyn, Anatoliy. *New Lies for Old: The Communist Strategy of Deception and Disinformation*. New York: Dodd, Mead, 1984.

Groothius, Douglas R. *Unmasking the New Age*. Downers Grove, Ill.: InterVarsity Press, 1986.

Halberstam, David. *The Best and the Brightest*. New York: Random House, 1972.

Heatherly, Charles L., and Burton Yale Pines. *Mandate for Leadership III: Policy Strategies for the 1990s*. Washington, D.C.: Heritage Foundation, 1989.

Henkin, Louis. *How Nations Behave: Law and Foreign Policy*. New York: Columbia University Press for the Council on Foreign Relations, 1979.

Higham, Charles. *Trading with the Enemy: An Exposé of the Nazi-American Money Plot, 1933–1949*. New York: Delacorte Press, 1983.

Hoffman, Stanley. *Primacy or World Order: American Foreign Policy since the Cold War*. New York: McGraw-Hill, 1978.

House, Edward Mandell. *The Intimate Papers of Colonel House*. Arranged by Charles Seymour. Boston: Houghton Mifflin, 1926–28.

———. *Philip Dru: Administrator; A Story of Tomorrow, 1920–1935*. New York: B. W. Huebsch, 1912.

Isaacson, Walter, and Evan Thomas. *The Wise Men: Six Friends and the World They Made*. New York: Simon and Schuster, 1986.

Jaguaribe, Helio. "World Order, Rationality, and Development" in *Conditions of World Order*. Edited by Stanley Hoffman. Boston: Houghton Mifflin, 1968.

Johnson, George. *Architects of Fear: Conspiracy Theories and Paranoia in American Politics*. Los Angeles: Jeremy Tarcher, 1983.

Johnson, Paul. *The Birth of the Modern World Society, 1515–1830*. New York: HarperCollins, 1991.

Koch, Adrienne, and William Peden. *The Life and Selected Writings of Thomas Jefferson*. New York: Random House, 1944.

Kennedy, Robert F. *To Seek a Newer World*. New York: Doubleday, 1967.

Kurtz, Paul, and Edwin H. Wilson. *Humanist Manifesto* (1933) and *Humanist Manifesto II* (1973). New York: Prometheus Books, 1984.

Ledeen, Michael A. *Grave New World*. New York: Oxford University Press, 1985.

Lemesurier, Peter. *This New Age Business: The Story of the Ancient and Continuing Quest to Bring Down Heaven on Earth*. Moray, Scotland: Findhord Press, 1990.

Levinson, Charles. *Vodka Cola*. London: Gordon and Cremonesi, 1978.

Mann, Thomas E., ed. *A Question of Balance: The President, the Congress, and Foreign Policy.* Washington, D.C.: Brookings Institution, 1990.

McCormick, Thomas J. *America's Half Century: United States Foreign Policy in the Cold War.* Baltimore: Johns Hopkins University Press, 1989.

McHale, John. *The Future of the Future.* New York: George Braziller, 1969.

Mehring, Franz. *Karl Marx: The Story of His Life.* Ann Arbor: University of Michigan Press, 1962.

Methvin, Eugene. *The Rise of Radicalism.* New Rochelle, N.Y.: Arlington House, 1973.

Miller, Elliot. *A Crash Course on the New Age: Describing and Evaluating a Growing Social Force.* Grand Rapids, Mich.: Baker Book House, 1989.

Miller, Merle. *Plain Speaking: An Oral Biography of Harry S Truman.* New York: G. P. Putnam's Sons, 1974.

Mullins, Eustace. *Secrets of the Federal Reserve.* Staunton, Va.: Bankers Research Institute, 1983.

National Center for Constitutional Studies. *The Real Thomas Jefferson.* Washington, D.C.: NCCS, 1983.

Neuhaus, Richard John, and Michael Cromartie, eds. *Piety and Politics: Evangelicals and Fundamentalists Confront the World.* Washington, D.C.: Ethics and Public Policy Center, 1987.

Nisbet, Robert. *The Present Age: Progress and Anarchy in Modern America.* New York: Harper & Row, 1988.

Padover, Saul. *Karl Marx: An Intimate Biography.* Abridged. New York: New American Library, 1980.

Perloff, James. *Shadows of Power: The Council on Foreign Relations and the American Decline.* Appleton, Wis.: Western Islands, 1988.

Pfaff, William. *Barbarian Sentiments: How the American Century Ends.* New York: Hill and Wang, 1989.

Pike, Albert. *Morals and Dogma of the Ancient and Accepted Rite of Scottish Freemasonry.* Richmond, Va.: L. H. Jenkins, 1871, 1921.

Pryce-Jones, David. *The Closed Circle: An Interpretation of the Arabs.* New York: HarperCollins, 1989.

Quigley, Carroll. *The Anglo-American Establishment: From Rhodes to Cliveden.* New York: Books in Focus, 1981.

————. *Tragedy and Hope: A History of the World in Our Time.* New York: Macmillan, 1966.

Ravenal, Earl C. "The Price of Defense" in *An American Vision: Policies for the 90s.* Edited by Edward H. Crane and David Boaz. Washington, D.C.: Cato Institute, 1989.

Reich, Robert B. *The Work of Nations: Preparing Ourselves for 21st Century Capitalism.* New York: Alfred A. Knopf, 1991.

Reichley, A. James. *Religion in American Public Life.* Washington, D.C.: Brookings Institution, 1985.

Roberts, Paul Craig, and Karen LaFollette. *Meltdown Inside the Soviet Economy.* Washington, D.C.: Cato Institute, 1990.

Robison, John. *Proofs of a Conspiracy.* 1798. Boston: Western Islands, 1967.

Russett, Bruce, and Harvey Starr. *World Politics: The Menu for Choice.* San Francisco: W. H. Freeman and Co., 1981.

Schlafly, Phyllis, and Chester Ward. *Kissinger on the Couch.* New Rochelle, N.Y.: Arlington House, 1975.

Schleicher, Charles P. *Introduction to International Relations.* New York: Prentice-Hall, 1953.

Schulzinger, Robert D. *The Wise Men of Foreign Affairs: The History of the Council on Foreign Relations.* New York: Columbia University Press, 1984.

Shoup, Lawrence H., and William Minter. *Imperial Brain Trust: The Council on Foreign Relations and United States Foreign Policy.* New York: Monthly Review Press, 1977.

Sklar, Holly, ed. *Trilateralism: The Trilateral Commission and Elite Planning for World Management.* Boston: South End Press, 1980.

Skousen, Cleon. *The Naked Communist.* Salt Lake City: Ensign, 1961.

Solzhenitsyn, Aledsandr, "Difficulties in the West with the Study of Russian History" in *Thinking About America: The United States in the 1990s.* Edited by Annelise Anderson and Dennis L. Bark. Stanford, Calif.: Hoover Institution, 1988.

Steinbrunner, John D. *Restructuring American Foreign Policy.* Washington, D.C.: Brookings Institution, 1989.

Still, William. *New World Order: The Ancient Plan of Secret Societies.* Lafayette, La.: Huntington House, 1990.

Sutton, Anthony C. *Wall Street and the Bolshevik Revolution.* New Rochelle, N.Y.: Arlington House, 1974.

Thompson, William Irwin. *Evil and World Order.* New York: Harper Torchbooks, 1980.

Tinbergen, Jan, Antony J. Dolman, and Jan van Ettinger, eds. *Reshaping the International Order: A Report to the Club of Rome.* New York: E. P. Dutton, 1976.

Toms, Michael. *At the Leading Edge: New Visions of Science, Spirituality, and Society.* Burdett, N.Y.: Larson Publications, 1991.

United Nations. *Global Outlook 2000: An Economic, Social, and Environmental Perspective.* New York: United Nations Publications, 1990.

Von Daniken, Erich. *Gold of the Gods.* Translated by Michael Heron. New York: G. P. Putnam's Sons, 1973.

Webster, Nesta. *Secret Societies.* New York: E. P. Dutton, 1924. Republished in a book club edition for Christian Book Club of America.

Wien, Barbara J., ed. *Peace and World Order Studies: A Curriculum Guide.* Fourth edition. New York: World Policy Institute, 1984.

Wormser, René. *Foundations: Their Power and Influence.* Second edition. Hollywood, Calif.: Angriff Press, 1977.

Wurmbrand, Richard. *Marx and Satan.* Westchester, Ill.: Crossway Books, 1986.

Journals: Selected List

"New World Order." Special Issue. *New Perspectives Quarterly.* Published by the Center for the Study of Democratic Institutions, Spring 1990.

Blumenthal, Sydney. "April's Bluff." *The New Republic,* August 5, 1991.

Brooke, Tal. "The Emerging Reality of a New World Order." *SCP Journal,* Summer 1991.

Brookhiser, Richard. "Two Centuries of New World Orders." *Time,* May 6, 1991.

Foreign Affairs (Journal of the Council on Foreign Relations). Volumes 1–5. April 1974–Spring 1991.

Gerson, Michael, and Gary North. Debate. "George Bush's Vision of New World Order: International Stability or Another Babel?" *World* magazine, February 5, 1991.

Global 2000 Report to the President: Entering the Twenty-First Century. Volume 1. Summary Report. Washington, D.C.: U.S. Government Printing Office, 1980.

Kondracke, Morton. "The Fine Print." *The New Republic,* February 25, 1991.

Kraft, Joseph. "School for Statesmen." *Harper's* magazine, July 1958.

Novak, Jeremiah. "The Trilateral Connection." *Atlantic Monthly,* July 1979.

Roper Organization. "The Two World Orders." *The Public Pulse,* June 1991.

Russett, Bruce, and James S. Sutterlin. "The U.N. in a New World Order." *Foreign Affairs* (Journal of the Council on Foreign Relations), Spring 1991.

U.S. Congress, House Committee on Foreign Affairs, Res. 211, the 99th Congress. "U.S. Policy in the United Nations: Hearings and Markup Before the Committee on Foreign Affairs and Its Subcommittee on Human Rights and International Organizations." Volume 3. Washington, D.C.: United States Government Printing Office, 1986.

Index

off